ONLINE

TRADING

SURVIVAL GUIDE

AN INDISPENSABLE HANDBOOK FOR TODAY'S WIRED INVESTOR

JACK GUINAN

DEARBORN™
TRADE

A **Kaplan Professional** Company

This publication is designed to provide accurate and authoritative information in regard to the subject matter covered. It is sold with the understanding that the publisher is not engaged in rendering legal, accounting, or other professional service. If legal advice or other expert assistance is required, the services of a competent professional person should be sought.

Associate Publisher: Cynthia A. Zigmund
Senior Managing Editor: Jack Kiburz
Interior Design: Elizandro Carrington
Cover Design: Design Solutions
Typesetting: the dotted i

Published by Dearborn Trade, a Kaplan Professional Company

Printed in the United States of America

01 02 03   10 9 8 7 6 5 4 3 2 1

Library of Congress Cataloging-in-Publication Data
Guinan, Jack.
    The online trading survival guide : an indispensable handbook for today's wired investor / Jack Guinan.
       p.   cm.
    Includes bibliographical references and index.
    ISBN 0-7931-3962-7
    1. Electronic trading of securities.   2. Investments.   I. Title.
HG4515.95.G85   2000
332.64'0285—dc21   00-010105

This book is dedicated with tremendous love to:
My Mom and Dad, Nancy and Harry Guinan,
and Kathy, Ed, Casey, Katie, Nancy, Laura, Samantha, Kelly,
Margie, Ashley, Bridgette, and Kelly.

CONTENTS

Chapter 4 ■ Funding Your Account.. 67

Chapter 5 ■ Understanding Account Balances and Margin Basics.. 89

ACKNOWLEDGMENTS

Thanks to Associate Publisher Cindy A. Zigmund, Senior Managing Editor Jack Kiburz, copyeditor Lois R. Sincere, Ph.D., and the other professionals at Dearborn for believing in this book and for working so hard to see it through to its successful completion; Wendy Sundsted, Joe DeLuca, Mary Helen Gillespie, and Cheryl Marconi, who encouraged me from the beginning; Albert H. Manwaring IV, whose input was critical in getting the ball rolling; Fidelity Investments Spartan Brokerage, especially Bruce MacAlpine, Bruce Chanenchuk, Jay Owen, Maura Gomes, Wilson Gomes, James Meyer, Bob Dacey, Bob Tashjian, Lynn Fortier, all of the traders, and the entire sales team; my friends and former colleagues at Brown & Company, who were always there when I needed them.

On the research end, special thanks to Mike Shirer at Forrester Research; Mark St. Marie at Credit Suisse First Boston; Jason Lind at U.S. Bancorp Piper Jaffray; Grace Toto at the Securities Industry Association; Teresa Horney at the American Association of Individual Investors; Chief Economist Evelina Tainer at Econoday Inc.; John Nester at the Securities and Exchange Commission; Meg Sharp and Brooke Adams at the Nasdaq/AMEX Market; and Steve Herrmann, specialist extraordinaire, at the New York Stock Exchange.

Also, thanks to Lori Kalahar and Wendy Reservitz, two special friends who supported me nonstop and who always knew just what to say; Telecom Company Professional Services Inc. of Philadelphia for the use of their offices while I was in town; my family, who were there every step of the way and made me realize once again just how lucky I am to have them; and last, but not least, the hundreds of thousands of online brokerage customers who over the years challenged me each and every day to become a better brokerage representative.

INTRODUCTION

Congratulations! Give yourself a tremendous pat on the back. You have just taken a big step to becoming a better online investor. After reading this book, you will have acquired an advantage over the millions of online investors who have gone before you. Whether you are a first-time online trader or a savvy old-timer, this book can help you. *The Online Trading Survival Guide* should enhance your online investing experience.

How does this book differ from the other books in the marketplace today? As the title points out, I'm going to give you insights from an insider's perspective. I'll take you inside your online brokerage firm and share with you critical information that will make your online investment experience more rewarding—and I hope more profitable. You will have an advantage over millions of online investors who have already made *their* mistakes by knowing how to avoid making them yourself. Having worked on the front lines of two of the largest discount online brokerage firms for more than ten years, I know what you'll be up against and will do my best to guide you through the online trading maze.

It's no secret that in today's fast-paced and volatile market environment, investing can be downright overwhelming. Markets are up one minute and down the next. One day they're yielding terrific gains, and the next, they're producing tremendous losses. In 1991, the average daily changes in the Nasdaq and Dow Jones Industrial Average were a mere 0.7 percent; today these market swings are 2.3 percent and 1.2 percent, respectively (Source: State Street Global Advisors). On top of this, everyone seems to have an opinion about what you should do with your money: Buy this, sell that; technology is king; the old economy blue chip stocks rule; on second thought, put your cash in money markets! Everything is racing toward you from all directions.

Following the markets and picking stocks is a tough enough task without the added distraction of running afoul of your online brokerage firm. I won't be so bold as to predict whether you'll make money in the market—that's up to you and your stock selection acumen. But with my years of professional experience, I will try to make online investing easier for you by removing the obstacles that will impede your route to success. I am aware firsthand of the trouble spots that you will likely encounter. Many of my days were spent resolving these very issues. Thousands of my phone conversations involved addressing problems ranging from completing the online brokerage account application to recognizing and resolving trading disputes to helping customers understand account balances and margin.

Your time is too valuable to be wasted. You should dedicate yourself to more rewarding activities, such as researching your next stock picks, rather than pursuing the resolution of brokerage problems that need not have arisen in the first place. Finding the research necessary to make informed stock selections is out there; your online broker, along with the aid of the Internet, has taken care of that. The issues that face investors today are not how to get the information but when to get it, and, once having gotten it, having the time to analyze it. You certainly won't if you are spending precious hours of your day battling with your online brokerage firm. Avoiding problems that eat up your time is critical for achieving seamless trading with an online broker.

■ Sir, Can You Please Help Me? ■

The year was 1998, and I had just ended a conversation with one of our new online brokerage customers, who was complaining about an execution of a stock trade that he had placed earlier in the day. He believed that the price he received on the purchase was incorrect. He was adamant that the execution price could not possibly have been five points ($5) above the quote that he saw on his computer. How could that happen? Surely there was foul play. After a lengthy discussion, I explained to him the mechanics of how his trade had been executed and the fact that he was trading a stock that was in a "fast market" (you'll learn more about fast markets later in the book). Nothing improper was done by anyone involved and the end result was that the customer paid $5 more for each share of the stock he bought.

The fact that our firm had executed his order properly meant nothing in this conversation. The damage was already done. The customer had to pay more money for the stock then he could ever have imagined. Everyone involved lost. The customer was extremely unhappy and our firm had the potential of losing a very good client. On top of that, the customer's time and the firm's time were wasted discussing a topic that should have been understood by the client before he placed his first trade. After all, the customer should have been aware that there exist certain types of orders that reduce this type of trade risk. In addition, who knows how many people had to be put on hold and wait longer on the telephone because I had to explain this issue over and over again with this client? Remember once your account has been established, you could wind up being one of the customers waiting on hold, a situation in which no one wins.

My biggest concern, however, was that this was not an isolated incident. These types of inquiries as well as others were popping up more frequently with each passing day by both novice investors and sophisticated investors alike. Call after call seemed to produce another complaint. Yet inherent in all these calls was one common thread—an angry, frustrated, and confused customer. After many of these conversations, I would feel frustrated. How could people put their life savings into an online trading account without understanding how it worked?

Then I realized: It wasn't the customer's fault. Everyone— from those in television to those with Internet Web sites—was giving online investors advice on picking stocks but few were explaining the realities involved with trading online. In fact, most were discussing just the opposite—how easy point-and-click investing could be. That's when I realized that I had to write this book.

■ EVEN THE SECURITIES AND EXCHANGE COMMISSION AGREES ■

Since 1998, there appears to have been a gradual shift in the investment communities' thinking regarding online trading. Although simplicity and cheap commissions are still the buzzwords to attract online traders, more frequently you are hearing rumblings about better educating the online investor. It is no longer enough for brokerage firms to merely sign up customers. The industry recognizes its fiduciary responsibility to educate online brokerage clients.

Today you are seeing this reflected more often in online brokerage advertising. You seldom see ads declaring that you can own your own island one day as a result of trading online. In fact, two of the largest online firms' tag lines are "Invest Responsibly" and "Creating a Smarter Investor." The Securities and Exchange Commission (SEC) has also come out publicly to support the need to better educate the online trader—and is it any wonder why? In 1999, the SEC reported that the number of complaints concerning online investing had increased 330 percent. SEC Chairman Arthur Levitt has gone on record to say, "The majority of them [complaints] can be addressed through better education and investors ensuring that they have done their homework."

In a 1999 statement, Levitt and the SEC identified four issues they believe every online investor should be aware of:

1. Investors must understand the issues and limitations of online trading.
2. Investors may be surprised at how quickly stock prices actually move.
3. Investors buying securities on margin should fully understand the risks involved.
4. Investors should exercise caution before initiating the style of trading and risks undertaken by market professionals.

The SEC statement goes on to point out: "Investors need to remember the investment basics, and not allow the ease and speed with which they can trade to either lull them into a false sense of security or encourage them to trade too quickly or too often." The SEC is concerned, and rightfully so, about online investors getting in over their heads. After all, it is the SEC and the self-regulating organizations that are responsible for protecting the retail investor. However, this does not exonerate individual investors of their own responsibilities. Chairman Levitt states emphatically that "investor protection—at its most basic and effective level—starts with the investor. . . . [W]hether you invest online, on the phone, or in person—know what you are buying, what the ground rules are, and what level of risk you are assuming."

This is where *The Online Trading Survival Guide* comes in. I have done my best to compile a work that I feel strongly will educate you about the ground rules and inherent risks of opening and subsequently trading on your online brokerage account. But I can only do so much within these pages. In the end, as Chairman Levitt advises, it will be up to you. Your survival in the online brokerage arena depends in large part on how much you really want to learn. I do not want to be the bearer of bad news or make you nervous—but online investing is not easy!

It involves a great deal more than checking off a few boxes on an application form: It also entails such matters as understanding the type of account you want, the types of account features you need to have in order to trade, and the types of orders that you need to place to reach your investment goals. The simplest of tasks harbor the potential to turn into major problems. Do you understand what you are entering into when you open your online trading account? Don't be fooled; you are becoming your own broker. And although you are assuming this awesome responsibility, no one, neither your online brokerage firm nor the SEC, is requiring you to demonstrate a minimum standard of investing competence.

When I became a broker in 1987, I was fortunate enough to get extensive company training and education on a continuous basis. I was also required by the National Association of Securities Dealers (NASD) to pass numerous licensing exams. And I am proud to say that I currently hold the following five NASD licenses: Series 63 Blue Sky Laws; Series 7 Registered Representative; Series 8 Sales Supervisor; Series 4 Registered Options Principal; and Series 24 General Securities Principal. You, on the other hand, will probably not have had the advantages of extensive training and testing that my colleagues and I have had. Make no mistake about it: Trading online without a certain degree of this training will put you at a disadvantage.

■ THE ONLINE TRADING SURVIVAL GUIDE ■

I have done my best to organize this book to be both enjoyable and beneficial. Even though we will be discussing technical material, I have interjected basic concepts and terminology to explain details in clear and understandable language. This is not the only online investment guide you'll ever need; on the contrary, I feel that it is in your best interest to be as proactive as possible in pursuing knowledge about the securities markets. The world of online trading and the markets in which they operate are in constant change. Driven by technology, they race ahead, and you must thus do your best to keep pace with these changes so as not to fall behind.

The Online Trading Survival Guide is an indispensable part of your education. Although I cannot possibly cover every aspect of online trading (the breadth and scope of the industry is far too great), I have drawn on my experiences to cover subjects that I recognize as vital for your online trading success. These subjects are presented in chronological order beginning with an online industry overview, followed by opening an account, trading on the various exchanges, working with your broker, and ending with understanding the tax consequences of trading. At the time of this writing, the material covered was current, but because of the dynamics of online trading, you should always ask your online broker about its current policies and procedures.

CHAPTER 1—THE ONLINE BROKERAGE INDUSTRY. What actually is this phenomenon known as online trading? Where did it come from and who are the players? From deregulation of fixed brokerage commissions on May 1, 1975, to the popularity of the discount broker in the late 1980s and early 1990s, I explore the growth of online trading in a historical perspective but with an eye to the future.

CHAPTER 2—CHOOSING YOUR ONLINE BROKER. Are you really ready to take charge of your own investing? If so, selecting an online broker that meets *your* needs is crucial. There are more than 150 online discount brokers to choose from in today's market. What is the process involved in selecting the right one? Here you'll find helpful hints in sifting through the advertising fluff to get at the heart of what's important to you in your online brokerage account. An easy-to-follow checklist will enable the novice investor, the active trader, and the turbotrader to identify account features that are essential to trade online.

CHAPTER 3—OPENING YOUR ACCOUNT. Trading online starts with this first step: completing the online brokerage new account application form. Here I discuss the many hurdles that customers often trip over in getting started. Opening individual, joint tenancy, partnership, trust, and individual retirement account (IRA) accounts as well as others are covered. Easy to miss but critical sections on the application are highlighted to ensure attention and success. For the options investor, I also discuss the options application form from your perspective as well as from your online broker's.

CHAPTER 4—FUNDING YOUR ACCOUNT. It is time to place your first trade, but are you certain that your online firm will take it for you? Will your funds be available? Funding an account can be as easy as writing a check or as intricate as executing a Depository Trust Company (DTC) transfer. In this chapter I discuss all of your options. Depositing checks, sending bank wires, delivering physical stock certificates, executing partial and full broker transfers as well as "DTCing" stock shares; all have their pluses and minuses with some methods faster than others. We'll also cover guidelines for smoothly transferring your account from one broker to another (transfer of assets).

CHAPTER 5—UNDERSTANDING ACCOUNT BALANCES AND MARGIN BASICS. Now that your account is funded properly, how confident are you about reading and understanding your trading balances? The long and short of it is that you must be able to calculate such items in your portfolio as net worth, cash core, cash market value, and for some of you possibly margin market value, short market value, option market value, and buying power. Your firm's computer will do this for you, but are you sure the numbers are correct? You'll never know unless you understand the concepts involved in calculating your own account balances. The rules of margin are also discussed so that even a novice will understand its risks and its benefits, and calculating margin requirements on stocks as well as the best way to handle margin calls are discussed too.

CHAPTER 6—THE TRADING EXCHANGES. This chapter explains the various market exchanges where your stock and option trades are being executed. It covers the New York Stock Exchange, the American Stock Exchange, the Philadelphia Stock Exchange, the

Nasdaq market, electronic communication networks (ECNs), and the Chicago Board Options Exchange. There is a lot more to executing an order than what you see at your computer terminal. Here, with words and flow charts, you will see how it is actually done.

CHAPTER 7—GETTING STARTED: IT'S TIME TO TRADE. Now that you have completed the first six steps successfully, you've finally reached the moment of truth: placing trades. As with everything else pertaining to online trading, it's more than point and click. The markets operate under an umbrella of strict competition and regulation, and you need to have confidence in the execution process. Fast markets arise from time to time, and you must understand how trade executions on market, limit, or stop loss orders can be effected. Also, be alert for Internet fraud and don't allow your emotions to take command of your trading. Don't become the stubborn investor or the panicked investor.

CHAPTER 8—WORKING WITH YOUR ONLINE BROKER. As you will soon learn, investing online does not always mean that you are actually online. Problems arise with technology, or customer service issues come up that make speaking with your online broker representative inevitable. You should know how your online brokerage firm handles these calls and the tools they use in addressing your trade inquiries. Learn the three Ps—Professional, Prepared, and Prompt—as well as when to challenge a trade order. Remember, online brokerage firms want to keep you happy; working with them does not have to be unpleasant.

CHAPTER 9—THE TAX MAN COMETH. Don't forget about Uncle Sam. All the trading that you do through your online brokerage account needs to be accounted for at the IRS. Learn the basic concepts behind the tax consequences of trading and the difference in the tax treatment of long-term and short-term capital gains. Although you should always seek the advice of a professional tax advisor, you will learn how to calculate your tax basis on stock and option contracts. It is never too early to start thinking about your tax situation.

EPILOGUE—THE CLOSING BELL. Online trading is here to stay. The small retail investor has demanded it and the investment community is delivering it. Who knows where we'll be in the next five years? As you read this, new technologies could be underway that will change the face of the entire industry. But you are in the here and now, so trade wisely.

APPENDIX A—THE ONLINE TRADING CUSTOMER EXAM. Don't move on until you have tested your knowledge. This 50-question exam, while meant for fun, is a good gauge of whether you have a strong grasp of the information presented. Consider this your broker's exam, but don't fret over it. It's better to find out now that you don't understand a particular concept then to find out when you're trading for real. It will not cost you anything to be wrong on the exam. Above all, have fun and learn.

CHAPTER 1

The Online Brokerage Industry

■ SAME SONG BUT THE DRUM BEATS FASTER ■

Hallelujah, online trading is here. Miracle of miracles, wonder of wonders—everybody log on and be happy. Well, isn't that the way it is? Have I missed something? This certainly is what the news media and the advertisers would have us all believe. Let's thank our lucky stars for online trading; if not for it, where would we be? Left out in the cold, isolated from the markets, shut out from the means by which to achieve our financial independence. Don't get me wrong; online trading is a great innovation. It has opened the doors of investment opportunity for millions of individual investors. But this overexuberance is bordering on hysteria. And guess what? Computer investing is not new and trading on one's own account has been going on for years.

In fact, the actual ability to trade via your personal computer has been around since the mid-1980s. Although it certainly was not as ubiquitous as it is today, the bottom line is that you could trade at your computer 15 years ago. Back then, brokerage firms issued computer software that allowed customers to enter their own trades, thus planting the seed for self-directed computer stock trading. With this software, investors could place their own trades via their computer without a broker's assistance. Since then, new technologies have led to the development of systems permitting orders to be placed directly through the Internet. And it is these systems that have given rise to the current networks that we commonly refer to as *online trading*.

Why online trading? Why now? How did a once novelty software item that permitted only a handful of investors to trade on their PCs balloon into a phenomenon that consists of over 150 online brokerage firms. What has occurred over the past 20 years or so that has led us to this point? Did you know that there are an estimated 7 million (if not more) online brokerage accounts today? Did we suddenly wake up one morning and discover that online trading was our investment nirvana? Although at times it certainly appears that way, truth be told, we have been slowly investing to our own tune for some time. Only recently has the Internet cranked up the volume and quickened the pace.

Investing Goes Mainstream

Whether as a casual mutual fund investor or as a self-directed stock trader, the stock markets have always held a certain allure. With each passing year a larger portion of our everyday lives has become enmeshed in the security markets. Through retirement plans at work, personal mutual fund investments at home, and self-directed stock trading accounts on the Internet, more Americans today than ever before are coming in contact with the markets. A study by the Cato Institute of Washington, D.C., points out that in 1999 some 76 million Americans owned stocks or stock mutual funds, and that number is expected to rise to 80 million in 2000. In addition, about 43 percent of U.S. households owned stock either directly or through retirement plans. This represents a 126 percent increase in shareholder ownership over 15 years.

In the 1980s the buzzwords among the investing public were mutual funds. People could not get enough of them. They offered the average investor the ability to invest small amounts of money in diversified and professionally managed stock portfolios at minimal cost. By the decade's end, investing in the markets no longer seemed as foreign to the average American. Not only were people making deposits to fund accounts, but they were also beginning a rudimentary educational process. They took advantage of general mutual fund educational literature provided by their fund companies—information that helped them take charge of their own accounts and plan for their own financial future. Although these tutorials were not specific to individual stock trading, phrases such as *total return, capital gains, dividend yield, portfolio diversification,* and *net asset value* became everyday jargon. Little did investors know that they were laying the groundwork for the future of online trading. Americans had taken their first bite out of the investment pie and they liked it.

This love affair with the markets, however, was almost short-lived. On October 19, 1987, the Dow Jones Industrial Average (DJIA) experienced the most publicized stock market crash since the infamous crash of 1929. On that sullen day in 1987, the DJIA lost 508 points or 22.6 percent of its total market value. Many investors were caught off guard. Those who panicked sold shares immediately and experienced extreme losses, only to realize later that the crash was the advent of one of the greatest bull markets in history. The DJIA closed on that day in 1987 at 1738.74 and hasn't looked back since. Today, at the time of this writing, the Dow stands at just under the 10,500-point mark.

Yet the brush with disaster did not deter investors. Quite the contrary, it did little to dampen their spirits. Soon after, they were back in droves. The Cato Institute reported that from 1989 to 1995, direct ownership of mutual funds leaped 149 percent from 4.5 million to 11.2 million investors. Investor confidence in the stock markets had returned.

People considered themselves wiser for having gone through the 1987 economic catastrophe. Arising from the rubble sprang a thicker-skinned and more determined investor, one less susceptible to the pounding of the volatile marketplace. It was only a matter of time before many of these investors ventured away from the more general mutual fund instruments and into individual stock portfolios. All that they needed was a little push; and that push came in the form of the discount broker with its enticement of low commissions. Who would have thought that those first small investment steps taken in the mutual fund arena would turn into a full-fledged sprint to individual stock trading?

May Day and the Evolution of Online Trading

On May 1, 1975, an event took place that changed the face of the brokerage industry forever. It was on this day that the Securities and Exchange Commission's ruling prohibiting security exchanges from fixing brokerage commission rates went into effect. Today, we take for granted the dirt cheap trading commissions we now enjoy, and we think nothing of the sheer abundance of online brokerage firms from which we have to choose. However, the brokerage industry was not always like this.

Before 1975, the industry behaved like a cartel similar to the OPEC oil cartel of today. There was no sugarcoating its behavior; the long-entrenched brokerage house members negotiated together to fix commission prices. The agreement that member firms operated under was referred to as the Buttonwood Agreement and was signed by 24 brokers on May 17, 1792. The practice of commission price-fixing stood in place for over 180 years. When the SEC finally abolished it, deregulation of commissions promulgated tremendous competition among brokers and gave birth to an entirely new industry: the discount brokerage industry.

Maybe you remember the individual known as the full-service financial broker? You remember the one who dutifully hunted down the best stock picks for you, the one who tediously perused hundreds of company's financial statements in the quest for that illusive investment gem. This was the individual who could hold your hand during down markets while in turn celebrate with you during the up markets, the person who knew you, your family, your spouse, and your job, the one who gave you personal attention and at times acted as financial advisor, confidant, and friend.

It's not as if full-service brokers have gone away completely. They are still out there. It's only that they have faded from the limelight. In fact, with more full-service firms now entering the online brokerage business, you may soon see them back, once again taking center stage. But for today, the full-service broker does not dwell in the land of the online broker. The voices of online investors have been heard loud and clear: "I can do it myself and I don't need a broker!"

Time was that you absolutely, positively depended on the full-service broker to invest. There was no other way. Full-service firms were your lifeline to the markets. Before deregulation and the subsequent advance of the discount brokerage industry, no stock trading lexicon included the phrase *do it yourself*. All market information flowed from the broker to the customer. Public investors accessing real-time market data were unheard of. Such access could not be done. Need a quote on a stock? Call your broker. Need to get a company report? Call your broker. Need to get an account balance? Call your broker. Need to buy or sell a stock? Call your broker. The retail investor had no need for this information anyway; after all, the broker was making all of the trading decisions.

For this reason, full-service brokers held all the cards. They had the access to real-time quotes, news, company reports, analyst reports, and the trading exchanges. They also had a team of financial analysts at their disposal who tracked business sectors, followed company stocks, and dispensed buy, sell, and hold recommendations. It was your broker's responsibility to synthesize this real-time market data to generate stock selections in your portfolio. Individual public investors were not privy to timely information. They did not have the means to trade for themselves even if they wanted to. There were no discount brokers back then and the Internet as we know it today did not exist. As Figure 1.1 illustrates, the full-service brokerage model did not foster independent retail trading.

However, deregulation in 1975 and the arrival of the discount brokerage firm changed the characteristics of the model shown in Figure 1.1. The full-service trading model no longer applied and a new discount-trading model emerged (see Figure 1.2). Catering to investors who were tired of paying high commissions and who felt that they could pick stocks better or at least as well as their broker, discount brokerage firms staked their claim on the individual trader. These firms attracted customers by offering lower commission rates than their full-service brethren. By today's standards these early discount rates would be considered exorbitant, in the range of $100 to $300, but at the time they were a tremendous savings.

Yet discount brokerage customers still had difficulty accessing real-time data. Although new technologies were being introduced,

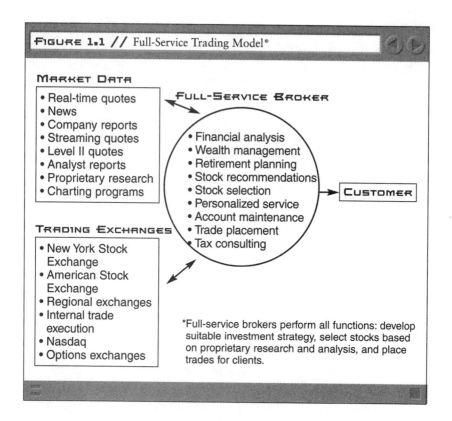

FIGURE 1.1 // Full-Service Trading Model*

MARKET DATA
- Real-time quotes
- News
- Company reports
- Streaming quotes
- Level II quotes
- Analyst reports
- Proprietary research
- Charting programs

FULL-SERVICE BROKER
- Financial analysis
- Wealth management
- Retirement planning
- Stock recommendations
- Stock selection
- Personalized service
- Account maintenance
- Trade placement
- Tax consulting

CUSTOMER

TRADING EXCHANGES
- New York Stock Exchange
- American Stock Exchange
- Regional exchanges
- Internal trade execution
- Nasdaq
- Options exchanges

*Full-service brokers perform all functions: develop suitable investment strategy, select stocks based on proprietary research and analysis, and place trades for clients.

such as Touch-Tone access and computer software, real-time trading was difficult, and thus discount brokerages were slow to gain popularity with investors. Many early discount customers still chose to maintain their full-service brokerage relationships while simply duplicating their full-service broker's trade recommendations in their discount brokerage accounts. Despite these limitations, discount trading did increase in popularity in the late 1980s and early 1990s. The stock market was continuing its steady climb upward (although with an occasional hiccup), and discount brokerage customers were enjoying the benefits of trading in an up market at lower commissions.

Keep in mind that getting a better deal on commissions versus a full-service firm's fees was only part of the story. Lower trading costs meant that individual investors could now move in and out of stocks more frequently with better opportunities to take profits. For example, full-service commissions charged on a buy trade of

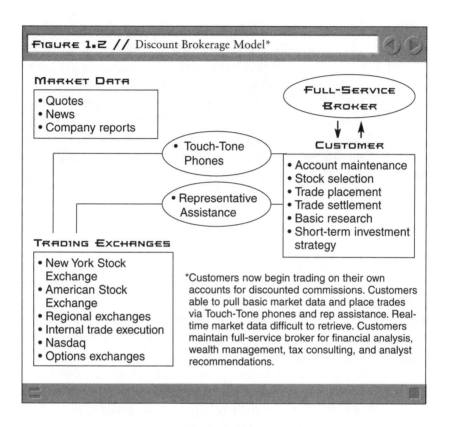

FIGURE 1.2 // Discount Brokerage Model*

MARKET DATA
* Quotes
* News
* Company reports

FULL-SERVICE BROKER

* Touch-Tone Phones

CUSTOMER
* Account maintenance
* Stock selection
* Representative Assistance
* Trade placement
* Trade settlement
* Basic research
* Short-term investment strategy

TRADING EXCHANGES
* New York Stock Exchange
* American Stock Exchange
* Regional exchanges
* Internal trade execution
* Nasdaq
* Options exchanges

*Customers now begin trading on their own accounts for discounted commissions. Customers able to pull basic market data and place trades via Touch-Tone phones and rep assistance. Real-time market data difficult to retrieve. Customers maintain full-service broker for financial analysis, wealth management, tax consulting, and analyst recommendations.

100 shares could have run about $300 each way. This meant that the stock would have to rise in value by $600 just to break even on the commission charges for one round-trip—a buy and sell. In other words, a stock purchased at $50 would need to gain a total of $6 to $56 to break even. On the other hand, if the discount broker's commission were only $50 each way ($100 round-trip), the stock needed to rise only $1 to recoup total round-trip commission costs. A discounted commission, therefore, changes a stock's breakeven point, in this case from $56 to $51. Under discounted commissions, at $56 the stock now garnered a profit of $500 (total cost $5,050–total sale $5,550) as opposed to just breaking even.

This realization marked a significant shift in the individual investor's retail investing strategy. It slowly pushed investors away from the long-held buy-and-hold strategy to a more short-term speculative buy-and-sell strategy. Still, however, discount trading was not considered mainstream. It was neither convenient nor streamlined, and real-time information was still hard to get. Although it was being delivered more efficiently, getting timely market information posed a challenge to the discount customer. For example, when I was a retail brokerage trader in the early 1990s, I can recall holding 30-minute conversations with active traders who were following a series of stocks looking for trading opportunities. These conversations were like a tennis match; the customer would ask for a stock quote and I would relay it back, then he would ask it again and I would return the quote again. This would play out over and over and over again. "What is the quote now? OK, and now what is it?" These volleys went back and forth continuously—certainly not an ideal way to trade.

As the brokerage industry continued to evolve, it found itself in transition. It was becoming extremely fragmented, giving retail customers three distinct choices for where they could trade. The first was a *full-service brokerage house* that offered all investment services, most notably proprietary research and stock recommendations. The second was a *discount brokerage firm* that offered order entry at lower trading commissions (usually on a sliding scale), mutual fund investing, cash management features, and 24-hour representative customer service. The third choice was a *deep discount broker* that offered no services other than deep flat rate trading commissions. Deep discount brokers were considered transaction-only brokers with no cost-effective way to deliver real-time market information fast and efficiently.

In 1995, online trading, as we know it, hit the scene and the brokerage trading model was again reshaped. However, this time it was not completely dismantled but rather rearranged and expanded. A new breed of nimble technology-driven brokerage firms entered the marketplace, offering the ease of Internet computer trading, unlimited real-time quotes and news, and ridiculously low commissions. Finally, investors could get the real-time market information they needed—and quickly. Once again individual investors seized the opportunity to distance themselves even further from their brokerage firms. No longer would brokerage customers trade on discount brokerage time; now they would trade on Internet time. Speed, convenience, lower costs, and information were the draw. The Internet usurped the brokerage firm as the individual investor's lifeline to the markets.

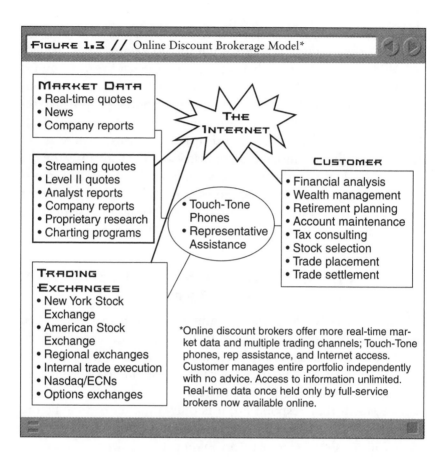

FIGURE 1.3 // Online Discount Brokerage Model*

MARKET DATA
• Real-time quotes
• News
• Company reports

THE INTERNET

• Streaming quotes
• Level II quotes
• Analyst reports
• Company reports
• Proprietary research
• Charting programs

• Touch-Tone Phones
• Representative Assistance

CUSTOMER
• Financial analysis
• Wealth management
• Retirement planning
• Account maintenance
• Tax consulting
• Stock selection
• Trade placement
• Trade settlement

TRADING EXCHANGES
• New York Stock Exchange
• American Stock Exchange
• Regional exchanges
• Internal trade execution
• Nasdaq/ECNs
• Options exchanges

*Online discount brokers offer more real-time market data and multiple trading channels; Touch-Tone phones, rep assistance, and Internet access. Customer manages entire portfolio independently with no advice. Access to information unlimited. Real-time data once held only by full-service brokers now available online.

As the online discount brokerage model shows in Figure 1.3, the key values in online trading lie in the real-time data and exchange access that did not exist before. Customers who made their own investment decisions could now go directly to the markets. They no longer needed to push buttons on a telephone or speak to a live representative. The Internet made online trading faster, cheaper, and more seamless. Today, the full-service brokerage model has come full circle with the customer now becoming the broker.

Online trading has leveled the playing field between professional traders and the general public. After the arrival of the discount broker, individual investors realized that it was possible to make their own stock picks and trade on their own accounts. Where the earlier discount brokerage firms provided direct access to basic market data (quotes, news, and company reports) and the trading exchanges via Touch-Tone phones and rep assistance, online trading now offered Internet access—and the floodgates were opened.

All of the information that was so out of reach five years ago is today readily retrievable with the click of a mouse: streaming quotes, Level II quotes, analyst reports, company reports, proprietary research, charting programs, and even initial public offerings (IPOs). The original musical score (self-directed investing) that was set down earlier by the mutual fund industry and then advanced by the discount brokerage industry is now being led by a new maestro—online trading. The underlying notes may still be the same, but at today's pace and volume, it certainly doesn't bear any resemblance to the tune we all started dancing to over 20 years ago.

■ THE ONLINE BROKERAGE INDUSTRY: A STATUS REPORT ■

It's hard to believe that online trading via the Internet has been with us for only about five years. Its impact on our lives has been extraordinary. It has literally become a part of our culture. Ask the men or women on the street if they invest online—whether in stocks or in mutual funds—and there's a good chance their answer will be yes. If they respond no, it is only a matter of time before they will. Your purchase of this book indicates that you either trade online already or plan on joining the ranks of the online trading community soon, and thus contributing further to the industry's unprecedented growth.

Depending on to whom you talk, there are from 6 million to over 10 million online brokerage accounts registered today (see Figure 1.4), an amazing statistic when you consider that we were at zero accounts not too long ago. Assets held in these accounts range from $400 billion to $600 billion, as shown in Figure 1.5. Where only a short time ago no one traded on the Internet, in early 1999, Credit Suisse First Boston estimated that approximately 16 percent of all equity trades took place online (see Figures 1.6 and 1.7). These numbers are quite astonishing; and the most remarkable aspect of this growth and change is that you—the individual investor—are the driving force behind this new market.

The individual investors trading from their computer terminals or wireless devices are the ones fueling the major changes taking

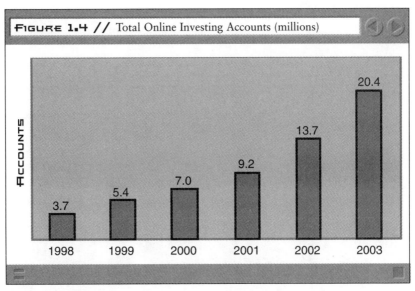

FIGURE 1.4 // Total Online Investing Accounts (millions)

Source: Forrester Research.

place. "If we build it, they will come" seems to be the online broker-age firm mantra. Online brokers are building more robust Internet trading sites to attract your business. Never forget that you are

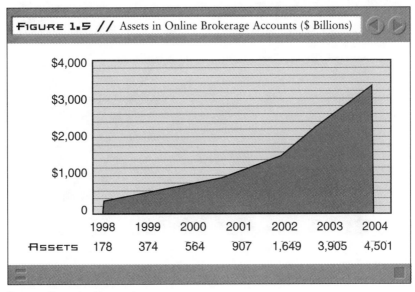

FIGURE 1.5 // Assets in Online Brokerage Accounts ($ Billions)

ASSETS	1998	1999	2000	2001	2002	2003	2004
	178	374	564	907	1,649	3,905	4,501

Source: Forrester Research.

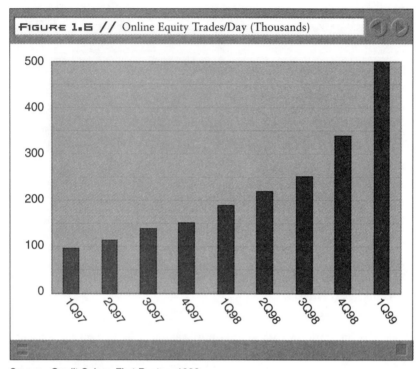

Source: Credit Suisse First Boston, 1999.

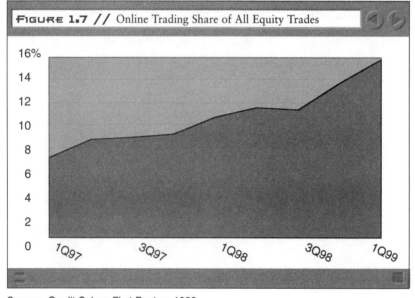

Source: Credit Suisse First Boston, 1999.

the catalyst for the changes that are sweeping through the discount brokerage industry.

This tremendous growth has attracted many firms into the marketplace. Today, you can choose from the more than 150 online brokerage firms listed in Appendix B. One hundred fifty online brokerage firms may seem excessive, and the number begs the question, "Are there too many?" I personally don't think there could ever be too many. Competition is good for the industry; it creates innovation and drives down prices. You as an online brokerage customer benefit directly from the aggressive tactics of competing brokers. Who can say what is in store for the online brokerage industry, but maybe, as I write this, a couple of kids in a garage somewhere are developing the next generation of online trading technology that will compete with today's firms.

Although there are many online brokers in the marketplace, recent data indicate that the majority of online brokerage customers are doing business with only a handful of companies. The statistics shown in Figure 1.8 are meant only to give you a specific snapshot of how the industry looks at the time of this book's writing. They are not meant to validate or recommend any one online brokerage firm over another but are included to give you a better understanding of the online brokerage landscape. I find that it's easier to follow the action if you know who the players are.

According to a U.S. Bancorp Piper Jaffray Report for December 1999 (shown in Figure 1.9), 4 firms out of the top 15 online brokers accounted for more than 75 percent of all online accounts

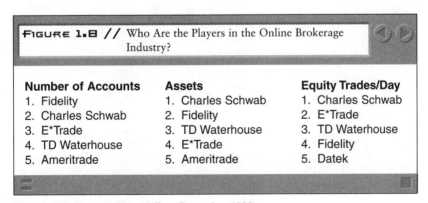

FIGURE 1.8 // Who Are the Players in the Online Brokerage Industry?

Number of Accounts	Assets	Equity Trades/Day
1. Fidelity	1. Charles Schwab	1. Charles Schwab
2. Charles Schwab	2. Fidelity	2. E*Trade
3. E*Trade	3. TD Waterhouse	3. TD Waterhouse
4. TD Waterhouse	4. E*Trade	4. Fidelity
5. Ameritrade	5. Ameritrade	5. Datek

Source: U.S. Bancorp Piper Jaffray, December 1999.

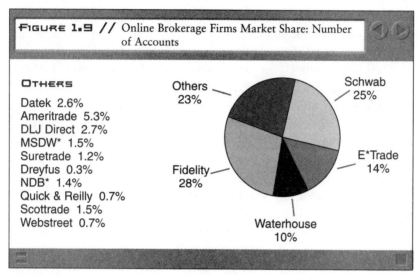

FIGURE 1.9 // Online Brokerage Firms Market Share: Number of Accounts

OTHERS

Datek 2.6%
Ameritrade 5.3%
DLJ Direct 2.7%
MSDW* 1.5%
Suretrade 1.2%
Dreyfus 0.3%
NDB* 1.4%
Quick & Reilly 0.7%
Scottrade 1.5%
Webstreet 0.7%

Others 23%
Schwab 25%
E*Trade 14%
Fidelity 28%
Waterhouse 10%

Pie Chart Source: U.S. Bancorp Piper Jaffray, December 1999.

(Fidelity Investments, Charles Schwab, E*Trade, and TD Waterhouse). Fidelity and Schwab held a combined 53 percent market share. In total assets (shown in Figure 1.10), there was no contest:

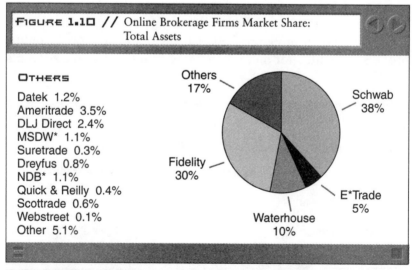

FIGURE 1.10 // Online Brokerage Firms Market Share: Total Assets

OTHERS

Datek 1.2%
Ameritrade 3.5%
DLJ Direct 2.4%
MSDW* 1.1%
Suretrade 0.3%
Dreyfus 0.8%
NDB* 1.1%
Quick & Reilly 0.4%
Scottrade 0.6%
Webstreet 0.1%
Other 5.1%

Others 17%
Schwab 38%
E*Trade 5%
Fidelity 30%
Waterhouse 10%

Pie Chart Source: U.S. Bancorp Piper Jaffray, December 1999.

Schwab and Fidelity combined to take 68 percent of the market. The picture changes somewhat when we focus on which firms are actually executing online trades—that is, their market share. As shown in Figure 1.11, Schwab led the pack with a 23 percent market share, and companies such as E*Trade, TD Waterhouse, Fidelity, and Datek rounded out the leaders.

What is interesting about these pie charts is the relatively small market share that some of the more publicized online brokers like Ameritrade, Datek, DLJ Direct, and Scottrade hold in assets and number of accounts. All of these companies figure prominently in newspaper, television, and online banner advertisements. If you didn't know better, you would think that these companies were the "biggies" in the industry. I don't mean to imply that bigger is better, for all of these firms perform their fiduciary responsibilities admirably; it's just that these companies command a large presence in the public eye, and before looking at the numbers, I had thought that their share of the market would be larger. But then again, that's precisely why they are advertising so heavily.

In defense of the smaller market share firms, they do hold their own when it comes to equity trades per day. Although Fidelity and Schwab dominate the industry in total number of accounts and

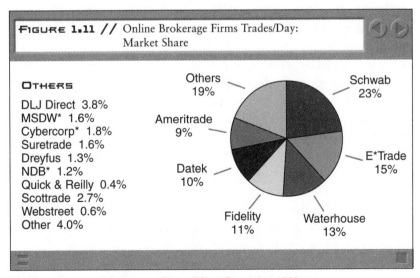

FIGURE 1.11 // Online Brokerage Firms Trades/Day: Market Share

OTHERS

DLJ Direct 3.8%
MSDW* 1.6%
Cybercorp* 1.8%
Suretrade 1.6%
Dreyfus 1.3%
NDB* 1.2%
Quick & Reilly 0.4%
Scottrade 2.7%
Webstreet 0.6%
Other 4.0%

Others 19%
Schwab 23%
Ameritrade 9%
E*Trade 15%
Datek 10%
Fidelity 11%
Waterhouse 13%

Pie Chart Source: U.S. Bancorp Piper Jaffray, December 1999.

total assets under management, the playing field levels off when it comes to trade execution. There you find that many firms that are smaller in relation to the big two's market share maintain significant trading market share in relation to their size. This makes sense when you consider that Fidelity and Schwab have been around longer (Ameritrade opened its doors—or should I say portal—in 1997, Datek in 1996) to collect assets and thus had a large pool of assets already under management before online trading went mainstream. When it comes to trading, these smaller firms originally attracted customers who simply wanted to trade more at lower flat rate commissions. Fidelity and Schwab, on the other hand, were late entrants to the deep discount arena and therefore missed out somewhat on capturing the active trader segment.

However, this type of industry polarization is fading fast. More online brokerage firms are diverging toward the middle ground in hopes of capturing both the casual investor and the active trader. The Fidelitys and Schwabs of the world are now offering deep-discounted commissions and active trader Web sites. The Ameritrades, Dateks, DLJ Directs, and Scottrades are no longer mere transaction brokers. They serve up a plate of stocks, options, mutual funds, and bonds. Even such old-line full-service firms as Merrill Lynch and JP Morgan now have online trading capabilities.

In the short term, major changes in the online brokerage landscape should not be significant. Down the road however, there could be more consolidations of smaller firms into larger ones such as Schwab's recent acquisition of Cybercorp, a smaller niche player for extremely active traders. Instead of building market share, they can acquire it, catering to everyone. Newer entrants in the marketplace will most likely target the more active traders (the ones who place more than 100 trades annually), attracting them with better day trading technologies. Two points to consider as you look at the online broker landscape: (1) the dot-com online brokerage industry is still in its infancy as evidenced by the fact that the majority of online brokers mentioned above did not exist before 1996; and (2) the online brokerage industry will continue to operate in an environment of constant change. No one can predict what the industry will look like in the future, but change in the industry will be good for you, the small investor.

■ ONLINE TRADING—WHY NOW? ■

Seriously, have you ever seen anything like it? The number of people who have online brokerage accounts today is incredible and even more incredible is the sheer number who will be opening accounts in the future. How many of you would have thought of trading individual stocks for your own account two years ago? My guess is that the majority would not have thought about it but you're not alone.

As mentioned earlier, you've had the ability to trade on your own account for some time now; why is it that all of a sudden you have the urge to participate? What factors have influenced your decision? I'm sure that you have your own personal goals for wanting to invest online, but, in addition to these, three prominent factors are most likely driving you to online trading: the Internet, the media, and the bull market.

The Internet

It's no surprise that the Internet is driving online trading. It is safe to say that the Internet *is* online trading. Would it be possible to have one without the other? I don't mean to be the master of the obvious, but the acceptance by the general public to transact business on the Internet has pushed online trading to new heights. It is a natural progression that as more households purchase personal computers and go online, the more they will shop online and the more they will conduct their finances online, including trading.

Here is an interesting fact from a Morgan Stanley Technology Research study in 1997. It took 38 years for radio to reach 50 million households; it took television 13 years and cable only 10 years, but it has taken the Internet less than 5 years to reach that many households. That's pretty amazing. Forrester Research points out that in 1994 there were 33.9 million U.S. households with personal computers. PC penetration in U.S. households grew by 58 percent in 1999 to 53.6 million. As PCs become less expensive and more accessible to lower-income and middle-income households, that number is expected to hit 64.1 million households by 2003.

Forrester also reports that the number of U.S. households on-line will increase to over 59 million by 2003 from 38.8 million in 1999. Of these households, 38.4 million will shop online in 2003, an overall increase of 193 percent from 1999 levels. By contrast, only 0.8 million U.S. households shopped online in 1995. Growing confidence in the Internet has also pushed U.S. households into using online financial services (investing, banking, electronic bill payment). Households using the Internet for financial services went from 0.2 million households in 1995 to 5.3 million in 1999 and the number is forecast to reach 22 million households by 2003. Pure online investing is also following suit with the 3.1 million U.S. households trading online in 1999 anticipated to grow to 9.7 million by 2003. The Internet is clearly no longer a gadget or novelty item. It is a venue for conducting serious business, and increasingly it is becoming a mainstay for the personal investment strategies of U.S. households (see Figure 1.12).

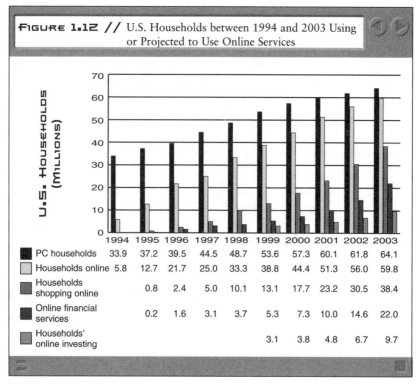

FIGURE 1.12 // U.S. Households between 1994 and 2003 Using or Projected to Use Online Services

	1994	1995	1996	1997	1998	1999	2000	2001	2002	2003
PC households	33.9	37.2	39.5	44.5	48.7	53.6	57.3	60.1	61.8	64.1
Households online	5.8	12.7	21.7	25.0	33.3	38.8	44.4	51.3	56.0	59.8
Households shopping online		0.8	2.4	5.0	10.1	13.1	17.7	23.2	30.5	38.4
Online financial services		0.2	1.6	3.1	3.7	5.3	7.3	10.0	14.6	22.0
Households' online investing						3.1	3.8	4.8	6.7	9.7

Source: Forrester Research.

The Media

Am I the only one who thinks that every other television commercial is an advertisement for an online brokerage company? Or that when you surf the channels you inevitably land on a TV station that covers the markets? You know the station where the well-dressed man or woman is standing on the floor of the New York Stock Exchange or at a computer while the consolidated stock tape runs along the bottom of your screen. What about newspapers, where every article about the Nasdaq or the Dow is interspersed with online broker print ads?

The enthusiasm that the media have shown for disseminating stock market news while promoting brokerage advertising has been unbridled. *USA Today* reported in a January 2000 article that cable networks were devoting enormous chunks of time to business news. Cable networks with the most business shows per day were CNN*fn* (18 hours); CNBC (15.5 hours); CNN (5.5 hours); FOX News (4 hours); and USA Network (3 hours). In the same article, the Center for Media and Public Affairs found that even on mainstream ABC, CBS, and NBC nightly newscasts, the number of business stories rose 19 percent in 1999 to 1,175 from 989 in 1998. I'm sure you noticed this trend on your local news telecasts also.

On the advertising front, the numbers are more prodigious. According to a *Business Week* article dated April 3, 2000, that cited a New York research firm, Competitive Media Reporting, advertising skyrocketed 95 percent in 1999 to $1.2 billion—now three times the ad spending of five years ago. U.S. Bancorp Piper Jaffray's numbers are even more amazing. Are you ready for this? In the fourth quarter ending December 1999, Schwab spent $77 million, E*Trade over $95 million, and Ameritrade over $58 million on brokerage advertising.

Is it any wonder why online trading is so prominent in our consciousness?

The Bull Market

You have heard it said before, "We are living during one of the greatest economic expansions of all time." Strong corporate earnings, strong economic growth, low interest rates, declining inflation, and unwavering consumer confidence are fueling unprecedented prosperity. The new economy is what many professionals are calling it, but, regardless of its moniker, it has been a boon for the securities industry. Individuals are flocking to the markets with abandon, and investor participation in the stock markets is at an all-time high. Can you blame investors for their exuberance?

Since 1995, when Internet trading was introduced, the Dow Jones Industrial Average (DJIA) has posted a cumulative return of approximately 200 percent. It had a remarkable streak of three consecutive years with returns of 20 percent or higher—33.5 percent in 1995, 26 percent in 1996, and 22.6 percent in 1997. The 1998 number was not too shabby either, returning 16.1 percent. In 1999, the Dow again posted returns above 20 percent at 25.2 percent. The S&P 500 Index, which is a broader measurement of market performance, has turned in a 220 percent cumulative return since 1995. The Nasdaq composite, which includes most of the technology issues (the dot-com companies), has returned an unbelievable 441 percent since 1995.

The overall markets have consistently been posting positive percentage changes for more than two decades now. Going back as far as 1980, the Dow had 17 up markets with an average percentage change per year of 14.6 percent. The S&P 500 was also in the black 17 times, while the Nasdaq totaled 15 years on the plus side. The S&P 500's average annual percentage change was 14.68 percent; the Nasdaq's was 20.08 percent. These numbers do not guarantee that you would have profited had you traded during the best market cycles. These are broad averages for the *entire* market, but not every stock in the DJII, S&P 500, or Nasdaq posted positive returns. In fact, in 1999 half of the Nasdaq-listed stocks lost money!

It is the perception of turning a profit by trading in the markets, however, that has attracted so many to online investing. In July 1999, Paine Webber and the Gallup Organization released findings under the Index of Investor Optimism. They discovered that the average investor expects to receive a 16.6 percent return from investing. Novice investors with five years or less of experience anticipate a 21.1 percent return. It doesn't matter whether these returns are sustainable or not. Right or wrong, if people believe that the markets will pay such high returns, then that is

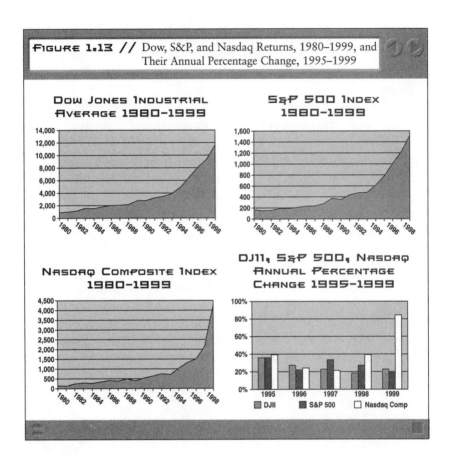

Figure 1.13 // Dow, S&P, and Nasdaq Returns, 1980–1999, and Their Annual Percentage Change, 1995–1999

Dow Jones Industrial Average 1980–1999

S&P 500 Index 1980–1999

Nasdaq Composite Index 1980–1999

DJII, S&P 500, Nasdaq Annual Percentage Change 1995–1999

where they are going to put their money. And what is being sold by the media and the brokerage industry as the easiest way to join in on the good fortunes? You got it—online trading.

▪ Putting It All Together ▪

I bet you never realized that online trading had so much history. Most of us know it only by its recent stardom. It is as if the entire online brokerage phenomenon miraculously appeared overnight out of thin air. Looking back, you begin to realize that such is not the case. Many pieces of the puzzle have fallen nicely into place to account for online trading's success. It makes perfect sense that online trading is so popular today. Mutual fund investing started us off in the 1980s; the onset and popularity of the discount brokerage industry in the early 1990s came next; top this off with a rising stock market, an unending media blitz, and the increasing popularity of the Internet, and all of it points in one direction: online trading.

Technology has made investing more accessible to the average person. Many who never conceived of investing for themselves are now taking the plunge. It's OK to get excited about online trading. Investing for yourself and managing your own finances is exciting. There is never a dull moment in the stock market. In addition, the brokerage industry has done a tremendous job of serving small investors. But don't be fooled by online trading. Keep everything in proper perspective.

Who's to say when or if this phenomenon will ever cease? Online trading is hot. Even more important to remember is that it is big business. The media have delivered online trading right to our front door and we have welcomed it with open arms. As a small investor, it must feel pretty good to have so many people—advertisers, newscasters, brokers, journalists—vying for your attention. But remember that they want something from you in return—your business.

CHAPTER 2

Choosing Your Online Broker

■ ARE YOU REALLY READY TO MAKE YOUR OWN INVESTMENT DECISIONS? ■

However odd it may seem to ask you to suspend your thoughts about online trading (after all, you *are* reading *The Online Trading Survival Guide*), it's important to do it for the moment. Too many people have jumped into online trading without thoroughly analyzing their decision. I don't want the same thing to happen to you.

Just because millions of investors have rushed to the Internet to implement their investment strategies does not necessarily mean that online trading is right for you. You have purchased this book, so I know you intend to trade online. But I hope that you are not basing your decision on what everyone else is doing and taking a "me too" attitude. You need to assess your own situation before you shift your life savings and investments to the Internet. Ask yourself:

- Do I feel comfortable conducting business online?
- Do I have the time to devote to online investing?
- Do I possess the market knowledge to make my own investment decisions?
- Do I need help from a professional investment advisor?

These are the kinds of questions that you need to ask before rushing to select an online firm.

No doubt about it, online trading is enticing. It is promoted as the best way to save money on commissions, gain access to the equity markets, and to trade profitably. Firms tout how easy it can be and how much *fun* you can have trading online. They portray online investors as happy-go-lucky individuals relaxing at their computer terminals. With images like these, is it any wonder that everyone wants to be a part of this online trading juggernaut? The prevailing thought seems to be, get aboard now before it is too late. Slow down! The markets aren't going anywhere. Investing is for life; it's not a fad.

Many newcomers have signed on for the wrong reasons, only to discover that this online ride is not nearly as comfortable as they had anticipated. It is crowded and bumpy. It races off at breakneck speeds only to stop suddenly, reverse course, and speed away again. The bandwagon that everyone refers to as online investing suddenly doesn't seem like such a good idea anymore. Newcomers begin to question their decision: "What have I gotten myself into? This is not at all what I had anticipated."

The biggest question you must answer is: *Am I prepared to manage my own investments?* That is really the bottom line. Online trading is not magic. You don't all of a sudden open an online trading account and instantaneously become a portfolio manager. Managing your own money is hard work and the convenience of trading on the Internet is merely a tool to help you achieve your financial goals. Like fax machines and telephones, the Internet is a mechanical device. Granted it's a powerful device, but a device just the same.

In today's new online brokerage model, as pointed out in Chapter 1, online trading allows market information and trade orders to be transmitted between individual customers and their brokerage firms without the middleman, a live broker. Instead of talking through telephone handsets, individual investors now communicate with their brokerage houses via desktop PCs or handheld wireless devices. The quotes, news, company reports, financial charts, IPOs, and broker recommendations that once flowed from a live broker are now downloaded directly from the Internet by customers sitting at their computer. Yet there is one component of this new model that is missing: personalized broker recommendations.

Although there is some talk regarding online firms disseminating some form of investment recommendations to customers in the future, such information will most likely be generic or very broad.

Make no ifs, ands, or buts about it; if you decide to trade online, you are on your own. The Internet has given you the same investment tools that were once only available to professional money managers—real-time quotes, news, charting programs, research, and company reports—and you are expected to use them to formulate your own trading strategy *on your own*. Once you are comfortable with this new model, then and only then will it truly be time to look for an online broker.

▪ Don't Get Caught Up in Online Brokerage Advertising ▪

We have all seen the newspaper advertisements and the television commercials used recently by online brokerage firms to sell their accounts. "Rated Number 1 by . . . ," "Trades for Only $5," "IPOs at No Extra Commissions," or "Join Now and Get Free Trades." These ads are very catchy, but you must not let yourself be mesmerized by them. I'm sure each advertisement is true in its claims, but to sign on with a particular firm solely because it has a catchy slogan or a giveaway is dangerous. Opening an online account is not like signing up with a long-distance phone carrier or your local Internet service provider. You are talking about entrusting your life savings to a financial institution.

If a particular ad strikes your interest, call the firm directly. Ask questions:

- If it's a relatively new online firm, how long has it been in operation?
- Is it signing up many customers from the current ad campaign?
- Does it have enough capacity to handle all the new business?
- Has its online trading system crashed or been delayed recently?
- If its system goes down, how else can you trade?
- What is the average hold time to speak with a trading representative?
- Will it charge you extra fees for trading on a Touch-Tone phone or with a live broker?

Commission Advertising

Commission rates are not always what they appear to be. Firms may charge higher commissions than they advertise based on the types of orders entered, small versus large orders, market versus limit orders, or listed versus Nasdaq stocks. For instance, a firm may advertise a rate of $10 for online trading, but this trade commission may apply only for a buy or sell trade of 1,000 shares or less. The commission on trades of more than 1,000 shares could actually be accessed a surcharge of .01 cent per share. Buying 2,000 shares would result in a total commission charge of $20 ($10 on the first 1,000 shares, .01 × 1,000 on the second 1,000 shares), $10 more then the advertised commission rate.

Also be aware of what are known as "roll-up" commission rates. Some firms charge a flat rate commission per transaction, whereas others roll up their commissions. Let's say a firm charges $14.95 per transaction up to 1,000 shares—no roll-up. Two identical trades buying 100 IBM in the same account during the same day would be charged $29.90 ($14.95 × two trades). A firm that rolls up commissions would only charge you $14.95 for those same two orders—that is, they roll the two trades into one. Sometimes a firm with an advertised lower rate can actually cost you more than a firm with a higher rate. Here's how it works. If Firm A offers a $14.95 rate per transaction with no roll-up, and Firm B quotes a $20 rate but rolls up commissions, Firm B will actually wind up being cheaper for three identical trades of 100 shares. Firm A's cost would be $44.85 ($14.95 × 3), but Firm B's cost would still be only $20 because the three trades would be rolled into one for commission purposes. You would like to have a roll-up commission schedule whenever possible.

If saving money on commissions is a high priority, request a commission schedule from your online brokerage firm so you can run through different scenarios to compare brokerage costs. Some firms may already supply commission calculators on their Web site that compare brokerage commissions with other firms, but I would rather calculate these commissions myself just to be sure.

Initial Public Offering (IPO) Advertising

IPOs are extremely hot in today's equity marketplace. They are considered by many to be a risky investment, but if you hit it right, the rewards outweigh the risks. The companies being offered in an IPO are generally younger, fast-growing companies. They normally do not have a long track record of earnings. Actually, some of the recent dot-com IPOs have no positive earnings at all nor do they project them in the near future. Earnings and profits are anticipated sometime down the road. Needless to say, investing in IPOs is speculative at best.

The mechanics of an IPO work like this. Acme Company needs cash. It contracts with an investment bank to both create stock shares and determine an initial value for the shares. The shares then get registered with the Securities and Exchange Commission and are then available for sale to the public. The underwriting firm puts together a selling team made up of brokerage firms to sell the stock to the public. You must have an account with one of these selling firms to purchase the stock at the initial offering price set by the underwriter. The good news is that your online brokerage firm sometimes participates as a member of the selling group and you can request to buy shares from them. The bad news is that most often your online firm only gets a very small amount of shares to sell.

For instance, if the underwriter creates 5,000,000 shares to sell to the public in an IPO, those shares are then distributed to the selling group. Your online broker, however, may only get 300,000 shares to sell, which means that only 300,000 shares are available to the entire customer base of your online firm. You can see the problem—too few shares for too many customers. Because the supply is small versus the demand, your online firm must prorate the amount of shares that you are permitted to purchase. You may ask to buy 2,000 shares, but in the end you may get only 200 shares. This is not your online broker's fault; it's just the way the IPO market functions in the current online brokerage world.

The investing public has a tremendous appetite for IPOs, and therefore online brokerage firms are advertising their availability. But as you can see, if you are going to open an account based on an online broker's advertisement proclaiming the availability of IPOs, you'd better think twice or at least call the firm to inquire more thoroughly.

"Rated Number One" Advertising

Online brokerage firms are extremely happy to advertise that they have garnered the top spot on an online broker survey, and rightfully so. If they deliver services better then anyone else, then they should be proud to declare that they are the best. But you need to dig deeper. What are they best at and are their product offerings best suited for your needs? If not, selecting a broker from a ratings list is meaningless. It is like purchasing an automobile because it ranks number one in a survey, only to find out that the survey measured durability and cargo space, when what you really wanted was a automobile with high engine performance. The result is inevitable; you will be disappointed in your purchase.

Online broker ratings are no different. They are discussed at length later in this chapter, but for now, understand that all rating surveys are not alike. The criterion that one survey implements to measure performance is not the same as another's. You could be looking at the number one–rated online firm in trade execution when you are actually searching for a firm that offers a large range of financial services. The trick is to find a survey that measures online broker performance according to the same criteria that you deem important. The closer you can get, the more relevant the survey rankings will be for your individual needs and the more satisfied you'll be with your online broker selection.

"Sign Up Now—Get Free Trades" Advertising

Sounds great, doesn't it, but will your online broker respect you in the morning? As I mentioned earlier, we are talking about your financial future, so don't rush into a decision based on gimmicks. I am not saying that an online firm that participates in this type of promotion will not be appropriate for you. Who knows, it could turn out to be your best choice and you could wind up saving yourself money at the same time. It's just that you need to do your due diligence first. Ask questions! Does its account services meet your requirements?

A problem that many individuals have is thinking too much in the short term. The market is returning tremendous gains, and they believe they must sign on with an online firm immediately. They never assess how this decision may affect their investment strategy in the long run. What happens after you have exhausted your free trades? Will a particular online broker be able to service your financial growth? If you do well in the market, will you be able to park profits into more secure investments like money markets or certificates of deposit (CDs)? On the flip side, will this online firm offer alternative investment products other than stocks if the market turns bearish? Consider this also: If the firm's campaign is successful and it signs up thousands of customers, will it have the capacity to handle this new volume of business?

It is vital to get to know your online broker before signing on for its services. It is inevitable that you will need to speak with your online firm. It doesn't matter whether you're getting a few free trades or not; when you have a problem, you must—and you have every right to—expect your online firm to be responsive. Call an online broker randomly and talk to the representatives. You will know from these interactions whether that firm is right for you. If the representatives are not courteous or do not seem knowledgeable when they're supposed to be putting on their best face to get your business, how do you think they will treat you when you call with a trade problem?

Once you have committed your money and assets to a firm, transferring them to another institution is not an easy process. If your online broker ends up being an inappropriate match, it could take you as long as six weeks to transfer an account to another institution. Be as confident as possible in your selection. Be inquisitive. Go to the Web site and "demo" its trading screens. Make sure you are comfortable with the format. Request a sample copy of the monthly statements to ensure that you can read and understand them. Do they tell you the purchase price of shares and gains or losses? If you have the luxury, test the waters first. Open an account with the least amount of money possible and trade. See how the firm does. The goal is to not have to transfer your account to another firm.

■ WHAT'S IMPORTANT TO YOU IN YOUR ONLINE BROKERAGE ACCOUNT? ■

Have you ever heard of needs-based selling? In the financial services business this selling technique is used quite often. In a nutshell, it refers to the practice of discovering what people's financial needs are before making a sales pitch. It is an interactive approach by which the sales representative asks a client a series of questions to uncover the client's hidden needs. Once those needs have been brought to the surface, then the representative can present products whose features and benefits best fulfill the client's specific requirements.

If you were to contact my office and request information about a brokerage account, how could I know what to send you unless I asked you a few questions? If I were trying to convince you that my firm's products were superior to a competitor's, how could I do that if I didn't know what was important to you? How would I know if our firm's services were appropriate for you? What are your hot buttons? Initiating a sales pitch by touting low commissions or low margin rates may fall on deaf ears. Your interests may be vastly different. Your only criterion for an online brokerage firm may be that it maintains local branch offices or a 24-hour representative-assisted phone service. You may not even care about commissions or margin rates!

The point is that only you know what you are looking for in an online brokerage firm. Whether it's the cheapest commissions, free research, free real-time quotes, technical chart analysis, the availability of representative assistance or a no-nonsense Web site, only you know what works for you. Choosing your online broker is the first decision of many that you alone must make. You need to take an inventory of what you need by asking yourself this question, "What is important to me in my online brokerage account?"

Most of your requirements will include the basics: low commissions, free research, free real-time quotes, and a reliable Web site. Novice investors may also want 24-hours-a-day, 7-days-a-week telephone representative assistance, mutual fund or fixed income products such as CDs or Treasuries (U.S. Treasury bills, bonds, and notes), cash management features (checking or bill payment), or an interactive Web site for financial planning; or they may want to do business only with a well-known, nationally recognized online brokerage firm. The list for active and turbotraders, who trade at least once a week, could be much shorter, including such items as the cheapest commissions, the lowest margin rates, advanced option-trading capabilities, international stock trading, or a no-frills Web site.

▪ Online Brokerage Account Features and Why You May Need Them ▪

Cash Management Features

CHECK WRITING. How will you get cash from your account? Without checks you must request the money be sent by mail. This can take several days and assumes that the representative will process your request properly. You can have the money wired to your local bank, but there are higher dollar minimums and additional fees. The ability to write a check on the account is worth having, especially if you need cash quickly.

CREDIT CARDS, DEBIT CARDS, BILL PAYMENTS, AND BANK WIRES. Planning to use your online trading account for all of your financial needs? Then these services can be of value. They often have no fees and enable you to consolidate all of your investments under one roof, giving you the added convenience of receiving all your financial information in one statement.

INTEREST-BEARING CORE ACCOUNTS. Make sure your online broker is paying you interest on your cash balances. Interest usually begins when your total cash core balance meets a specified minimum. Smaller balances earn less interest than larger balances. Also, ask if the cash balances can be swept into a money market mutual fund. These funds almost always pay higher interest than the house interest paid on cash core accounts. Interest on core accounts is usually not a major concern for active traders because they seldom keep cash balances. Their money is usually in stocks or options.

INTEREST ON SHORT ACCOUNTS. If you don't sell stocks short, don't worry about short interest. If you do, understand that most online firms will not offer you short interest unless you ask for it. They may require a higher short credit balance minimum, but if you are successful and they grant short interest, you will earn extra cash.

SECURITIES INVESTOR PROTECTION CORPORATION (SIPC) INSURANCE. Online trading accounts are not insured by the Federal Deposit Insurance Corporation (FDIC), but they are insured by the SIPC. The SIPC is a private fund supported by member broker-dealers that insures cash and securities in accounts up to a total of $500,000 ($100,000 cash). It does not insure your account against loss of value from market risk. It kicks in only if your firm becomes insolvent. Most online brokers take out additional private insurance policies in the millions. If your assets are over $500,000, check how much additional insurance your firm carries.

Account Products and Services

FREE REAL-TIME QUOTES. Real-time quotes tell you what the current prices are for a stock at the time that the quote is displayed on the screen. You must have real-time quotes in order to trade. Delayed quotes, which can be as old as 15 minutes, are worthless. Updating a real-time quote is known as "refreshing" the quote. If a quote is not refreshed, it becomes old—that is, no longer current. For example, if you have received a real-time quote and then leave your computer but return five minutes later, the real-time quote is now five minutes old.

STREAMING QUOTES. These are real-time quotes that do not need to be refreshed. They are updated continuously on your screen on their own. Leaving and returning to your computer five minutes later still results in a current real-time quote. Many active traders prefer streaming quotes to refreshing real-time quotes.

LEVEL II QUOTES. These quotes display prices on the Nasdaq. Level II prices indicate the number of shares being offered for purchase and for sale, aka the bid and ask price respectively. Level II quotes also display the names of the market makers entering the bid and ask prices. Unless you are trading in and out of Nasdaq stocks daily, Level II quotes will not be a major consideration.

FREE MARKET NEWS AND RESEARCH. These features are available in abundance all over the Internet so you should not have to pay for them. They are convenient if you are able to access them at your online broker's Web site. This way, if you are researching a company, you don't have to leave the site and navigate back to place a trade, which will cause a delay and perhaps result in your missing the trade.

MULTIPLE INVESTMENT PRODUCTS. These are mutual funds, corporate bonds, and Treasuries used for diversification and for buying on margin. Instead of investing only in stocks, with these products you are able to diversify your portfolio and also combine all of your assets under one roof. There is no need to maintain your mutual funds in a separate mutual fund company, thus making your recordkeeping easier. All of your assets are reported on one statement. Some firms offer no-fee mutual fund investing, but others don't. Inquire about extra fees if your portfolio will consist of mutual funds.

INTERNATIONAL TRADING. International stock trading is becoming increasingly popular with active investors. Although these securities are considered risky, some individuals like to diversify by investing overseas. It is an added bonus if your online firm offers international trading at lower commissions.

24/7 TOLL-FREE CUSTOMER SERVICE/TRADING TELE-PHONE CENTER. Whether you trade once or over one hundred times each year, you will eventually talk to your firm's representatives, and chances are it will be when you have a problem. Don't underestimate the value of a quality telephone center. Telephone representatives (reps) must be able to answer the phones in a timely matter for trading and servicing your account; must be knowledgeable and competent enough to resolve your problem; and must be professional. Investing can get stressful. Conversations between reps and customers can get tense. A telephone representative who performs professionally can help you through many difficult situations.

WIRELESS TECHNOLOGY. Although some firms are offering Palm Pilots, pagers, and Internet-ready telephones, these services are seldom free of charge. Such devices permit investors to access their accounts and the stock markets from virtually anywhere. They will alert you when the market or a predetermined stock reaches a certain level. They deliver real-time stock quotes, news, balances, and executed trade reports. Some even allow trading. For investors who are on the road during market hours and not at a computer, these devices may be worth the cost.

DIRECT DOWNLOAD CAPABILITIES FOR ACCOUNTING PURPOSES. The more you trade, the more records you will need to maintain. Every trade you make during the year has to be reconciled with Uncle Sam come tax time. Some firms today are offering account interface with products such as Quicken and Microsoft's Money.

LOCAL BRANCH PRESENCE. Your check got lost in the mail and your buy transaction settles today, so what do you do? If your online firm has a local branch office, you can walk in and simply deposit the cash—problem solved. Branch offices are also useful for picking up checks, dropping off share certificates, completing application paperwork, resolving problems face-to-face, consulting with a financial representative, or even placing trades. The ability to walk into your online broker's branch office is a tremendous asset.

Trading Features

DIRT CHEAP COMMISSIONS ($0 TO $10). Your first instinct may be to get the cheapest rate available, but remember that lower commissions are often accompanied by fewer services and higher account minimums. It's great to save money, but at what cost?

REASONABLY LOW COMMISSIONS ($10 TO $30). The good news is that every firm has reasonably low commissions. The average online brokerage commission is about $15.75. How low are you comfortable going? There is no longer a need to give up valuable account services just to save a few dollars.

LOW MARGIN RATES. For you margin traders out there, reducing your margin rate by just one-half of a percent on a $50,000 debit balance can save you $250 per year. The larger the debit balance, the greater the savings. Depending on the size of your debit balance, lower margin interest charges can often be a better deal than lower trade commissions.

MULTIPLE TRADING CHANNELS. These are a must for all traders. Make sure your online broker provides you with alternative trading channels, such as representative assistance, and allows you to trade via a Touch-Tone instrument and online computer or wireless devices. If one channel is down, you must be able to place an order some other way.

ONLINE OPTION TRADING AND SHORT SELLING. If these instruments are part of your trading strategy, your online broker's Web site should offer you the ability to buy and sell options and to sell stock short. Otherwise, you may be forced to trade through a representative and subsequently be charged higher rep-assisted commissions.

INTRADAY ACCOUNT BALANCE UPDATES. You just made five trades and want to know how much money you now have in your account. Immediate intraday account updates give you this information. Each buy and sell trade is reflected immediately in your online account balances. If you are planning on trading more than once a day, ask your broker if it has this feature. Many on-line firms update balances only after the market closes.

DEDICATED TRADING TEAM. Active traders don't want to call in on a central phone site. Customer conversations on these general phone lines tend to be much longer and thus create longer hold times. A dedicated trading team's only role is to enter trades and handle trade-related issues. The representatives are more knowledgeable. Do you need to enter a ten-time "butterfly" option spread or a 1:2 ratio call spread? If so, you need a dedicated trading team that knows what it's doing.

EXTENDED TRADING HOURS. Traditional trading hours for stocks are from 9:30 AM to 4:00 PM EST. Some brokers are offering extended trading hours from 8 AM to 8 PM EST. Preopening or extended-hour trading is mostly on the Nasdaq and over the counter. Transactions in securities listed on the New York Stock Exchange (NYSE) are limited. After-hours trading is not for everyone as it is still somewhat new and volume so far has been light. But if you're not getting your fill of the markets during regular business hours and you're up for it, then there is no harm in having this option.

Web Site Features

EDUCATIONAL WEB SITE. How much help will you need without a broker? The novice investor should look for a Web site that not only transacts trades but also educates. The Web site should offer tools that assist you in making investment decisions. Deciding to go it alone doesn't mean that your online broker can't help you direct your investment strategy. These Web sites can help you set up mock portfolios interactively in accordance with your financial goals. They can substitute to some extent for the old-style broker who once held your hand.

STREAMLINED ACTIVE TRADER WEB SITE. This type of Web site is designed for speed with no frills. Get In and Get Out is this site's motto. The last thing you want as an active trader is to search a site for the trading screen. Evaluate an online broker's Web site for simplicity. Are there too many distractions? The more graphics offered, the slower it tends to be. You should be able to monitor real-time stock quotes and place trades from the same screen. Backing out of multiple screens erodes precious time. Remember that stock prices move quickly.

SYSTEM REQUIREMENTS. Confirm with your online broker that you have the proper system requirements. The high-speed Internet technologies to which firms are upgrading today are often not supported by the older systems you may have at home. Don't assume that an online broker's Web site will be compatible with your particular computer or browser.

■ WHAT FEATURES ARE RIGHT FOR YOUR SITUATION? ■

Now that you have a better understanding of the particular features that are being offered by online brokerage firms, which ones might you need? To answer that question, you must figure out what type of investor you are or will be. No two investors are alike, but all investors tend to fall within certain investment groups. I have classified three types of investors: the novice investor, the active trader, and the turbotrader. Accompanying these classifications is a checklist indicating the features that each investor category may need (see Figure 2.1). I developed this list from my experience dealing with online traders. Use it as a guide. If you find you need individual features that don't fall under your trading type, that's

OK. Most important is that you identify the services that you need *before* you open an account. If you open an account with an online firm that doesn't offer a service that is important to you, is it the firm's fault or didn't you research the firm as thoroughly as you should have? You will only have yourself to blame if you sign on with a firm that doesn't meet your needs.

Types of Investors

NOVICE INVESTOR (TRADES LESS THEN 30 TIMES PER YEAR). I consider a novice to be someone who is just starting out and has never traded individual stocks before. The novice is looking more for long-term investments and overall money management rather than to strictly trade in and out of stocks but would like to learn more about investing.

ACTIVE TRADER (TRADES 30 TO 100 TIMES PER YEAR). The active trader is more knowledgeable than the novice and looks forward to the challenge of trading individual stocks. The active trader wants to make money but also enjoys the thrill of investing, trading about once a week or from 30 to 100 times per year. This type of investor wants to be as independent as possible but needs help occasionally. Online investing consumes more time for active traders than for novice investors, and their trading is slightly more sophisticated. They dabble in margin and option buying as well as short selling. Active traders seldom want educational programs clogging Web sites.

TURBOTRADER (TRADES OVER 100 TIMES). The turbotrader spends all day trading. Following the markets is not a hobby—it is a way of life. Trading every day, turbotraders will make well over 100 trades each year. Give these investors what they want and just leave them alone.

The good news is that the majority of online brokerage firms have come a long way in meeting all of your needs whether you are a novice investor, an active trader, or a turbotrader. Even traditional full-service firms like Merrill Lynch are now offering online trading. The online brokerage market is intensely competitive and in order to survive, firms realize they need to compete at all

FIGURE 2.1 // New-Account Checklist for Three Types
of Investors

	Novice	Active trader	Turbo-trader
CASH MANAGEMENT FEATURES			
Check writing	X	X	
Credit cards, debit cards, bill payments, and bank wires	X	X	
Interest-bearing core accounts	X	X	
Interest on short accounts		X	X
SIPC insurance	X	X	X
ACCOUNT PRODUCTS AND SERVICES			
Free real-time quotes	X	X	X
Streaming quotes		X	X
Level II quotes		X	X
Free market news and research	X	X	X
Multiple investment products (mutual funds, bonds, Treasuries)	X	X	
International trading, IPOs			X
24-hour toll-free customer service and trading phone center	X	X	
Wireless trading technology		X	
Direct download capability for accounting		X	X
Local branch offices	X	X	
TRADING FEATURES			
Dirt cheap commissions (less than $10)			X
Reasonably low commissions ($10 to $30)	X	X	
Low margin rates		X	X
Multiple trading channels (rep assistance, Touch-Tone phones, Internet and wireless access)	X	X	X
Online option trading and short selling		X	X
Intraday account balance updates			X
Dedicated trading team		X	X
Extended trading hours		X	X
WEB SITE CHARACTERISTICS			
Educational/interactive Web site	X	X	
Streamlined active trader Web site		X	X
System compatibility	X	X	X

levels for all of your online business. Some small niche players that do not wish to be all things to all people are still out there, but their numbers are dwindling.

The American Association of Individual Investors, or AAII (800-428-2244), in its Discount Broker Survey 2000, reviewed product offerings of more than 90 discount online brokerage firms. Of the 65 firms that the AAII designated as discount firms, the average representative-assisted trade commission on a trade of 100 shares at $50.00 per share was only $40.62, with the lowest fee a mere $15.00. The 34 firms designated as primarily online brokers (deriving most of their business from the Web) had an average commission of only $14.62. The lowest commission was as little as $5.00. In addition, 55 firms permitted trades to be made through multiple channels: representative assistance, Touch-Tone phones, and the Internet. Sixty-five firms offered some type of free Web research, 61 firms provided free real-time quotes, and 43 firms offered everything (multiple trading channels, free Web research, and free real-time quotes). These numbers demonstrate that the majority of online firms are catering to all of your needs.

As you move forward with your search for an online brokerage firm, some standards you should not discount. At the minimum, your online broker should offer low commissions, free real-time quotes, free Web research (or at least links to research sites), and multiple trading channels. If not, you should reconsider giving it your business. Pay particular attention to firms that offer multiple trading channels. The ability to contact your online broker via several means is extremely important. If, for example, your firm's Web site should crash or your Internet service provider is having problems or you just aren't at a computer, you must have an alternative means of getting in touch with your online brokerage firm so you won't be locked out of the market.

Don't make choosing an online broker any harder than it needs to be. As the AAII numbers bear out, the majority of firms are giving clients what they need: lower commissions and access to market information. The majority of firms are also delivering similar trade executions, thanks in large part to stock exchange competition and the National Association of Securities Dealers' (NASD) new-order handling rules (discussed in a later chapter). The bar for online brokerage services has been raised. Customers have been demanding more from their online brokers and the online firms have been delivering. Today, the quality of online brokerage services has improved to the point that it is difficult to pick a firm that is an outright dog.

Looking at the category of primarily online discount brokers in the American Association of Individual Investors Discount Broker Survey 2000, it is evident that the majority of firms are offering basic account features. Below is a snapshot of the commission rates being charged and the services rendered. If the online brokerage firm that you are currently investigating falls outside the following numbers, then maybe you should consider doing business with someone else:

Commission rates: Highest $39.95 Lowest $4.95 Avg. $15.27

Avg. minimum balance to open account	$3,500
Firms offering no-load mutual funds	76%
Firms trading bonds and options	76%
Firms offering Touch-Tone phone trading	73%
Firms offering rep-assisted trading	100%
Firms offering free Web research	88%
Firms offering free real-time quotes	65%

■ RATING SERVICES AND SELECTING YOUR ONLINE BROKER ■

Online broker rating services offer a quick and easy way to narrow your online brokerage search. With over 150 online and discount brokerage firms to choose from, using a rating service can save you a tremendous amount of time. By no means are the services perfect, but they do give you a better understanding of who is actually delivering on their claims for low commissions, Web reliability, responsiveness, and trade execution. Reviewing these surveys is an excellent place to start your search for an online broker.

Be careful, because online rating services are not all alike. Each varies in the methodologies used to measure online broker performance. Some services give more weight to certain criteria than do others. One rating service may emphasize low commissions and

Web reliability, whereas another may weigh more heavily customer service or breadth of products. The trick is to find a survey that looks at online firms the way that you do.

Take out your list of criteria that you developed earlier, the one that answered the question, "What's important to me in my brokerage account?" and match it to a firm in the survey that offers those same account features. Whether you are a novice investor, an active trader, or a turbotrader, try to cross-reference your criteria list with an online broker survey to see the best match with your profile. This is not an exact science. The alternative, however, would be to research all 150 plus brokerage firms individually. Remember that the majority of online firms will be able to meet your physical trading requirements for commission costs, real-time quotes, news, and research.

Select a firm that has consistently demonstrated the capacity to deliver on its features and services. Keep in mind that this month's winner could be next month's loser. Look for consistency in the rankings. Once you have spotted firms that you believe are suitable, call them a few times and ask more questions. Online brokerage firms, like people, have personalities. It is important that your personalities don't conflict.

Keep in mind that most recent surveys do not reflect the full-service firms that are now offering online trading at flat rates. These new rates can be as low as $29.95 or less depending on your wealth and trading activity. The surveys also do not take into account premium trading accounts that are offered by firms such as Charles Schwab and Fidelity. These types of accounts, which are based on higher minimum balances and greater trading activity, offer cheaper trading commissions than those that are published and subsequently used in survey calculations. Consequently, firms may be ranked lower in a survey because their standard accounts, not their *premium* trading accounts, are being measured.

When you go directly to a survey's Web site, you'll note that each survey is accompanied by commentary, which you should read. You'll find comments from customers who are actually trading with these online firms. Their insights are extremely helpful and will give you a personal perspective on the ability of these firms to deliver on their promises. A list of online rating service Web sites is shown below:

Online Rating Service Web Sites

American Association of Individual Investors	<www.aaii.com>
Gomez Advisors	<www.gomez.com>
J.D. Power and Associates	<www.jdpower.com>
Kiplinger's Personal Finance	<www.kiplinger.com>
SmartMoney	<www.smartmoney.com>
Money	<www.pathfinder.com/money/onlineinvesting>
Keynote Systems	<www.keynote.com>
TheWhiz.com	<www.thewhiz.com>
Forrester Power Rankings	<www.forrester.com>
Barron's	<www.wsj.com/articles/barronscovermain.htm>
CNNfn	<www.cnnfn.com>
Worth Magazine	<www.worth.com>

■ HAS YOUR ONLINE BROKER BEEN IN ANY TROUBLE? ■

You obviously want to avoid any online brokerage firms that have a disciplinary history. If individual investors are constantly filing complaints against a particular firm or a firm's representatives, that should immediately raise a red flag. The NASD can provide information on any disciplinary actions that have been taken by securities regulators against online brokerage firms. The information can be retrieved by going to the NASD Public Disclosure Program at <www.nasdr.com> or by calling 800-289-9999.

CHAPTER 3

Opening Your Account

■ GET IT RIGHT THE FIRST TIME ■

It was the artist Billy Joel who in the late seventies belted out the lyrics, "Get it right the first time, that's the main thing." I know he wasn't referring to setting up an online brokerage account, but his words could just as easily apply to filling out your online brokerage application. Pay very close attention to what I'm about to say: To avoid unnecessary headaches now and well into the future, be sure to fill out your online brokerage application correctly—the first time!

A simple recommendation, but if not followed precisely, you will run into problems that you could never have foreseen that could cost you both financially and emotionally. Filling out your application incorrectly will disrupt your trading patterns and waste valuable hours of your time, not to mention drive you crazy.

I cannot begin to count the number of customers who have run up against the roadblock called the new-account application. You would think that opening an account would be fairly simple. First, you decide to establish an online brokerage account. Second, you pick an online brokerage firm. Third, you contact the firm and request an application, or better yet you go online and download one for yourself. Finally, you complete and sign the application, fund the account, get an account number, and, presto, you are open for business.

Ah, if life were that easy. The truth is that for many customers this unfortunately is not the norm. People generally have difficulty filling out their new account application. Whether it is an individual account, a joint tenancy account, or a more complex account, such as a trust or partnership, people trip over this first step.

While researching this issue, I had the pleasure of speaking with one of the new account managers at a major online discount brokerage firm. I discovered that roughly 40 percent—almost one-half—of all applications submitted to this particular firm were considered not in good order. Look closely at this percentage because it emphasizes a very good point: It's very easy to make a mistake when filling out your application.

What does "not in good order" mean? An application falling within this category is lacking a number of items. It is either incomplete, filled out incorrectly, or missing additional paperwork. Bottom line: Your online broker's new account department will most likely not be able to set up an account for you under these circumstances. This will put both you and your brokerage firm in an undesirable position. Without an account, you will be locked out of the market, unable to implement any trading strategies and possibly missing some timely trading opportunities. The brokerage firm, in kind, cannot accommodate your trading needs and therefore will be unable to collect trade commissions.

Once your account application has been labeled "not in good order," your brokerage firm needs to contact you, either by phone or by mail, to request more information and thus causing the firm's costs for setting up the account to increase. And you, who have already taken time out of your busy schedule to fill out the original application, now need to fill out even more paperwork.

■ MR. SMITH OPENS AN ACCOUNT ■

For several years my primary responsibility was to bring in new brokerage business to my firm. I spent countless hours conversing with potential clients like you in an attempt to convince them that our firm was the place to trade. (By the way, I could do this wholeheartedly because I was convinced of that fact.) When a potential client decided to open an account with us, it was a great feeling. The worst feeling? Having a client choose our firm and get mired down in the new account process.

The scenario would play out this way. My phone would ring and on the other end would be Mr. Smith, who days before had agreed to open an account. He was now inquiring if his new account had been set up. He was calling on this particular day at this particular time because he wanted to place an order on a stock, which he had been following for weeks. He informed me that he had sent his application in a few days earlier, so it was reasonable to assume that his account should have been set up. After contacting our new accounts department, I was told that his application was not in good order and additional information was needed. His account could not be established. There would be no trading for Mr. Smith on this day!

It was left up to me to inform him of this fact, as well as to tell him that he would now need to supply us with additional information and paperwork. Can you see where this is heading? Let's just say that for the next 15 minutes, a very angry Mr. Smith enthusiastically (and very loudly I might add) made me aware of his displeasure with our organization. Although he raised some very good points in his verbal barrage, the fact remained that he did not fill out the paperwork correctly and, subsequently, his account could not be opened that day and he could not trade. It was his responsibility to complete the application and he had not fulfilled his obligation.

▪ TRYING TO MAKE IT EASY ▪

Online brokerage firms do not intentionally try to make opening an account a difficult process. To the contrary, when you go online or receive your application in the mail, be confident that your online broker has done everything possible to simplify the procedure. It may not always seem that way when you peruse a brokerage application, but brokerage firms go to great lengths to make opening an account as easy as possible. They would like your introduction to their firm to be as enjoyable and seamless as can be. This first encounter sets the tone for your future business relationship. Believe me, they want to put their best foot forward.

You may have noticed a lot of online brokerage advertisements recently, in the print media, on television, and via online banners. Their messages ring loud and clear—these firms want your business. But keep in mind that getting your business comes with a price tag. Online brokerage firms are spending millions of dollars on technology upgrades and advertising to get you to notice them. In 1999 alone, brokerage firm advertising reached $1.2 billion according to Competitive Media Reporting. Firms understand that you have many choices in the marketplace. The last thing an online brokerage firm wants to see is your committing to opening an online account with it, and then reversing that decision because its application process is too difficult.

Online brokers are faced with a dilemma. They are caught in the middle between making the application easy for you and making sure that they get the vital "know your customer" information they need to have. When establishing your account, your online brokerage firm must exercise due diligence. It is required by the Securities and Exchange Commission's New York Stock Exchange (NYSE) Rule 405 (which I'll discuss in more detail later) as well as its own in-house compliance regulations to get and maintain on file such data as your name, legal address, Social Security number, date of birth, citizenship status, employment status, income, net worth, and investment objectives. You may think that this information is unimportant but your firm doesn't, and frankly that's what counts. Remember, brokerage firms would not request information from you if it was not necessary. They too would like to make their lives a little easier.

■ THE APPLICATION: YOUR BROKER'S PERSPECTIVE ■

Technology has done wonders for the world of online investing, but when it comes to setting up your online brokerage account, it's still done the old-fashioned way—by people. Brokerage firms have come a long way in streamlining the application delivery system. Filling out applications online and downloading applications to your desktop are two quick and easy methods of getting brokerage applications into your hands.

The firms would love to see these methods become standard procedure because they would reduce the firm's set-up costs for a new account and would enable you to get up and running more quickly, thereby permitting you to implement your trading strategies sooner. Such quick methods allow the online broker to close your business in a timely manner and garner valuable customer satisfaction points. Brokerage firms want to see you happy. It is a popular doctrine in business, including the online brokerage business, that it is much cheaper to keep you as a customer than it is to acquire a new one. Online brokerage account acquisition costs have run up as high as $627 per new customer account, according to Credit Suisse First Boston.

Rest assured that your online broker is doing everything imaginable to develop ways to shorten the time period between your decision to open an account and its ability to establish it. But there is one aspect of opening an account that cannot be bypassed. People ultimately review the information you submit on your account application. This is no small task. The broker's representative needs to be a General Securities Principal (a person who has successfully completed the Series 8 NASD exam). If you also wish to trade options on your account, your option agreement must be reviewed and approved by a Senior Registered Options Principal (a person who has successfully completed the NASD Series 4 exam). Approving an application takes time.

It has been my experience that firms do a tremendous job in setting up your brokerage accounts. The average turnaround time from the moment an application is received in the new accounts department until an account is established on the system has normally been between 24 and 48 hours. This is a respectable turnaround time when you consider that each section of each application needs to be scrutinized, reviewed, and approved before any account can be opened and approved for trading.

It's a Numbers Game

To give you some idea about what is going on in these departments, let me throw some numbers at you. According to a Piper Jaffray report for the second quarter of 1999, online brokerage firms opened the following number of accounts for that quarter: National Discount Brokerage (NDB), 23,000 accounts; Datek, 49,000 accounts; Ameritrade, 77,000 accounts; Waterhouse, 155,000 accounts; Schwab, 300,000; E*Trade, 332,000 accounts; and Fidelity Investments, 339,000 accounts. This is a snapshot of one moment in time, but when you do the math, you realize that these representatives are opening a heck of a lot of accounts on a daily basis, and these numbers do not even reflect the applications that were rejected.

These statistics should make it clear what you are up against. It is a numbers game. At these levels, firms have tried to design their applications so that a representative can review your information quickly and thoroughly. These new-account representatives do not have the luxury of spending an inordinate amount of time with each application. They look for the information in the required fields to be filled out completely (and they hope legibly) and if it is not, the account is designated not in good order, and they move on to the next application. That's just the way it is. It has to be. Brokerage firms could never process all of the applications that they receive if they did not stick closely to this system. Take note: Brokerage firms do not take joy in rejecting your application. It is not good for business. They will only reject your application if they have no other choice.

Regulations and Rule 405

The Securities Exchange Act of 1934 established the Securities and Exchange Commission (SEC), which is entrusted with regulating the securities markets and protecting investors (that means you). The act of 1934 encompasses a wide area of regulatory oversight, including the regulation of the exchanges and over-the-counter markets, the regulation of broker-dealers, the regulation of credit (also known as margin) by the Federal Reserve Board, the regulation of client accounts, and customer protection rules. Your online brokerage firm under NYSE Rule 405, Know Your Customer, requires that all exchange members exercise due diligence to learn essential facts about every customer and account. Below is an excerpt of NYSE 405 taken from the *New York Stock Exchange Guide, Constitution and Rules.*

Diligence as to Accounts

Rule 405. Every member organization is required through a general partner, a principal executive officer or a person or persons designated under the provisions of Rule 342(b) (1)[#2342] to

(1) Use due diligence to learn the essential facts relative to every customer, every order, every cash or margin account accepted or carried by such organization and every person holding power of attorney over any account accepted or carried by such organization.

Firms need you to give them all the information requested on the application because your firm is acting in your best interest. It uses the information to make informed decisions about your online trading account. Will you be permitted to trade on margin? What options level will you be eligible to trade? Will it be covered call writing, spreads, naked equities, or naked index options? Firms need you to give them accurate and truthful information if they are to set up a suitable account for you. Otherwise they cannot.

▪ THE APPLICATION: YOUR PERSPECTIVE ▪

I hope you now have a better understanding of what your online brokerage firm is looking for and why. But what items should you consider and how can you avoid falling into the various new-account application traps? After all, when all is said and done, completing the application is your responsibility.

In most cases, except for special circumstances, such as a trust, a corporation, a partnership, or an investment club account, you will be filling out a standard application form. You may also decide that you would like to have options trading on the account or have a friend trade for you; or you may need to transfer an account from another brokerage firm or bank. For these reasons, you will need additional paperwork, such as an option agreement, a trading authorization form, and a transfer of assets (TOA) form.

If the firm can get the proper paperwork into your hands and make sure that you fill out the application correctly, it can get you up and running without a hitch. Well, that certainly sounds simple enough. What type of an account will you be opening and what type of paperwork will you need?

■ ACCOUNT REGISTRATION TYPES ■

Online brokerage firms offer two standard accounts: cash accounts and margin accounts. A *cash account* is exactly what the words imply; all security transactions will be settled in cash—in other words, cold hard dollars. When you purchase a security in a cash account, you must have the entire amount of the purchase available at the time of the trade settlement. If you're buying $25,000 worth of stock, then you must have $25,000 in the account to cover the trade.

A *margin account* allows you to borrow money from your broker to pay for a security purchase. A margin account provides a loan from your broker that is charged interest and eventually must be paid back. Your stock is used as collateral for the loan. Your online broker has strict policies regarding the amount of money it requires from you in a margin transaction. For example, if you purchased $50,000 worth of securities on margin (borrowing money) and the broker required a 50 percent margin requirement, you would need to deposit $25,000 (50 percent of the trade) and the broker would loan you the rest. This is not just a paper transaction; you owe the firm money if you do not pay for the stock in full. A margin loan is a demand loan and can be called in at any time. As in any form of borrowing, do not overextend yourself. Borrowing money against your stock can be risky, as I will explain in more detail in Chapter 5.

The Margin Agreement

The margin agreement is actually pretty straightforward. At this point, you just need to decide if you do or do not want margin capability. This section of the application is not asking you if you want to trade on margin, that is, to borrow money from your broker to buy stocks on margin; it is simply asking whether you want a cash account or a margin account. (Again, I'll discuss margin in more detail in Chapter 5, but for now I'm only concerned with getting you through the application process.) Actually, when you sign your brokerage application, there is a very good chance that you are also signing a margin agreement. In fact, some firms require that you open a margin account just to do business with them.

Don't take offense; this is simply the way some online brokerage firms conduct business. Although they would prefer that you maintain a margin account, it is ultimately your choice. During my 12 years of working in the industry, I have never heard a colleague suggest to a customer that the customer open a margin account simply so the firm could collect margin interest. It is unethical and is just not done. Simply having a margin account does not mean that you will pay margin interest. As in the case of credit cards, you pay margin interest only if you owe your brokerage firm money! Interest kicks in only when you buy stocks or make cash withdrawals that exceed the cash balance in your account.

The decision to have margin or not is yours. However, I can tell you from my experience that by giving you more investing flexibility, it may be easier for you in the long run to agree to maintain a margin agreement on file.

Here is a quick example. Say, for instance, that you have $10,000 in cash in your online brokerage account. You sent a check the day before for $5,000 to get your balance up to $15,000, but the check has not been deposited yet. The stock you have been following for a week is finally at your desired price. It's time to make the purchase. You would like to buy 1,000 shares at the current market price of $14, but your account only has $10,000 in it. You go online to trade, but the system tells you that you have insufficient funds. When you originally opened your account, you checked off that you did not want margin. So now what do you do? You contact your broker and explain your predicament (not enough cash and no margin); the representative calmly explains that he can only take a trade up to your $10,000 cash balance because you don't have a margin account.

Had you had a margin agreement on file, your order for 1,000 shares could have been taken. You would have received the number of shares that you wanted and at the price you targeted. Your check would probably have arrived before the three-day trade settlement and you would not have been charged any margin interest. Even if the check arrived after the trade settlement, the worst situation would have been that you would be charged interest on the amount owed on the trade. Compare this small interest charge to the cost of missing out on the trade altogether. With only a cash account on file, you may have missed the trade that you so patiently awaited.

Of course, nothing is ever this cut and dried. If you were a long-standing customer with your firm, it may have taken the trade for you or you could have had your bank wire the additional money into the account. But the point is that if you simply keep a margin agreement on file, even if you never use margin (borrow money), it will give you greater flexibility, as noted above. It should also be noted that if you check off that you would like a margin account, your brokerage firm will run a cursory credit check, which is done for all margin accounts.

Individual Accounts

These accounts are also known as single accounts. Only one individual, who is considered the account holder and whose name appears on the registration, can exercise control over the account. This person needs to be at least of majority age in the state where the account will be registered. Most brokerage firms will not allow you to open an account unless you are 18 years or older. (Some firms may require you to be 21 years or older.) An individual account has only one beneficial owner. Unless trading authorization is granted to a third party, the registered owner is the only person who can execute buy and sell orders on the account. This person is also the only individual who can request cash or security distributions from the account. An individual account is eligible for margin and options trading. The individual whose name will appear on the account registration as the registered owner must sign the account application.

Individual	Mr. Harry Smith
	1 Main Street
	Boston, MA 02110
Individual New-Account Application	yes
Margin Agreement	yes
Option Agreement	if desired (all levels)
Transfer Paperwork	if needed
Trading Authorization	if desired (ltd. or full)
Signature(s)	owner

Joint Accounts

This type of registration typically has the names of two or more individuals as registered owners on the account. Some firms, but not all, will permit three names to appear on the registration. If you want to open an account with four or more individuals, I suggest you contact your broker because it may not allow four. As with the individual account, registered owners appearing on the account registration under joint tenancy must be at least 18 years or older; you are not permitted to open a joint account with a minor. If you wish to establish an account with a minor, you would more likely consider a Uniform Gifts to Minors Act account (discussed in the next section).

The persons appearing on the registration of a joint account have the ability to control the investments in the account as well as request distributions of cash and stock from the account. Any check or stock certificate requests will be distributed in the name of all joint tenants and mailed to the address of record. All owners of a joint account must sign the new account forms. It is customary for brokerage firms to use the tax ID number or Social Security number of the individual whose name appears first on the account registration for year-end tax reporting.

Joint accounts permit margin and options trading. If options trading is requested on the account, all registered owners must complete and sign the option agreement. In determining option eligibility levels, a firm's Registered Options Principal will look at all owners' backgrounds but will focus primarily on the account owner who has the highest trading qualifications and experience.

Owners of joint accounts need to be designated at the time of application generally as either joint tenants in common or joint tenants with right of survivorship. These two categories have different consequences on the death of one or more of the registered owners.

JOINT TENANTS IN COMMON (JTIC). This designation stipulates that a deceased tenant's ownership in the account is fractional and retained by that tenant's estate. It is not passed on to the surviving tenant(s). For example, if under a JTIC agreement ownership interest is divided 70 percent for one owner and 30 percent for the other, this is the fractional percentage of the account, which would pass into the deceased owner's estate. Assets enter into the deceased's will and are distributed accordingly.

JOINT TENANTS WITH RIGHT OF SURVIVORSHIP
(JTWROS). Under a JTWROS agreement, each owner of the account has an equal and undivided interest in the cash and securities in the account. Unlike JTIC, a JTWROS designation stipulates
that a deceased owner's interest in the account passes to the surviving tenant(s). This transfer of assets escapes probate, although
estate taxes may be due depending on the amount of assets transferred. Under this circumstance the surviving tenant(s) need to
supply verifying documentation of the death of the deceased tenant as well as fill out new application forms to have the account
reregistered under the surviving tenant(s) ownership.

Joint Account	Mr. Harry Smith
	Mrs. Nancy Smith
	1 Main Street
	Boston, MA 02110
Joint Tenant New-Account Application	yes
Margin Agreement	yes
Option Agreement	if desired (all levels)
Transfer Paperwork	if needed
Trading Authorization	if desired (ltd. or full)
Signature(s)	all owners

Uniform Gifts to Minors Act (UGMA)/Uniform Transfers to Minors Act (UTMA) Accounts

These accounts are used primarily by individuals as a means of
transferring taxable income and capital gains to a child who at the
time is usually in a lower tax bracket. This is accomplished by setting up the account with the child's Social Security number, which
you must supply for the minor. The account requires an adult to
act as custodian for the child or minor. The person who makes a
gift to the minor is known as the *donor* of the securities. All gifts
by the donor to the minor are registered in the name of the custodian for the benefit of the minor. The minor is considered to be
the beneficial owner of all cash and securities in the account. The
donor and the custodian do not have to be the same person nor
necessarily have to be a family member.

The custodian manages all gifts to the minor until the minor reaches the age of majority. All gifts under a UGMA/UTMA account are *irrevocable,* meaning that the donor may not take back the gift! The assets become the sole possession of the minor at the time the minor reaches the age of majority for the appropriate state. The donor cannot stipulate how the assets should be used after the minor reaches the age of majority at the time the property is transferred into the minor's name.

In completing the UGMA/UTMA account application, you must fill out the custodian's name and legal address and the minor's name and Social Security number. You do not need to have the minor sign the application. In most cases this will be impossible because the minor may not even be old enough to know how to write.

The custodian has full control over trading in the minor's account. Firms do not permit margin trading and most likely will restrict options trading to the most conservative level. There can be only one custodian and one minor or beneficial owner for each account. You are also not permitted to have two persons acting as custodians for one minor or a single custodian acting on behalf of two minors. Each account must benefit only one minor.

Custodial Accounts	Mrs. Casey Jones, CUST
	FBO Katie Jones, UGMA
	2 Main Street
	Boston, MA 02110
UGMA/UTMA New-Account Application	yes
Margin Agreement	not permitted
Option Agreement	if desired (level 1)
Transfer Paperwork	if needed
Trading Authorization	if permitted by firm (ltd. or full)
Signature(s)	custodian's

Trust Accounts

Trust accounts are also known as fiduciary accounts. Cash or securities are placed in the account under trust for someone else. The manager or trustee of the account is considered the fiduciary.

A fiduciary is any person legally appointed and authorized to represent another person and to make any decisions necessary for the prudent management of the account. Fiduciaries can be trustees designated to administer the trust, executors who are designated in a decedent's will to manage the affairs of the estate, administrators appointed by the courts to liquidate the estate of a person who died without a will, receivers appointed by a judge in a bankruptcy, or conservators for persons incompetent to handle their own affairs.

Online brokerage firms permit margin and options trading for your trust account if the trust agreement itself allows it, which is why firms require you to complete special paperwork. A specific trust application has been developed by some firms to avoid the need to fill out a separate Trust Certification of Investment Power (TCIP) form. If your firm does not have this type of application, you must complete a separate TCIP form. Your TCIP form is kept on file in place of your entire trust document. All trustees must take care in signing the application and/or TCIP form if required.

Trust Account	Nancy A. Doe, TTEE
	Smith Cardiology Pension
	Plan 5/6/99
	FBO Laura Anne
	3 Main Street
	Boston, MA 02110
Trust New-Account Application	yes
Margin Agreement	if permitted by trust
Option Agreement	if permitted by trust
	(all levels)
Transfer Paperwork	if needed
Trading Authorization	if desired (ltd. or full)
Trust Certification of Investment Power	yes (if needed)
Signature(s)	all trustees

Business/Corporate Accounts

It will take a little more work on your part to get this type of account set up properly. Besides the new-account application form, the most important form required is the corporate resolution.

Unless you are an unincorporated business and your online broker requires a resolution of unincorporated business form, you must complete the corporate resolution.

Corporate or business accounts permit margin and option trading. The level of option trading that would be granted is commensurate with the client information submitted by the officers of the corporation. This account will also allow third-party trading if a trade authorization form is completed. A unique aspect of the application requirements is that you must affix or stamp the application with your corporate seal. If a corporate seal is unavailable, you most likely will be required to send in your articles of incorporation. Do not forget to affix your corporate seal to avoid unwanted delays in setting up the account.

The signature requirements for this type of account are also a little different. Most firms request that you identify the officers or individuals who will be authorized by the corporate resolution to transact business on the account in one field, while in another they will request the signature of a person whose name does not appear in the aforementioned field, unless, of course, you are the sole officer of the corporation. It is extremely important that you read through this application very carefully and execute the specific requirements asked by your firm.

Corporate	Samantha Lynn, Inc.
	One Main Street
	Boston, MA 02110
Corporate New-Account Application	yes
Margin Agreement	yes
Option Agreement	if desired (all levels)
Transfer Paperwork	if needed
Trading Authorization	if desired (ltd. or full)
Corporate resolution	yes
Signature(s)	all officers

Partnerships and Investments Clubs

A partnership is an unincorporated association of two or more individuals. Most online brokerage firms permit partnership accounts to trade on margin and trade options. Opening a partnership account requires a new-account application and a partnership agreement form. The partnership agreement stipulates which partners can make transactions for the account and requires the signatures of either all general partners or, at the minimum, a number sufficient to open the account.

The general partners are those individuals who are directly responsible for the day-to-day management of the partnership's activities. Individual acts by general partners are binding on the other partners. General partners are usually liable for the partnership's total liabilities as opposed to limited partners, who invest only money and are not involved in management decisions. Limited partner liabilities are just that—limited to partners' dollar investments.

Partnership	Ashley and Kelly Partners
	One Main Street
	Boston, MA 02110
Partnership New-Account	
Application	yes
Margin Agreement	yes
Option Agreement	if desired
Transfer Paperwork	if needed
Trading Authorization	if desired
Partnership agreement	yes
Signature(s)	all partners

An investment club is a group of people who have pooled their assets and ideas to make joint investment decisions. Investment clubs can be a great way for you to get involved in the markets if you are a small investor. Not only are you combining your assets to possibly make bigger investments, but you are also commingling your knowledge to learn more about investing from other club members.

Online firms differ in their treatment of investment clubs regarding what is permissible when trading. Some firms allow you to trade on margin, whereas others don't. Some may permit unlimited option trading levels, but others may not. The one commonality with all firms is their requirement that you fill out specific investment club new-account paperwork. You need to have the names of all the investment club members on the application. Be sure to follow your particular firm's application instructions to the letter when it comes to signing these documents.

Investment Club	Bridgette Investment Club
	One Main Street
	Boston, MA 02110
Investment Club New-Account	
Application	yes
Margin Agreement	if permitted by firm
Option Agreement	if permitted by firm
Transfer Paperwork	if needed
Trading Authorization	not applicable
Investment Club Formlet	yes
Signature(s)	members

Individual Retirement Accounts (IRAs)

IRA accounts are tax-qualified retirement plans. Except for Roth IRAs, they allow you to make tax-deductible contributions if you qualify and earn interest, dividends, and capital gains tax-free. These accounts must be opened with a retirement brokerage application only! Many customers request an application but don't specify that it is for a retirement account and inevitably are sent a standard application. Customers then simply cross out the words "Brokerage Application" and replace them with "Retirement Account" in the belief that this is sufficient; it isn't.

Firms have recently designed new application forms to accommodate standard IRAs, Roth IRAs, and rollover IRAs. One application can be used for all three account types. You merely check off which account you desire. These accounts permit third-party trading (limited trading authorization only) but not margin trading. Because you are not permitted to trade on margin, your option-trading level is limited. Online firms differ in the option-trading level they permit in a qualified retirement account. Your online brokerage firm's in-house regulations dictate at what option level you can trade. Some firms allow only the purchase of options, whereas others allow selling options. Check with your broker for its specific policy.

You will need to complete *all* sections of the application. (Remember no margin). It is important that you designate a beneficiary on your IRA; if you forget, call your firm to ask for an additional beneficiary form. As with all individually registered new brokerage accounts, the registered owner must sign the application.

IRA, Roth IRA, Rollover IRA	Online Broker CUST IRA
	FBO Mr. Kelly Gilbert
	One Main Street
	Boston, MA 02110
Retirement New-Account	
Application	yes
Margin Agreement	not permitted
Option Agreement	if desired
	firm decides level (1 or 2)
Transfer Paperwork	if needed
Trading Authorization	if desired (limited only)
Signature(s)	account owner

■ THE OPTION AGREEMENT ■

The option agreement is normally a separate application form in addition to your new-account application. You must complete this form in its entirety. You need to be aware of several levels of options trading. Each level allows you to implement the various options trading strategies. The option trading levels can range from a simple buy of options contracts to putting on more sophisticated options spreads or combinations (see Figure 3.1).

For those of you who may not be familiar with options trading, here is a brief overview. Options are considered derivative investments, which means that their value is based on an underlying instrument such as a stock. An options contract gives the owner (the person who bought the option) the right to either buy or sell the underlying stock at a specified price (strike price) until a specified date in the future (expiration date). Call options give the options owner the right to buy stock (call away) at the strike price, whereas put options give the options owner the right to sell stock (put to) at the strike price. For either right the owner pays the option seller a cash premium. Options contracts have a limited life and expire on what is known as the expiration date.

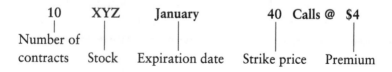

Figure 3.1 // Option Level Chart

Level 0 or A	Covered call writing	Margin not required
Level 1 or B	Level 0(A) plus purchases of calls and puts (equity/index) and purchases of straddles and combinations (equity/index)	Margin not required
Level 2 or C	Levels 0(A) and 1(B) plus equity spreads	Margin typically required
Level 3 or D	Levels 0(A), 1(B), and 2(C) plus index spreads, uncovered (naked) equities, uncovered (naked) straddles/combinations on equities	Margin required
Level 4 or E	Levels 0(A), 1(B), 2(C), and 3(D) plus uncovered (naked) index and uncovered (naked) straddles/combinations on indexes	Margin required

In this example, 10 represents the number of contracts, XYZ is the underlying stock, January is the expiration date (equity options expire on the third Friday of the specified month), 40 is the strike price at which XYZ stock can be bought in the case of calls, and $4 is the premium paid by the owner to the seller for the option contracts. Each contract represents 100 shares of stock; therefore this contract gives the owner the right to buy 1,000 shares (10 × 100) of XYZ at $40 anytime until the third Friday of January. The customer pays a total of $4,000 for this right (10 × 100 × $4 premium).

Buying calls are considered bullish, and buying puts are considered bearish. In the above example, the owner of the call option hopes the stock trades well above $40 in the open market, say up to $50. The call option owner anticipates a rise in XYZ's price. At that point the owner can exercise the option contract and buy XYZ at $40, then turn around and sell it in the open market at the higher price of $50. The reverse applies to put options. An owner of a put option wants to see the price of the underlying stock fall. The basic trading philosophy behind put and call options can be summarized in the following chart.

	Options Buyer	Stock Price	Options Seller	Stock Price
Calls	Bullish	↑	Bearish	↓
Puts	Bearish	↓	Bullish	↑

Trading options can be complicated and risky. As the Option Level Chart (Figure 3.1) indicates, your online broker may allow you to buy options, sell covered options, sell uncovered options, or buy and sell spreads and straddles. If these terms are unfamiliar to you, don't complete the option agreement. You should understand these strategies fully before trading any of them. There are many educational books and Web sites that can assist you in better understanding the complexities of options trading. I have found that the Options Institute at <CBOE.com> is a terrific free resource for learning more about the basics of options. It teaches how the various options strategies can help you reach your unique investment objectives.

Getting back to the option application, online brokerage firms designate the different option levels in many ways. Some firms assign numbers from 0 to 4, others use a scale from 1 to 5, and still others may use a combination of numbers and letters. The thing to keep clear is that the lower levels, Levels 0 or A for example, refer to the most conservative option strategies. The higher levels, Levels 5 or E, pertain to the riskier option strategies. The Option Level Chart in Figure 3.1 does not reflect any specific brokerage firm's option levels. All firms are different. The chart merely shows the progression in labeling option levels from the most conservative to the riskiest.

It is the responsibility of the firm's Registered Options Principal (ROP) to grant you an option level that is suitable according to your investment objectives, financial situation, and your investing experience. Specific factors that firms consider are your income, your liquid net worth, your total net worth, and your trading experience (both in options and equities). Although firms review these criteria differently, they must all use some type of guideline to approve your option level for trading purposes.

A common mistake by an investor filling out the option agreement application would be to forget to check off an investment objective or check off a more conservative objective, such as preservation of capital, while requesting a more aggressive option level. An ROP may deny this customer the riskier option level under these circumstances. It is the ROP's responsibility both to you and to the firm to be certain you are not trading at an option level that is not supported by your investment objectives, your finances, and your investing experience, which you have indicated on the option agreement form.

Your online brokerage firm approaches the business of trading options very seriously. If there is any doubt concerning your option application, your firm's decisions will lean to conservatism. For example, when an option agreement came up for review at one of my old firms and the customer met all net worth and income criteria but failed to indicate an investment objective, the account was approved for a more conservative option level, regardless of what the customer requested. The level could not be upgraded until we could verify the client's investment objective. It is for this reason that I have been so emphatic about the importance of completing *all* sections of an application *accurately* and *truthfully*.

To give you a better understanding of how your firm may actually review your option agreement, I have put together the following chart. It is not to be used to obtain an option level greater than the one suitable for you. In fact, looking over this chart may warn you that you are considering an option strategy that is too risky in light of your investment objectives, your financial background, and your investing experience.

	Income	Liquid Net Worth	Net Worth	Experience	Investment Objective
Level 0 or A	$25,000	$10,000	$20,000	investing 1 year	conservative
Level 1 or B	$25,000	$20,000	$30,000	investing 1 year	conservative
Level 2 or C	$30,000	$20,000	$40,000	1 year investing options	conservative/ moderate
Level 3 or D	$50,000	$35,000	$50,000	1 year investing options	aggressive/ speculative
Level 4 or E	$70,000	$50,000	$100,000	1 year investing index options	more aggressive/ speculative

This chart is for your informational use only and is not brokerage firm specific. Some firms may not permit any clients to trade the riskier option levels, whereas other firms may require an income level above $25,000 just to open a standard brokerage account merely to trade stocks. Meeting any or all of these criteria at your current online brokerage firm will in no way guarantee that you will be approved for your desired option level.

■ OTHER THINGS TO CONSIDER ■

Online Brokerage Account Insurance

Your online brokerage account is insured. The Securities Investor Protection Corporation (SIPC) provides the insurance that online firms carry, but brokerage firms are not banks and are therefore not protected by the Federal Deposit Insurance Corporation (FDIC).

Under the Investors Protection Act of 1970, Congress established the SIPC. All online brokerage firms registered with the Securities and Exchange Commission (SEC) and with national stock exchanges are required to be members of the SIPC. The SIPC insures the cash and securities in a brokerage account up to a maximum of $500,000, with a limit of $100,000 on cash and cash equivalents. Most firms carry additional private insurance into the millions of dollars on your accounts. Sorry to tell you, but SIPC won't insure you against lousy stock picking. It is important to understand that *SIPC insurance does not protect you against market risks*. It insures your account only against the failure of your online brokerage firm. In the event that your firm fails and becomes insolvent, the SIPC will attempt to merge your firm into another or liquidate your firm's assets in order to pay you off up to the SIPC's coverage maximums.

Signature Guarantees

From time to time your online broker may request documentation that requires a signature guarantee. If you want to change ownership of assets held in an account (moving assets from an individually registered account to a corporate account, for example) or if you are giving someone else trading authority on your account, a signature guarantee may be required. The signature guarantee is a security measure to protect you from fraud. A notarized signature by a notary public, however, is not a signature guarantee.

You can get a signature guarantee at your local bank, your online broker's office, or any other firm that is a member of the New York Stock Exchange or National Association of Securities Dealers, a credit union, or a savings association. Unlike a notary public, these institutions are financially liable for the authenticity of your signature. You present a representative of one of these institutions with valid identification and sign the documents in the representative's presence. Some banks or brokerage firms may charge a small fee for this service unless, of course, you have an account in good standing with them, in which case they may waive their fee.

Verify Your New Account Information

We have covered a lot of ground in this chapter and thus I'm confident that you will make it through this first step of setting up an online brokerage account more smoothly! But your work is not yet over. After you receive confirmation of your new online brokerage account, be sure to verify that all the information is correct.

As we learned earlier, online firms process thousands of applications each day. You are responsible for entering your information correctly, but sometimes mistakes are made (remember, to err is human). A digit on your Social Security number may be transposed, your mailing address or telephone number may be off, or you may not have been approved for margin or at the option level you desired. Correct these mistakes *immediately,* before you enter your first trade, because by then it could be too late. Discovering mistakes now will save you time—and money—in the future.

▪ TROUBLESHOOTING THE ONLINE BROKERAGE APPLICATION ▪

A standard brokerage application for a new account is shown in Figure 3.2. Your online brokerage firm needs you to fill out each section accurately, completely, and truthfully. Remember too that setting up your account is not automatic. You must do your job by completing the proper application completely, and your brokerage firm will do its part by setting up your account correctly and in a timely fashion. You cannot control what happens at your brokerage firm, but you certainly can control what *you* do.

FIGURE 3.2 // Customer New-Account Application

Section 1—Account Ownership
Account registration
___ Individual   ___ Custodial Account (UTM/
___ Joint Tenants—Rights of Survivorship under the State

Do you have all the paperwork necessary? Trading authorizations forms, option agreements, and TCIP form. Do you have the correct application? Corporate, Investment club, Trust, IRA.

In most cases, you must be over 18 to open an account.

t Tenants in

Keep correct contact information updated. Statements and confirms sent to record address. Keep phone number current so broker can contact you in case of emergency!

Name___
nt Street
ddress

r's Name___

State

phone Number ___

Account Owner/Minor

Social Security number and tax ID used for year-end IRS reporting! Some firms may not permit online trading without a valid tax ID number.

Date of Birth   ___/___/___
Social Security Number ___
Tax ID Number   ___
Citizenship ___ U.S. ___ Resident Alien ___ Non-resid
Employment Status ___ Employed ___ Self-Employed
Occupation ___
Employer's Name and Address ___
Affiliations ___ Employed for a stock exchange, a member firm of an exchange of the NASD
___ Director, 10% shareholder or policy making executive of a public company?

They're not checking to see if you are a good employee. If you work in the industry, duplicate statements may need to be sent to your employer.

Section 2—Financial Information
Bank Reference ___
Investment Objectives:
___ Conservation of capital ___ Income
Annual Income: ___ Less than $20k ___ $20,00
___ Over $101,000
Estimated Net Worth: ___ Under $30k ___ $30,001–$50,000 ___ $50,001–$100,000
___ $100,001–$500,000 ___ Over $500,000
Liquid Net Worth: ___ $25,001–$50,000 ___ $50,001–$100,000 ___ $100,001–$500,000
___ Over $500,001

This section is key. It determines your eligibility for margin as well as your approval for options trading. Your broker is not selling this information. It needs it to perform its fiduciary responsibility. Fill this out, completely!

Section 3—Investment Information and Options Tra
Overall Investment Experience: ___ Limited ___ Good ___ E
Years Trading: ___ Stocks ___ Bonds ___ Equity Options ___ Inde
Years Option Experience: ___ Purchasing ___ Covered Writing ___ Spreads ___ Naked Equity
Puts/Calls ___ Naked Index Puts/Calls ___ Other Combinations
Trading Plans: _ Covered Writing _ Purchases _ Spreads _ Uncovered Wriiting. Combinations
and Spreads _ Uncovered Writing (Index Options) and Combinations

Don't get burnt here. Make sure your investment objectives match the option level you are seeking. Be truthful and honest.

Section 4—Margin

Endorse certificates properly. For transfer of assets, attach copy of latest statement.

you like to be eligible for margin transactions? ___ YES ___ NO

n **5—Funding Your Account**
___ WITH CERTIFICATES ___ TRANSFER OF ASSETS ___ Full or ___ Partial

No one is asking you to borrow any money here. This simply gives you margin capabilities. Check yes and move on.

n **6—Customer Agreements and Signatures**
ner must READ the Customer Agreement and SIGN this
re of Owner   Date   Signature of Joint O
___/___/___

Don't forget to sign the application. Be certain ALL owners sign!

CHAPTER 4

Funding Your Account

■ WHY CAN'T 1 JUST WRITE YOU A CHECK? ■

Every application will ask you, "How will you be funding your new account?" Easy enough, right? You'll just give your online broker a check and be up and running. Many times it is that simple but not always. What if, after depositing your check, you immediately wish to trade stocks, bonds, or option contracts? Maybe you would like to leverage those deposited funds to trade on margin or possibly buy shares of an initial public offering (IPO). You could be in for a rude awakening if you attempt these types of transactions, because some firms may not permit them right away.

Unfortunately, you would not know this unless you attempted your first online trade and were denied. Fund-clearing policies are stated in the customer agreement, but if you're not specifically looking for them, they won't jump out at you. Discovering that you cannot trade at just the time you're attempting to enter the trade could make you miss the market, especially if the stock price is moving. As with most aspects of online trading, things are not always as simple as they appear.

If you can't deposit a check, then what can you do? How will you fund your new online brokerage account if all of your assets are held in stocks? What is the correct way to deposit physical shares or transfer stocks from one broker to another? How long will these types of transfers take, and will they keep you out of the market?

These are the issues that I'll tackle in this chapter. You have completed your application successfully, so your next step is to fund the account in a manner that will afford you the best opportunity to trade when you decide to. Who knows, your first trade may be in two months, but if it's sooner, what particular funding method will allow you to trade now? You don't want to lose money by being locked out of the market because you funded your new account in an inappropriate manner. You need to be aware of your funding options and the pluses and minuses of each one. Choose a method that meets your trading needs.

■ REMEMBER, ONLINE BROKERS ARE NOT BANKS ■

Before I proceed with the various ways to fund your account, it is important to understand that online brokerage firms are not banks. Although they receive deposits, offer check-writing accounts, and provide debit and credit cards to customers, they are still online brokers. One of the main differences between banks and brokerages was pointed out in Chapter 3: Online brokerage firms are *not* insured under the Federal Deposit Insurance Corporation (FDIC).

It was the Glass-Steagall Act of 1933 that attempted to erect a barrier between investment banking and commercial banking. The purpose of the act was to protect bank depositors from the inherent risks when commercial banks engaged in investment banking and underwriting activities in the early 1930s. The act was a direct result of the collapse of many securities firms and commercial banks during the Great Depression. Among other things, the act originally forbade commercial banks from owning brokerage houses. Today, the distinction between banks and online brokerage firms is becoming noticeably less clear. The Glass-Steagall Act is slowly losing its teeth. In fact, there is a very good chance that your online brokerage firm may be owned by, or is an owner of, a commercial bank. However, subtle differences still exist, and by recognizing them, you will be able to trade more efficiently.

Clearing Your Deposited Check

Online brokerage firms take longer to clear checks than do banks. It can take up to 7 days for a personal check to be collected at your online brokerage firm, whereas most banks can clear these same checks within 48 hours. This slower clearing process may affect your ability to trade options, buy into IPOs, or engage in margin transactions. Also, for example, if you deposited $10,000 into your new online account, purchased $20,000 of marginable securities, and immediately sold them for $30,000, most online brokerage firms would put a hold of up to ten days on any request for proceeds from this sale. They would not release any funds from the account until they had collected the original deposit of $10,000. This means that a quick trading profit does not always translate into quick cash in hand.

Bounced Checks

The unfortunate occurrence of bouncing a deposited check into your online brokerage account has potentially greater ramifications than merely bouncing a check from your checking account at a bank. It happens to everyone at one time or another and is usually an honest mistake, but with your online broker the issue is cut and dried. Mistake or not, if you bounce a check, the game is over; that check is history. Where your commercial bank would redeposit the check (and of course charge you a fee), your online broker may not. By not redepositing the check, you would now be open to two alarming problems.

First, if the check had been submitted to cover a purchase of stock and subsequently bounced, there is a high probability that you would not be able to make another payment to cover the trade by its settlement date. (Equity trades settle under the terms of trade date plus three business days.) If you did not sign a margin agreement (covered in Chapter 3) and the trade was therefore executed in a cash account, you would be in jeopardy of reneging on the trade. When buying stock in a cash account, you are telling the broker that you will pay for the trade in full by settlement. Not having cleared funds in the account by the trade's settlement date could lead to an additional late charge of up to $20 or, even worse, the shares could be sold with commission in the open market and you would absorb any losses that resulted.

As I suggested in Chapter 3, had you signed a margin agreement and had available margin from your existing stock positions, a bounced check would have been a nonissue in terms of the trade settlement. The stock purchase would have been covered by your margin account (the loan from your broker) and you could then have merely resubmitted another check to cover the trade. Margin in this case would have performed much as your reserved credit account does on your bank checking account. And like reserve credit, you would have been liable for interest charges for borrowing money from your broker.

The second problem with bouncing a check is that your online brokerage firm does not take kindly to bounced checks. Make no mistake about it; regardless of how warm and fuzzy some online brokerage advertisements may be, your online brokerage firm wants you to uphold your end of the agreement with it. If you purchase a stock, you're expected to meet your obligation and settle the trade. Firms don't want to hear that you can't balance your checkbook. Even if they wanted to give you a break, most times they can't. Online brokerage firms are accountable to the SEC and the NASD as well as to various regulations. Bouncing one check will not put you in disfavor with your online broker, but bouncing several checks, innocently or not, could lead to more serious penalties. I'll put it to you bluntly; if you continuously bounce checks, your firm will not want to do business with you. The simple solution: Don't bounce any checks.

This Is Not Your Local ATM

Moving cash around in an online brokerage account is not as simple as moving balances around in your commercial bank account. This is the hardest concept for most customers to understand. It is very convenient for customers of commercial banks to visit their ATM and within minutes successfully complete multiple monetary transactions. With a few touches of the keypad, customers can transfer money between savings and checking accounts, pay down mortgage balances, or pay off credit card debts. These transactions are usually confirmed at the ATM and completed prior to the next business day.

The mechanics in your online brokerage account are quite different. Online brokers operate with one core cash account where your cash sits; the balance of your portfolio is held separately as stocks, options, bonds, or mutual funds. Every cash transaction is executed through the core account. When you deposit a check, receive a cash dividend, sell a security, purchase a security, write a check, or receive cash from a maturing bond, all settle in the core account. However, instead of a 24-hour maximum settlement as is the case with your bank's ATM, funds in the core account have settlement periods anywhere from 24 hours up to 5 business days. In a cash account the funds from a stock sale executed on Tuesday the 1st would not settle in the core account until Monday the 7th. The stock trade actually settles at market close on Friday and the funds are available on Monday. Problems arise when you attempt to access these funds prior to settlement dates.

For example, many investors write checks from their online brokerage accounts too soon. They attempt to pay bills and make mortgage payments, car payments, and even down payments on homes. To generate the cash to pay these bills, they will sell off part of their portfolio. Unfortunately, many investors submit their checks before their trades have actually settled, assuming that because they had sold $25,000 worth of securities on Tuesday, their money would be available as early as Wednesday. As a result, their checks bounced.

Remember, too, that your broker will not resubmit that bounced check. So you see, it's important that you understand how your particular online brokerage firm handles its core accounts. How quickly and by what means can you access your cash? The next time you want to pay a bill, be certain that the funds are available. The best way to do so is simply to ask your online broker what his or her clearing policies are.

■ When You Absolutely, Positively, Must Execute Your Trade Now! ■

Funding your account with a personal check is the most convenient way to get started. However, this method will not guarantee you 100 percent access to the trading markets. Let me repeat this point for emphasis: Depositing a check into your account does *not* mean that you will be able to execute all trades in your account immediately.

The only types of deposits that allow you to execute trades immediately are deposits known as federal funds, which are considered immediate and cleared money. With federal funds you are able to trade stocks on margin and trade penny stocks, option contracts, IPOs, or anything else that your account allows. In general, the term *federal funds,* as it relates to the Federal Reserve System and commercial banking, is described as "all money deposited by commercial banks at a Federal Reserve Bank, including any money in excess of the reserve requirement." For our purposes the term has a more basic and pertinent meaning: immediate funds for trading.

Most online brokerage firms will accept Federal Reserve checks, Treasury checks, postal money orders, and bank wires as federal (or fed) funds. Note, however, that cashier's checks are not considered federal funds and thus do not clear immediately. Many customers have deposited cashier's checks under this assumption, only to discover that they could not purchase the IPO or the option contract that they so desperately wanted and subsequently ended up missing their trade.

Bank wires are the most commonly used type of fed funds. They are easiest to execute and are the timeliest. For instance, if you wanted to buy 1,000 shares of a stock tomorrow when it hit your price of $15, you could easily call your bank and have it wire $20,000 to your online account. In most cases, the money would be available the same day.

Of course, there are some restrictions. The account from which the money is coming (your bank) must have the same registration (or ownership) as the account where the money is being sent (your online broker). For instance, you could not wire funds from a corporate account to a joint tenant account. Some banks and brokerage firms also require bank wires to be of a certain minimum balance (e.g., $3,000). It is highly unlikely that you could wire $100. It goes without saying that you must have available funds in the account before your bank or brokerage firm will wire the money. Under normal circumstances, bank wire requests made before 10:00 AM EST are received in your account by 3:00 or 4:00 PM EST the same day. Banks and brokerage firms normally charge a small fee for this service. It is your responsibility to supply wiring instructions to the sending institution. A typical wiring instruction that you would give to your bank to wire cash to your online broker would look as follows (your online broker will give you these instructions):

> **Wire to:** Name of your online broker's bank
> **ABA number:** Account number of your online broker's bank
> **For credit to:** Name of your online broker or clearing firm
> **Account number:** Account number of your online broker's clearing firm
> **Benefit of:** Your name (the way the online account is registered)
> **Account number:** Your online brokerage account number

In addition to the benefit of receiving cleared funds, bank wires are easily traceable. They do not get "lost in the mail." Once a wire has left your bank, a federal reference number is generated. This number guarantees that the money has been delivered out of your bank account in accordance with your wire instructions. If you receive a federal reference number and the funds don't show up in your brokerage account, there is a problem and you should contact your bank to verify your instructions. There should be no gray areas when it comes to bank wires. Once the money has left the sending firm's account, it should be deposited into the receiving firm's account.

■ Funding Your Account by Check ■

The easiest of all funding methods is simply to write your online broker a check. Although I have mentioned some of its limitations, it is still one of the most common means used by online investors. Most of you may never trade options, purchase IPOs, or execute a margin trade within the first 24 hours of opening your account, so starting off with a personal check deposit is perfectly fine.

Because of its simplicity, you should not encounter many problems, but, I do have a few suggestions. Make sure that you write your online brokerage account number somewhere on the face of your check before depositing it, even if it is accompanied by a deposit slip. Online brokerage representatives process thousands of checks each day, and if your check and deposit slip become separated without an account number on the check, it will be extremely difficult to credit your account.

Also, be certain to verify the mailing address where the check should be sent. Firms have many different departments, each with its own post office box number. Sending your check into a random address of the company is asking for trouble. For example, a check sent to your online broker's stock receipt department in California would perhaps have to be forwarded to the check receipt department in Dallas, which would obviously slow the deposit time and increase the likelihood that the check gets lost. Sending your check to the incorrect department may sound like a trivial matter, but, believe me, it causes enormous frustration for customers when they are waiting to place that first trade and the check is nowhere to be found.

Each online brokerage firm has its own policies regarding the types of checks that they will and will not accept. The following table gives you an idea of the kinds of checks you can and cannot deposit at most online brokerage firms:

CAN	CANNOT
Personal checks	Travelers' checks
Cashier's checks	Credit card checks
Federal Reserve/Treasury checks	Unsigned checks
Postal money orders	Altered checks
Certified checks	Third-party checks
Corporate, estate, partnership checks	Checks in a foreign currency
Second-party checks	Postdated checks

■ DON'T LEAVE THOSE STOCK CERTIFICATES LYING AROUND ■

Are you the type of person who likes to hold on to things? Let me tell you: Don't hold on to those stock certificates. Although you may feel more secure knowing that they are stuffed in a shoebox under your bed, they are doing you absolutely no good there. It is best to send those certificates to your broker for safekeeping. So if you're holding on to those certificates, gather them up and we'll talk about how you can safely deposit them into your online account.

The number of people who still cling tightly to their physical stock shares always surprises me. Maybe it's because of the assurance from investors knowing that at any time they could pull out the certificates, gaze at their name emblazoned across the face, hold them in their hands, and feel good about being a stockholder of XYZ Corporation. Or maybe it's because of the romantic notion of seeing a tangible reminder of their participation in the capital markets. Ah yes, owning a piece of a company like IBM; isn't that what our capitalist society is all about?

But do you really need to hold on to those shares? Besides your personal preference, I see no advantage in it. Now I know some of you may be thinking, "Of course that's his opinion; he works in the industry! Brokerage firms would love to get their hands on my stock." You're right. I am an industry insider and that's precisely why I'm telling you to deposit those shares—and not for the reason you may think.

Remember, your ownership will not cease when your online broker holds your stock. You still maintain beneficial ownership. Granted, getting a monthly statement with your stock share balances is not as romantic as holding on to your physical stock certificates, but it represents the same thing—stock ownership. Brokerage firms do receive a financial benefit by holding your stock certificates, but it is not at your expense. Sure, online brokers can make money by loaning your shares to other customers, whether in-house or at other brokerage firms, to facilitate trading, short selling, or margin borrowing, but this benefit doesn't cost you anything. What goes on behind the scenes is irrelevant as it pertains to your personal online brokerage account.

In fact, it's better for you to let the broker hold your shares because your online broker then assumes the responsibility for handling all service issues, such as collecting dividends, redistributing cash dividends, adjusting your shares for any stock dividends or stock splits, settling your sell orders, and safeguarding the certificates. The broker also handles reorganization items in the event your ownership in a company were to change because of a merger or an acquisition. Sometimes company takeovers can get quite confusing.

Where one day you owned 1,000 shares of ABC Inc., you may wake up the next day to find that you now own a combination of 700 shares of XYZ Corporation and some cash. ABC Inc. no longer exists. No need to worry: With your stocks held in street name (explained below), your online broker will handle the intricacies of the merger for you.

By holding the securities yourself, you risk losing or destroying them. If that happens, you will have a lot of work ahead of you (not to mention that it will also cost you money). If you misplace your 100-share certificate of IBM, you would need to journey down a long and arduous path to obtain new certificates. First, you would have to contact the *transfer agent.* (A transfer agent is a corporation, usually a commercial bank, that is responsible for maintaining the records of the names of the registered shareholders and bondholders of the company.) The name of the transfer agent usually appears on the stock certificate, but because you misplaced your shares, this information would not be available. So you would call IBM's investor relations department to get the name of the transfer agent and then call the transfer agent to verify your ownership. The agent would then reissue shares in your name, which could take up to three weeks for you to receive them, while you're crossing your fingers that the price of your stock will not plummet during the wait. This is certainly a lot of work and stress that you don't need.

Holding in Street Name

You will hear the term *hold in street name* frequently as you begin your online investing. It simply means that when you deposit stock certificates or buy shares in your account, these securities will be held in the name of your online brokerage firm. However, you will remain the beneficial owner. For all intent and purposes, you own the shares.

Trading online is inexpensive and convenient. It affords you the luxury of investing at your own pace according to your own schedule. Allowing your online brokerage firm to hold your securities in street name facilitates this ease and convenience. It allows the payment and delivery of your transactions to be executed in a timely manner. Stocks held in street name make settling trades much easier for you than if you personally held the shares. Could you imagine how the markets would operate if customers had to physically deliver stock certificates each time they bought and sold?

Two very important facts also come into play. First, if you are physically holding shares, you will not be able to sell them online. When you enter a sell order, the computer will not recognize the existence of the shares in your account and will deny the trade. Although you know that you own the shares, your online broker and its computer system don't. If you can't enter your sell order at a particular moment, you may miss the market and possibly lose money on the inability to trade. What good is trading online if you can't sell your shares online when you need to? Moreover, it doesn't make sense to hold the shares yourself because you will eventually have to send them in anyway if you intend to sell them. So do it now rather than later.

Second, if you are a customer who is trading on margin and is in physical possession of stock securities, you may be minimizing the margin borrowing that would otherwise be available if the shares were in the account. Margin is discussed in more detail in Chapter 5, but by depositing stock in street name, you increase your available margin-buying power. This in turn increases the leverage on your account to a maximum level, enabling you to implement more fully any margin strategies. Again, margin is not for everyone, but if you do use it, you are shortchanging yourself by holding shares at home.

Depositing Stock Certificates

There are three requirements for depositing stock certificates into your account: (1) the shares must be in negotiable form; (2) they must be endorsed properly to the receiving brokerage firm; and (3) they must be delivered to your firm in a safe and secure manner.

Just as with any U.S. currency, stock certificates must be in good physical condition. You would no more accept a shredded, torn, or defaced one-dollar bill than would your online broker accept stock certificates that are delivered in the same fashion. If you are sending in shares, do your best to deliver them in good condition. You would be surprised and amused at the shape of some stock certificates that have been sent to online brokers in the past.

NEGOTIABLE FORM. Negotiable stock certificates are shares registered in a form that allows you, the shareholder, the right to assign, give, or transfer ownership to another person (your online brokerage firm) without a third party's permission. It sounds technical but it's not. It just means that you have the authority to sign over the stock to your online broker without additional legal documentation. Rest easy; in the majority of cases, the stock certificates that you deliver will be negotiable.

PROPER ENDORSEMENT. After determining that your shares are indeed negotiable and before mailing the certificate to your online broker, make sure you endorse the certificate on the back. Endorsing certificates simply means completing two key sections of each certificate. Figure 4.1 shows you the front and the back of a typical stock certificate. Your online brokerage account registration must match the registration that appears on the face of your stock certificate. If your account registration is in joint name, as in Mr. Harry Smith and Mrs. Nancy Smith, your stock certificates must be registered in the same manner.

Turning the stock certificate over, you will notice two blank sections. This is where you must insert the name of your online brokerage firm—after the phrase "constitute and appoint." Some firms may request that you use the name of a separate clearing agent. Contact your online broker to confirm exactly what name it wants you to insert. After executing this section, turn to the signature lines at the bottom of the certificate. Sign the certificate in the name(s) of the person(s) exactly as it appears on the face. Failure to execute these two steps properly will result in delays.

SAFE DELIVERY. After the securities have been endorsed correctly, it is now a matter of getting them into the hands of your online broker in a quick and safe manner. Prior to delivery, I recommend that you place your online brokerage account number somewhere on the face of the stock certificate. Some online firms prefer that you place the account number at a particular location on the certificate to ensure that the representative receiving the shares will book them to your account properly.

Many people choose to send certificates by regular mail. Although an acceptable way of delivery, regular mail doesn't offer you security against lost certificates. I found that customers fared

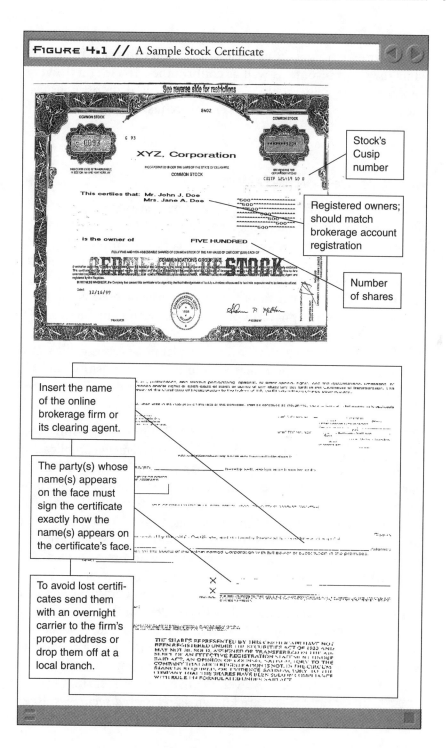

FIGURE 4.1 // A Sample Stock Certificate

Stock's Cusip number

Registered owners; should match brokerage account registration

Number of shares

Insert the name of the online brokerage firm or its clearing agent.

The party(s) whose name(s) appears on the face must sign the certificate exactly how the name(s) appears on the certificate's face.

To avoid lost certificates send them with an overnight carrier to the firm's proper address or drop them off at a local branch.

better and felt more secure when they used an overnight carrier. It is worth the extra expense to know that you can track the shares while they are en route as well as confirm their receipt on delivery. Another secure delivery alternative is to simply drop off your certificates at your local online broker's office (assuming, of course, it has one).

Additional Paperwork That May Be Required

UNSIGNED CERTIFICATES. If for some reason you send stock certificates to your broker unsigned, you will be asked to complete a separate document known as an *irrevocable stock power*—a power of attorney form transferring your ownership of the securities to the brokerage firm. Your firm, in what is called a legal position, will hold securities that have been deposited without an endorsement (your signature) on the stock certificate. Shares held in "legal" can't be sold and also don't generate additional borrowing power or margin buying power. Completing an irrevocable stock power form removes these shares from their legal position and allows you to sell them and borrow against them. Obtaining an irrevocable stock power form is as easy as contacting your online broker.

CONTROL AND RESTRICTED SECURITIES. Depositing and trading control and restricted stocks can be extremely complicated. Trading or borrowing against these shares on margin requires additional legal consultation between the corporate counsel of the company in which you own the shares and the control and restricted stock department of your online brokerage firm—a time-consuming and costly process. Not all firms accept control or restricted securities, so before sending them in, confirm that your online broker will accept them. It is beyond the scope of this book to make you a control and restricted stock specialist, but I am confident you can learn the basic concepts that will help you deposit these certificates.

The rapid growth of IPOs as well as mergers and acquisitions and the increased use of company stock options as a form of compensation increase the chances that you will come across control or restricted securities. However, the majority of securities traded in the United States today are known as *registered securities*. Registered securities are issued by a public company for sale to the general public under the guidelines set up by the Securities Act of 1933 and the Securities and Exchange Act of 1934. Registered securities have met all requirements of the Securities and Exchange Commission, are traded in the open market, and are not subject to the rules governing control or restricted securities.

Stocks owned by control persons—that is, company insiders or affiliates—are known as *control securities.* Control persons can be directors of the company, officers (people in a position to directly or indirectly control the management of the company), or major shareholders who own 10 percent or more of the company's outstanding shares. Restrictions on control securities also apply to family members, spouses, or other entities affiliated with control persons.

Restricted securities are unregistered securities that are acquired directly or indirectly from the issuer or from an affiliate of the issuer. You may have received these types of shares through a private placement, a merger, a partnership distribution, or a stock option or bonus plan. Restricted shares are not registered with the SEC and thus are not acquired through a public offering. They can be specifically identified by a legend that appears on the back of the stock certificate that restricts the manner in which the shares can be resold.

It is your responsibility as the shareholder to inform your online broker that you are in possession of control or restricted securities, as they require special handling by your broker. There may be certain holding-period requirements and volume limitations on the sale of these shares. You will need to complete either Form 144 and/or 144 Seller's Certification when depositing the shares into your account for resale or for margin purposes. The shares are subject to regulatory guidelines under SEC Rule 144, and it is imperative that you contact your online broker when you realize that you possess such shares. Your online broker will instruct you on what legal documents must accompany your certificates.

■ TRANSFERRING YOUR ACCOUNT FROM ONE BROKER TO ANOTHER ■

OK, you've had it with your current broker. The service is lousy, the commissions are too high, and its Web site is just too slow. You have given it every possible chance to keep your account, but your concerns fall on deaf ears. The broker just doesn't seem to care whether you stay or go. So you make the decision to go! The only problem is that you are still trading in your account, you have a large portfolio of stocks, and the market is taking more dips than a bag of chips at a Super Bowl party. What can you do?

Liquidating your entire portfolio and writing a check is out of the question. A partial transfer is not an option because you don't want to give the firm any more of your business. The only real choice is to execute a full broker-to-broker transfer. Does this sound familiar? Customers are continuously transferring assets back and forth between brokerage houses for many different reasons—and not always stemming from a conflict. Sometimes the reason is strictly business. Maybe you are at a bank and merely wish to diversify your portfolio into stocks, so you decide to open an online trading account. Whatever the reason, understand that you have a choice of how to execute the transfer. If you decide to move your assets from one institution to another, it can be done in three different ways: a partial transfer of assets, a full transfer of assets, or a DTC transfer (see below). Before moving on to the actual mechanics of the transfer process, let's look at a few key terms.

AUTOMATED CUSTOMER ACCOUNT TRANSFER (ACAT). ACAT refers to the electronic transfer system that brokerage houses use to expedite the transfer of assets between institutions. It was developed by the National Securities Clearing Corporation to facilitate requests for the full transfer of assets. Partial transfers of assets are normally not handled in the ACAT process. An ACAT transfer will occur when both firms participate in the ACAT system and when the securities being transferred are eligible for processing through an ACAT. Positions that may not be eligible for an ACAT include foreign stocks, U.S. Treasuries, certificates of deposit, and proprietary mutual funds. The majority of broker-to-broker transfers are processed through an ACAT.

DEPOSITORY TRUST COMPANY (DTC). The DTC is the world's largest securities repository, where securities are typically exchanged electronically. This computerized transfer network reduces the need for the physical transfer of shares. Its network links over 11,000 broker-dealers and custodian banks as well as transfer agents. The DTC is a member of the Federal Reserve System and is owned by most of the brokerage houses on Wall Street and the New York Stock Exchange. Each online brokerage firm has an identifying DTC number assigned to it in order to facilitate the transfer and clearing of securities transactions between brokerage houses.

COMMITTEE ON UNIFORM SECURITIES IDENTIFICATION PROCEDURES (CUSIP). A CUSIP number is assigned as a security identification number for each issue of common stock, preferred stock, corporate bonds, and municipal bonds. Online brokers use CUSIP numbers when recording all buy and sell orders. CUSIP numbers are often found on your confirmation tickets or your monthly account statements. They are used by brokerage firms to accurately expedite the electronic transfer of securities between firms. A CUSIP number is basically a bar code for identifying a publicly traded stock.

TRANSFER IN KIND. You may see the term *transfer in kind* on the application form for your transfer of assets. It simply notifies your online broker that you would like to transfer your stock positions without liquidating them. If you own 100 shares of IBM, 100 shares of General Electric, and 100 shares of Chrysler, you fully expect those shares to have been transferred into your new account. You don't want your old firm to sell your shares and transfer the resulting cash balances.

Partial and Full Transfer of Assets (TOA)

A copy of a standard transfer of assets form is shown in Figure 4.2. The information it requests is straightforward. Your completed form for a partial or full transfer must always be returned to the receiving broker (your new firm). Your assets will then be transferred from the rescinding broker (your old firm) to the receiving broker (your new firm) via an ACAT transfer for full-account transfers and non-ACAT transfer for partial-account transfers. Like you, your receiving broker wants the transfer to be completed as quickly and accurately as possible. The sooner the broker gets your account, the sooner it can start collecting commission revenues; but it is ultimately in the hands of the rescinding broker to deliver your account in a reasonable period. Your old broker or bank has

FIGURE 4.2 // Transfer of Assets Form

Have you thought out your TOA thoroughly? It will take a few weeks to transfer the account.

1 Brokerage Account Information

If opening a new account attach a copy of a compl

Brokerage Account Number _____

Account Owner/Custodian/Trustee _____

Joint Owner/Minor/Trust Name _____

Social Security Number/Tax ID Number_____

Home Phone #_____

Work Phone # _____

Indicate IRA Type __ Traditional __ Roth __ Rollover I

> If this is a new account, be sure to include new-account application. Again, the firm needs your SS# and telephone numbers. Don't forget.

2 Account to Be Transferred

You must enclose your most recent account statement to process this transfer.

Name of Firm currently holding account _____

Address _____

City/State/Zip_____

Account Owner(s) Names _____

Account Number _____

Firm's Phone Number _____

__ Check if account being transferred is margin ac

__ Account statements

__ Corporate resolution for business account

__ Trustee Certification of Investment Power for trust accounts

> You need to enclose a copy of your most recent statement.

> Review the TOA checklist. Make sure there are no open orders and no special margin requirements, and that all security positions will be accepted. Be sure to give the new firm the correct old account number and make sure account registrations are identical.

3 Account Instructions

1 Full-Account Transfers __ Transfer entire a proceeds

2 Partial-Account Transfers. List all investments to transferred below:

Description of assets   Number of share   Type of transfer

_____   In-kind Liquidate

_____

_____

__ Certificate of Deposit—Date of maturity __/__/__

__ Cash—Transfer all cash or __ Partial transfer of $_

> Executing full or partial transfer? In-kind or liquidating assets?— Be clear! If partial transfer, list securities on form. Remember, there is no need to transfer cash—ask for a check.

> Once you sign the application— you must stop trading. Unsettled trades cannot be transferred. Trading will delay the TOA. Be patient and check in with your broker to make sure the transfer is on schedule.

4 Owner Authorization—Signature of Owner(s)

Owner _____

Joint Owner/Plan Administrator _____

to transfer the account; and once the paperwork is filed, the ball is in its court.

Your transfer of assets will take between three and six weeks from the date that online brokers receive the paperwork, although non-ACAT partial transfers may take even longer. These are precautionary time frames that give your online broker some breathing room. However, it has been my experience that if you complete the transfer form correctly and completely while following a few basic rules, a full transfer should be completed in about eight business days from the receipt of the paperwork.

Keep in mind: While your account is in transfer you cannot trade! Under these circumstances eight business days may be too long, and six weeks could be totally unacceptable. For this reason, you need to thoroughly investigate your reasons for wanting to switch brokers. You need to weigh all of the advantages and disadvantages. I've seen too many customers transfer their assets only to realize that they are no better off at their new firm and in many cases worse off. Eventually, they wind up transferring back—what a headache. As we discussed, only you can answer the question, "What's important to me in my brokerage account, and will my new firm meet my needs?"

Transferring your account because you were enticed by a television advertisement or because you'll save a couple of dollars on commissions is not always a valid reason for transferring. Granted, if you are trading 100 times a year and you can save $5 to $10 per transaction, then a transfer may be worth looking into. But to move your account without significant reasons doesn't make sense. Besides, it's very possible that you could lose any small commission savings that you may have anticipated at the lower-cost firm simply by missing just one trade while your account is in transit. But then again, only you know whether the dollar savings are significant enough.

If you do decide to transfer, be confident about your decision. Even after you proceed with your transfer, most rescinding brokers will permit you to sell shares in the event of a market correction; but with each executed trade, you create an unsettled position that will cause major delays in your account transfer. Under this scenario, your transfer will be pushed out beyond six to eight weeks. I have witnessed firsthand several account transfers that took two months or more to complete because clients just would not stop trading. I always tried to instill in them that it is impossible to time the markets and therefore impossible to initiate a transfer in anticipation of a flat market. If you truly believe that the transfer is in your best interest, then you need to stop trading, be patient, and let the transfer happen. You cannot have it both ways—continue to trade and execute a quick transfer of assets.

A tip for those of you who are about to transfer your account and are holding both cash and stocks: simply withdraw the cash from your account first. You can do this by writing a check (if you have check-writing privileges), requesting a check be sent to you, or by wiring the cash to your new brokerage account. Once the cash is withdrawn, file your transfer paperwork as normal. That way you will have cash in your new account within a couple of days. The stock positions will still take about eight business days to transfer, assuming of course you stop trading in the old account. But at least you now have cash in the new account and therefore the ability to take advantage of any buying opportunities. You should always avoid transferring cash through the ACAT system; there is no need to do it.

Review the checklist in Figure 4.3 before you file your TOA paperwork. It will reduce the chance that problems will arise and will help expedite the time frame for the completion of your TOA.

DTC Transfer of Stock

Extremely active traders have the most difficulty when transferring assets between brokerage firms. A DTC transfer is a last resort for these customers. Transferring stock via the electronic vault of the DTC allows individual stock positions to be transferred within 48 hours. It is at the discretion of the rescinding broker whether it will execute this type of transfer. Normally, brokerage firms will only permit a few stock positions to be transferred through the DTC as a courtesy to the customer and rarely will it execute a full transfer via the DTC. Firms are not obligated to DTC shares and a refusal is not a reflection on you and is not cause for taking any action against your broker. If the firm can do it, great; if not, simply initiate a partial or full transfer.

Figure 4.3 // Checklist for Expediting Your Full Transfer of Assets

✓ Verify that account registrations at the rescinding broker and at the receiving broker match.

✓ Complete the Transfer of Assets Form (Figure 4.2) and return it to the receiving broker with your most recent account statement.

✓ Stop trading in your old account!

✓ Verify the receiving broker's acceptance of any questionable stock positions (foreign stocks, proprietary mutual funds).

✓ If your account carries a margin debit balance and has an equity percentage of 40 percent or less, confirm the receiving broker's margin requirements for stock or options positions. Avoid violating the credit policy of the receiving firm.

✓ If your account carries a margin debit balance, confirm the margin requirement on any concentrated stock positions, which account for 40 percent or more of the total market value of your account. Always avoid violating the credit policy of the receiving firm.

✓ Cancel any open orders that you previously placed at the rescinding broker.

✓ For *Option Traders!* Avoid transferring option contracts during option expiration week (the third Friday of each month).

✓ Remember: Stop trading in your old account! Be patient. You decided that the transfer was in your best interest.

Rescinding brokers that will transfer shares to another receiving broker via the DTC will frequently request the instructions in writing. Your letter should contain the name of the receiving broker, the DTC number of the receiving broker (obtained by calling the receiving broker), your online brokerage account number, and the stocks to be delivered, including the quantity, name, and CUSIP number. Also, be sure to include your daytime telephone number in case there are any questions or problems.

Transferring stock through the DTC is not problem free. The transfer of stock will reduce the available margin at the rescinding broker because there is an accompanying drop in total market value equal to the amount being transferred out. If, for example, your account was worth $100,000 and you transfer $40,000 in stock to another firm via the DTC, your market value drops to $60,000. For this reason you must confirm that you hold enough equity in your account to accommodate the loss of the margin resulting from the removal of the shares via the DTC. You must also cancel any open orders that you may have outstanding on the stock transferred via the DTC. And as with partial and full transfers, the account registrations need to be identical at the rescinding and the receiving brokers.

■ IT'S NOT ROCKET SCIENCE, BUT ■ ■ ■ ■

Depositing checks, wiring funds, or delivering stock certificates shouldn't be the most difficult things to accomplish in your online brokerage account—and now that you have read through this chapter, they won't be. Yet some of you will still not consider all of your funding options. For some, your funding method may not have an impact on your trading, but for others it can make the difference between trading today and trading next week. Remember, every day countless investors miss trades because of their funding method. It is a very simple relationship—Funds = Trading—but with no assets in the account, you can't trade. So before moving ahead, go back and reevaluate all of the funding methods: check deposit, bank wire, stock certificate deposit, full transfer of assets, partial transfer of assets, or a DTC transfer. Determine which one is right for your situation because you will not be able to move on to trading unless this step is accomplished.

CHAPTER 5

Understanding Account Balances and Margin Basics

■ KNOW HOW TO READ YOUR ACCOUNT BALANCES ■

Account balances are displayed online or via your monthly account statements. They give you a snapshot of both the amount of your cash holdings (or debit balance if you're trading on margin) and the market value of your securities positions. Trading activity and market fluctuations change these numbers daily. Balances can be accessed online 24 hours each day either as end-of-day or as intraday balances (as mentioned in Chapter 2). Your monthly account statements, on the other hand, are just that, a month-end report. It is your responsibility to keep track of what is going on in your account.

It is critical that you understand how your online brokerage firm calculates your account balances. In the end, you will employ these numbers to make vital investment decisions. You must have a reasonable level of confidence that the balances are correct, and the best way to ensure that they are is to calculate them for yourself. This does not mean that you are expected to maintain the knowledge and skill of a certified public accountant; you only need to look at your balances for overall accuracy. Do they add up? Are there any numbers that do not look right?

Your account balances divulge two critical pieces of information relating to (1) trading and (2) tracking portfolio performance. *Cash core* and *available to borrow* tell you how much you can buy, whereas *cash* and *margin market values* indicate how much you can sell. Through an account entry known as *net worth* or *total account balance,* you can determine the dollar value of your total account and whether this account value is going up or down. If you are unfamiliar with these terms now, don't worry; by the end of this chapter you will be familiar with them.

Your online broker updates the account balances for you. Its sophisticated computer programs account for all trading activity and stock price changes. When these programs are run, they should result in a true account balance. However, there are times when these computer programs don't update balances properly, which results in a false balance. Maybe a stock was not priced and resulted in a lower net worth figure, or maybe a check was credited to the wrong customer's account and inflated one customer's cash core while undervaluing another's. Online brokers and their computers are not perfect; mistakes can happen. Catching them early is critical.

Would you be able to quickly recognize what balances were incorrect? What particular item was throwing your account off balance? And, worse yet, would you place an incorrect trade based on erroneous information? Remember that you are ultimately responsible for ensuring that your balances are correct. This is one of the many duties you assumed by becoming your own broker. Besides, don't you want to be certain that your online broker is accounting for all of your assets properly? After all, it *is* your money.

Whether you're trading infrequently on a small account or trading actively on a large margin account, understanding your balances need not be difficult. There are basic accounting concepts that apply to everyone and I'll explore them in this chapter. Let's begin with a general overview of your portfolio and then drill down to the specific account categories that lead to the calculation of your overall balances. In addition, I'll discuss the role of margin, its benefits and risks, and how to avoid margin trouble. I suggest that you have a calculator and pencil handy so you can run through some of the examples with me. Although there won't be any heavy lifting, calculating the examples yourself will go a long way in helping you to master the necessary concepts.

▪ The Long and Short of It ▪

If you're going to be a broker, you need to think and speak like a broker; and the most basic way that your online brokerage firm approaches your overall account balance is in terms of *long positions* and *short positions*. What do you own and what do you owe? Looking at your account in this way gives you a better overall picture of your portfolio. Every transaction that you make results in an accounting balance that is either added or subtracted. Long positions are added; short positions are subtracted.

In this context, long or short positions refer only to stocks, bonds, and option contracts. You could say that a cash balance is a long cash position, or that you had a short cash position if you owed your firm money (margin debt), but in reality this terminology is not used for cash balances. The terms *long* and *short* refer only to the positions that online firms allow you to transact: stocks, bonds, mutual funds, or option contracts.

For example, if you had previously purchased 100 shares of IBM, 100 shares of Chrysler, 10 U.S. Treasury bonds, and 10 America Online call options, you would be said to be long those positions. You would regard these particular stock, bond, and option positions as a form of ownership—call them assets if you like. On the other hand, if you sold 1,000 shares of Ford Motor stock short (borrowing stock from your broker) or sold 10 General Motors call options, you would be short these positions. For account balance purposes, short positions represent liabilities, and, like general accounting principles, assets are added to balances while liabilities are subtracted.

Many of you may never sell stock short or sell an option contract in your account, but that does not relieve you of understanding these balances. Many individuals avoid learning new concepts simply because they don't understand them. Today, selling stock short or selling (writing) option contracts may seem foreign to you, but who knows what strategies you may implement down the road. It is easier to understand your account balances if you concentrate on both sides of the account balance ledger—the long side and the short side—rather than focusing only on the long side:

- *Long positions.* These represent ownership (assets). If you purchase stocks, bonds, mutual funds, or option contracts, you are said to be long these positions. As a result, the value of these long positions are added to your account balances.
- *Short positions.* These represent obligations (liabilities). If you sell stock short or sell option contracts, you are said to be short the stock or short the option contract. As a result, the value of these short positions are subtracted from your account balances.

■ LONG AND SHORT ACCOUNT TYPES ■

Online brokers use three main account types to organize your portfolio: cash, margin, and short stock. Each time you purchase or sell stocks, bonds, mutual funds, or option contracts, you are trading in and out of one of these account types. The two main types are cash and margin. When we refer to cash in this context, we are not speaking in terms of actual cash dollars that earn interest, and when we refer to margin as an account type, we are not referring to a margin debt resulting from borrowing money. Here, we are only focusing on the account types as they pertain to what your online trading screen prompts you to trade in—cash, margin, or short stock.

Long and short positions are labeled on the books of your online broker in the following three account types:

1. *Cash transactions.* These indicate to the computer that you intend to pay for the trade in full. No loan value available for borrowing will be generated from these positions. Stocks, bonds, mutual funds, and option contracts can be transacted in this type of account.
2. *Margin transactions.* These indicate to the computer that you can either pay for the stock in full or borrow money from your broker. Positions in margin generate loan value. Stocks, bonds, mutual funds, and option contracts can be transacted in this type of account.
3. *Short stock transactions.* These indicate to the computer that you are borrowing stock from your broker for sale. You are

not selling existing long stock positions. Most online brokers will allow you to transact only stock in this type of account.

CASH TRANSACTIONS.

Cash core $20,000   Total net worth $20,000

Let's assume that you already have deposited $20,000 into your account. Your beginning balance is $20,000 cash, giving you the same net worth shown above. You log on to your computer and begin to place a buy order for 1,000 shares of XYZ at $20. The computer asks if you would like to make the trade in cash or margin; you select cash. The trade is executed at $20 for a total of $20,000, and you are now long 1,000 shares of XYZ. After settlement (trade date plus three business days) and assuming the stock is still trading at $20, the account balance is now:

Cash core $0   Total net worth $20,000
                         Cash market value $20,000

The $20,000 purchase is taken from your cash core and the 1,000 shares of XYZ are long in your cash market value and reflected in total net worth (what you own). For online trades in cash transactions, you must have the full amount of the trade on hand before the order is placed. In the above example, the computer would not accept a cash trade for $30,000 because it is more than the $20,000 cash on hand.

MARGIN TRANSACTIONS. What if you intend to pay for the trade in full but decide to enter the trade in margin instead of in cash? Assuming that the stock price remains at $20 after trade settlement, the results are as follows.

Cash core $0   Total net worth $20,000
                         Margin market value $20,000

The stock purchase is now long in margin market value (no longer cash market value) and reflected in total net worth. As you can see, you have *not* created a margin debit balance. As mentioned in Chapter 3, you only pay interest on money that you borrow. As long as you have enough cash in your cash core account to cover the buy, you will not be charged any interest. However, what is not shown (but will be discussed later in this chapter) is the benefit of a resulting loan amount known as "available to borrow" that is generated by buying the stock in margin. This available-to-borrow figure can be used to take a cash loan or as a loan to buy more stock.

Margin transactions also allow you to purchase an amount of stock greater than your cash core balance. In the above example, instead of buying 1,000 shares, you decide to buy 1,500 shares at $20 totaling $30,000. You know that you have the extra $10,000 in the bank but you don't want to wait until that money can be deposited in your online brokerage account. You are convinced that the stock price will be higher if you wait until you actually deposit the funds. In the margin type of transaction, you do not have to wait. You could enter the order online immediately, which would create the following accounting.

Cash core	$ 0	Total net worth	$20,000
Margin debit	$10,000	Margin market value	$30,000

The $10,000 in margin debit is the loan amount ($20,000 original cash core + $10,000 loan = $30,000 long stock purchase) that must be repaid and is charged interest. However, this loan does not begin until settlement (trade date plus three business days). Therefore, if you know that you have the cash at the bank and you can get it to your broker before the trade settles, there will be no interest charges. For example, bank wiring $10,000 into your account the next day would result in the following balances.

Cash core	$0	Total net worth	$30,000
Margin debit	$0	Margin market value	$30,000

As you can see, you now have paid for the shares in full, you no longer carry a debit balance, but you were able to buy the stock when you wanted without having to wait. This is one of the main reasons why I suggested in Chapter 3 that you check margin on your application. Having margin affords you greater trading flexibility than a cash account.

SHORT STOCK. The mechanics of selling stock short is completely different than buying and selling long stock positions and thus has completely different accounting categories. First, your online broker must approve a short sale. The firm must have enough shares of the requested stock in inventory (stock held in street name) or available from another broker-dealer so you can borrow the shares and sell them short. Tracking down stock can be time consuming. If you know that you will be shorting stock one day, inquire about the availability of the shares in the morning. Then when you are actually ready to place a short sell order, you won't have to wait for the broker's approval—the shares will have already been approved for a short sale.

Selling stock in short types of transactions creates two account balances, a short credit balance and a short market value. The short credit balance reflects the proceeds of the short sale. Short sale proceeds are not released to your cash core (thus, you cannot withdraw them) because they are part of the margin requirement on the short sale. However, when calculating your total account balance or total net worth, this balance is considered an asset and added back to your account. The short market value reflects the current price of the short shares—the price that you need to pay to buy the stock back in the open market to deliver the shares back to the broker. Therefore, short market value is a liability and is subtracted from your account balances.

Cash core	$ 0	Net worth	$35,000
Short credit balance $15,000		Margin market value	$30,000
		Short market value	$10,000

In the above example, the customer owns $30,000 worth of long shares on margin and has received $15,000 from an earlier short sale reflected in short credit balance. The short market value reflects the current market value of the shares previously sold short. In this case, it looks as though the customer has made a profitable short sale; he has received $15,000 in the short sale but would need to buy the shares back at only $10,000 in today's market, representing a gain of $5,000. To calculate net worth, you add the margin market value and the short credit balance and subtract the short market value (I'll discuss this formula later). Be aware that if the price of the short stock should rise, the cost to fulfill the obligation to buy back the shares will rise too. Unlike a long stock purchase where the losses are limited to the purchase price of the stock, a rise in the price of short stock can create unlimited losses. Theoretically, the stock can rise to infinity.

■ DO YOU KNOW IN WHAT ACCOUNT TYPE YOUR POSITIONS ARE? ■

Some online brokerage firms have a policy whereby all stock positions that are purchased in a cash transaction are automatically transferred to a margin account at settlement. Your brokerage firm does this for two reasons: (1) it wants to be able to loan your stock to others—clients, banks, or broker-dealers—so don't be alarmed as this doesn't affect your stock ownership and is only done if you have taken a broker's loan; and (2) the firm wants you to have the ability to borrow money from it. The firm is not advising you to buy stock on margin or borrow money from it, but you may be more inclined to take advantage of loan privileges if you have loan value.

Knowing your firm's account policy is important when you sell your stock. Attempting to sell long stock out of a cash account after it has been transferred to a margin account may cause delays. You may have purchased the stock in cash, so it would seem to make sense to sell it from a cash account. Yet when you do, the computer informs you that you do not own the shares. By the time you figure out that the shares have been moved to a margin account, the market price of the stock could have changed. I've spoken to many a panicked investor who thought his or her shares were missing when they were sitting safely in a margin account. Confer with your online broker to find out if it has the policy described above, or, to make life easier on yourself, simply place all your trades in a margin account, even if you intend to pay for them in full.

Buying back stock in the correct account type to cover a short stock position is equally important. Occasionally, short sellers carelessly buy stock in a margin account when the purchase was actually intended for a short account to cover a short stock position and deliver the borrowed shares back to the broker. This causes account balance problems because the computer will still calculate the short market value as a liability even though it should no longer exist. The new balance will incorrectly reflect both the margin stock purchase and the existing short account and won't result in a true account balance.

▪ Calculating Total Account Value/Total Net Worth ▪

The following long and short categories appear on both your on-line balance and your monthly statements. Each day your online broker adjusts these categories to reflect transactions and market price fluctuations and is referred to as *marking to the market*. Online firms may use names different from the categories you see here. For instance, some firms use the term *net worth, net equity,* or *total account balance* to describe the same dollar value of your owner-ship in your portfolio. Such differences should not cause confu-sion. If you look at each category as a form of ownership (long) or obligation (short), you will have an easier time approaching these balances regardless of the terminology. After that, it's just a matter of doing the math.

CASH CORE BALANCE (CB). This balance reflects the amount of funds sitting in your core account as cash. Stock sales, interest payments, dividends, or any other cash deposits are held in the cash core account. An uncollected cash balance refers to check de-posits that are waiting to be cleared or trades awaiting settlement.

CASH MARKET VALUE (CMV). This account shows the bal-ance of all long positions in a cash account. For stocks it is all share balances in the cash account multiplied by the price of those shares. In the case of option contracts, it is the price of an option contract (its premium) times the number of contracts times 100. One contract represents 100 shares.

MARGIN MARKET VALUE (MMV). This category reflects the value of all positions held in a margin account. Eligible securities can be used for broker loans. Margin market value minus the debit balance equals margin equity. Calculating MMV is the same as calculating CMV: multiply the current market price of each po-sition by its quantity.

SHORT CREDIT BALANCE (SCB). This credit balance indi-cates proceeds from short sales of individual securities. It is not considered cash money. The money is available to you when you cover the short sale. Buying back the borrowed shares in the open market reflects a profit if it is done at a lower price than the original short sale.

LONG OPTION VALUE (LOV). Firms may separate options market values from your long stock market values. Each option contract represents 100 shares; therefore, the dollar balance of LOV is equal to the number of long option contracts times price (premium) times 100 (review Chapter 3 if needed).

DEBIT BALANCE (DB). This is the amount of money that you owe your online brokerage firm. However, because trades settle as far out as the trade date plus three business days, it is possible to have a debit balance and money in your cash core account simultaneously. When the trade settles, the cash will be drawn from your core cash balance to pay for stock purchases. Know when your trades are settling, and account for any unsettled debit balances. Only in the event that the purchase amount exceeds your cash core balance will you hold a settled debit balance. It is on this debit balance that margin interest is charged.

SHORT MARKET VALUE (SMV). This is the current market value of all short stock positions. It is the dollar amount that you would need to pay to buy back the short shares in the open market. A rise in this market value means that you have bet "wrong." Instead of the stock going down in value, the stock price is rising. Under these conditions you are losing money.

SHORT OPTION VALUE (SOV). This balance reflects all short option positions. It is calculated in the same manner as LOV.

NET WORTH/LIQUID NET EQUITY (NW). This balance tells you what you would walk away with in cash if you were to sell all long positions (ownership) and buy back (i.e., cover) all of your short positions (obligations) while paying off any outstanding debit balance. Tracking the ups and downs of the net worth figure indicates just how well your portfolio is performing. The following formula can be used to arrive at your net worth or net equity balance:

Net Worth/Net Equity Formula

$$NW = (CB+CMV+MMV+SCB+LOV) - (DB+SMV+SOV)$$

Net Worth/Net Equity Formula Example:

Cash core (CB)	$ 0	Net worth (NW)		$109,900
Margin debit		Cash market value		
(DB)	$ 5,000	(CMV)		$ 16,500
Short credit		Margin market value		
balance (SCB)	$15,000	(MMV)		$125,000
		Short market value		
		(SMV)		$ 18,600
		Long option value		
		(LOV)		$ 12,000
		Short option value		
		(SOV)		$ 35,000

▪ CASH DIVIDENDS AND STOCK SPLITS ▪

Cash dividends will change your long stock position values. There are three important dates for a stock's cash dividend: the ex-dividend date, the record date, and the payable date. The ex-dividend date is normally two business days prior to the record date. All shareholders who own the stock on the record date are entitled to receive the dividend. On the ex-dividend date, the stock trades without the dividend and its stock price reflects the loss of value. For example, a stock priced at $30 would lose 50 cents in value on the ex-dividend date if it were paying a 50 cent dividend. As an owner of this company, you would receive the cash dividend on the payable date (usually three to four weeks after the record date).

The stock price in this example would drop by the amount of the dividend to $29.50 on the ex-dividend date. Owning 2,000 shares of this stock would result in a drop of $1,000 in value. The stock price is still affected by market conditions, but on the ex-dividend date it loses the value of its dividend. Technically, however, you haven't lost any money because your cash core account eventually will be credited with $1,000 (2,000 shares × 50 cents) cash dividend on the payable date (in three to four weeks).

Stock splits have an even greater effect on your stock's long market value. A company can declare many split combinations, 2 for 1, 3 for 1, 3 for 2, or even a 1 for 3 reverse split, but let's look at a simple 2 for 1 stock split when you own 2,000 shares of a $50 stock totaling a $100,000 market value. After the 2 for 1 stock split, you now own 4,000 shares at $25—still $100,000 market value. You now own 2 shares for every 1 share and the stock price drops in half, thus the term *split*. Unlike a cash dividend, the ex-dividend date for a stock split is the day after the payable date. For example, the record date on a stock split could be October 28, the payable date (when the new shares are distributed) November 11, and the ex-dividend date (the day the stock trades at the split price) November 12.

Confusion often arises because your online brokerage firm's computers may not credit your account with the new split shares until after the ex-dividend date. Therefore, continuing with the example above, on the ex-dividend date, your account may still show the original 2,000 shares of stock but at the split price of $25. You log on to your account balance to see that your market value has dropped in half; 2,000 shares at $25—$50,000 market value. This is not a correct balance but can obviously give you a scare. Normally, the split shares are credited within 48 hours after the ex-dividend date and everything is back in order—4,000 shares at $25, or $100,000 market value. Therefore, if you notice a major discrepancy in your long market value, whether in a cash account or margin account, confirm that all cash dividends and stock splits have been adjusted properly.

■ BORROWING MONEY FROM YOUR BROKER ■

Up to this point our margin discussion has focused primarily on account balance categories. Margin until now has been referred to only as an account type where stocks, bonds, mutual funds, or option contracts were traded and held. No broker loans were actually secured. From this point on, however, when we speak of margin, we will in fact be talking about the rules and requirements involved in taking out a broker's loan. This loan can be used to either buy more securities or withdraw cash, and it changes your relationship with your online broker from agent-client to creditor-debtor. You, of course, are taking on the role of the debtor.

Margin transactions are governed by the Federal Reserve, the New York Stock Exchange (NYSE), the National Association of

Securities Dealers (NASD), and your online broker's own policies. The Federal Reserve Board was granted the power to set minimum initial margin requirements by the Securities Exchange Act of 1934. The NYSE, the NASD, and your online broker set minimum maintenance requirements. You must understand the difference between these two requirements—initial requirements and maintenance requirements—if you are to grasp the rules of margin.

The material that follows is basic and doesn't cover the entire scope of margin, although it gets to the heart of margin trading. Margin trading is not something that you want to fool around with—it is not a game. If you have questions regarding your particular margin situation, then contact your online broker. And I hope you have selected one whose representatives can answer your particular margin questions.

■ The Language of Margin ■

Margin trading has a language all its own. The first thing you need to do is familiarize yourself with basic margin terminology because when you speak to your online broker, it will be using "margin speak." Without learning the terminology, you will not have a clue as to what your broker is talking about.

MARGINABLE SECURITY. This is any stock, bond, mutual fund, or other security deemed by the Federal Reserve Board to be eligible for margin trading; these securities can be used as collateral for margin loans.

MINIMUM MARGIN EQUITY. A margin account must be established with a minimum margin equity of $2,000 in cash or securities; otherwise, it cannot be a margin account.

MARGIN EQUITY. This refers to the current net worth in a customer's margin account. It is equal to the value of all long marginable securities less the debit balance. An account with $40,000 of marginable stock less a debit of $10,000 would have a margin equity of $30,000.

MARGIN. This is the amount of cash or securities that must be deposited to secure a broker's loan. Stock purchased for $10,000 with a 60 percent margin requirement would require margin of

$6,000 ($10,000 × 60%). Margin is also referred to as margin equity.

INITIAL MARGIN REQUIREMENT. This is the amount of margin that must be deposited to meet the higher of the Federal Reserve Board's Regulation T, the NYSE's requirement, or your online broker's house requirement for initial security purchases or short stock sales.

MAINTENANCE MARGIN REQUIREMENT. Expressed as a percentage or as a dollar value, this is the level of margin equity required to be maintained on the account throughout the duration of your broker's loan and is based on house maintenance requirements (see below).

REGULATION T. This is the minimum initial margin requirement established by the Federal Reserve Board on securities purchases or short stock sales. Although this requirement can change at the discretion of the Federal Reserve Board, it is currently set at 50 percent. Every margin transaction must satisfy this initial margin requirement within the period of trade date plus five business days. With Regulation T at 50 percent, a margin purchase of $20,000 would have an initial Regulation T requirement of $10,000 (50% × $20,000).

EXCHANGE MAINTENANCE REQUIREMENT. This requirement is a maintenance requirement in effect throughout the duration of an outstanding broker's loan. It is set by the NYSE at the current margin of 25 percent, which is the lowest margin requirement that needs to be maintained by your online broker. Buying or owning marginable securities worth $50,000 would have an exchange requirement (margin equity) of $12,500 (25% × $50,000).

HOUSE MAINTENANCE REQUIREMENT. This is an initial and maintenance requirement that is set by your online broker. Most online brokers set house maintenance requirements at 30 percent. However, firms can raise the margin percentage as high as they wish but no lower than the NYSE requirement of 25 percent. It acts as an initial margin requirement when its percentage exceeds the initial Regulation T requirement. Buying or owning marginable securities worth $50,000 when house requirements are set at 30 percent requires margin (equity) of $15,000 (30% × $50,000). As a maintenance requirement it is in effect throughout the duration of an outstanding broker's loan.

REGULATION T CALL (FED CALL). This is the initial cash or security margin requirement issued under the Federal Reserve Board's Regulation T. A fed call is generated each time you enter into a margin transaction. The call is equal to the Regulation T requirement, which is currently set at 50 percent. A fed call must be met by the trade date plus five business days. Once the fed call is met, that particular trade is no longer bound by the Regulation T requirement, although any new trades would fall under Regulation T.

MAINTENANCE CALL (HOUSE CALL). A house call is a violation issued by your online broker because of a decrease in stock prices (margin market value) that causes margin equity to fall below minimum house maintenance requirements. For example, if margin equity is $10,000 and the house maintenance requirement is $15,000, then a house call is issued for $5,000. House calls must be met *promptly* by deposits of cash or marginable securities. Although most firms require house calls to be met within the period of the trade date plus three business days, your online broker can request that you meet this call on demand.

REGULATION T EXCESS EQUITY. This is the amount by which margin equity exceeds the Regulation T requirement. If margin equity is $10,000 and the Regulation T requirement is $8,000, then Regulation T's excess equity is $2,000. This figure is sometimes called the special memorandum account (SMA).

HOUSE EXCESS EQUITY (HOUSE SURPLUS). This is the amount by which margin equity exceeds house maintenance requirements. If margin equity is $10,000 and house maintenance requirement is $4,800, then house surplus is $5,200 ($10,000 − $4,800 = $5,200).

AVAILABLE TO BORROW. This is the amount of loan money available to a customer for cash withdrawal or for additional securities purchases. The loan amount is the lesser of the Regulation T excess equity (SMA) or the house surplus amount. If Regulation

T excess equity is $2,000 and house surplus is $5,200, then $2,000 is available to borrow.

BUYING POWER. This is the dollar amount available to purchase additional marginable securities. The amount is equal to the lesser of an account's available-to-borrow figure divided by the Regulation T requirement or the house maintenance requirement.

■ MARGIN TRADING ON YOUR ONLINE BROKERAGE ACCOUNT ■

Buying Stock on Margin Using Cash Deposits

In the following example, let's assume that Regulation T requires 50 percent and the house maintenance requirement is 30 percent. Because the NYSE requirement at 25 percent is always below the house requirement, I will not figure it in our examples. If your margin equity falls below 30 percent, you have violated your house requirement. If your margin equity should fall below 25 percent, you're in deep trouble.

Cash core	$20,000	Net worth	$20,000
Margin debit	0	Margin market value	0
Available to borrow	0	Regulation T (50%)	0
Regulation T excess	0	House requirement (30%)	0
House surplus	0	Buying power	40,000

The figures above show the beginning account balance for a customer who has deposited a check of $20,000. We'll assume that the check has been collected (cleared) and the funds are available. $20,000 is in cash core and is the account's net worth. Cash is 100 percent marginable, so the customer can borrow 100 percent of the cash core value to buy more stock as reflected by the buying power figure of $40,000. Let's assume that the customer decides to borrow money from the firm to buy $40,000 in marginable stock. What happens to the account balance after the trade?

Cash core	$ 0	Net worth/Margin equity	$20,000
Margin debit	20,000	Margin market value	40,000
Available to borrow	0	Regulation T (50%)	20,000
Regulation T excess	0	House requirement (30%)	12,000
House surplus	8,000	Buying power	0

Each marginable transaction initiates a fed call (the Regulation T 50 percent initial transaction requirement). When a trade is initiated, the computer searches cash core or available-to-borrow balances to meet the fed call. In the example here, the purchase of $40,000 of stock shares initiates a fed call for $20,000 ($40,000 margin market value × 50% Regulation T initial requirement = $20,000) and the computer finds the funds in cash core. The initial requirement has now been met, and after the trade has settled, there is no longer any cash core balance. All of the cash was applied to the purchase. You own $40,000 in stock (margin market value), your debit (the money you borrowed) is $20,000, and your margin equity is $20,000 ($40,000 margin market value – $20,000 margin debit). Now look at the margin requirements. Regulation T requires you to pay for 50 percent of the trade initially. You have satisfied this with your initial $20,000 deposit. The house requirement states that you must maintain at least 30 percent margin equity to secure your loan ($40,000 × 30% = $12,000). Your margin equity is $20,000, so you have more than the required amount. With margin equity at $20,000 and the house requirement at $12,000, you have a house surplus of $8,000. However, because you take the lesser of Regulation T excess (SMA) or house surplus, the available-to-borrow figure tells you that no more funds can be borrowed for cash withdrawals or additional stock purchases. Your account is considered fully margined.

What would have happened if you did not want to purchase the $40,000 maximum amount in your buying power? Let's go back and look at a purchase of only $25,000 of marginable stock. What happens to the account balances this time?

Cash core	$ 0	Net worth/Margin equity	$20,000
Margin debit	5,000	Margin market value	25,000
Available to borrow	7,500	Regulation T (50%)	12,500
Regulation T excess	7,500	House requirement (30%)	7,500
House surplus	12,500	Buying power	15,000

A fed call is issued for $12,500 ($25,000 × 50% = $12,500). The computer finds this balance and more in the cash core. Because you did not buy up to the maximum amount, the margin excess shows up in Regulation T excess ($20,000 margin equity – $12,500 Regulation T = $7,500 Regulation T excess). Your margin debit is only $5,000 ($20,000 cash core – $25,000 purchase = debit $5,000). Margin equity has not changed; it is still $20,000 ($25,000 margin market value – debit $5,000 = $20,000). The difference in this scenario is that you now can borrow additional cash of $7,500 or buy more stock on margin up to $15,000. The account is not fully margined. When you borrow money from your firm, the main categories that you want to focus on are your margin equity balance ($20,000) and your two margin require-ments—Regulation T ($12,500) and house requirement ($7,500). The questions that you must ask yourself are: Have you met Reg-ulation T and the house maintenance requirements? Do you have enough equity to collateralize the broker loan? In this case, the an-swer to both is yes.

Remember that Regulation T does not have to be met over the entire life of the loan, only at the initial transaction. House re-quirements need to be met for as long as the loan is outstanding. If this account falls below 50 percent margin equity after the trade, you have not violated Regulation T. However, this account is called a *restricted account*, which basically means that you need to make additional deposits to buy more stock. You don't have to bring in cash or sell stock to get the margin equity in the account back to 50 percent.

Continuing on with this example, what will happen to the ac-count balances if you decided to borrow the Regulation T excess by writing a check off of the account? Remember, you can borrow $7,500 because the account is not fully margined. Say you with-drew $4,000 more dollars. What happens?

Cash core	$ 0	Net worth/Margin equity	$16,000
Margin debit	9,000	Margin market value	25,000
Available to borrow	3,500	Regulation T (50%)	12,500
Regulation T excess	3,500	House requirement (30%)	7,500
House surplus	8,500	Buying power	7,000

Your debit balance increases by $4,000 to $9,000 and your mar-gin equity decreases by $4,000 to $16,000. This makes sense be-cause your margin market value minus your margin debit equals your margin equity ($25,000 margin market value – $9,000 debit balance = $16,000 margin equity). Increasing your debit in the equation decreases your equity; available-to-borrow and buying power have also been reduced. The $9,000 debit balance is not free money; you pay interest on the loan. Also, you must maintain a margin equity balance equal to or greater than the house requirement for the duration of the loan. If your stock should fall in price causing margin equity to fall below the house maintenance requirement (a violation known as a house call), you must bring in more cash or marginable securities to get your equity back to maintenance levels. (I'll examine house call violations a little later.)

Buying Stock on Margin Using Marginable Securities

Going back to our original example where $20,000 was deposited, what would the account look like if you paid in full for a purchase of $20,000 of marginable stock but executed the trade in the margin account instead of borrowing money? Assuming all margin requirements stay the same, let's take a look at what happens:

Cash core	$ 0	Net worth/Margin equity	$20,000
Margin debit	0	Margin market value	20,000
Available to borrow	10,000	Regulation T (50%)	10,000
Regulation T excess	10,000	House requirement (30%)	6,000
House surplus	14,000	Buying power	20,000

This is the flexibility that I was referring to earlier. Under these circumstances, you create buying power by placing marginable stock trades in the margin account rather than in the cash account. Look closely, you do not have a margin debt on the account. But you can borrow $10,000 in cash (the lesser of the Regulation T/SMA or the house surplus amount) or buy $20,000 in additional marginable stock (the lesser of available to borrow divided by the Regulation T percentage or the house requirement percentage). Say you researched a stock, found it to be a great buying opportunity, and wanted to buy shares right now. You have the funds elsewhere, perhaps at your bank, so you just need to get the trade in today and pay for it later. However, the computer won't allow you to buy any more stock in cash because you have no money in the cash core account. But you can borrow money to buy an additional $20,000 with the margin account. Here is what would happen if you purchased an additional $20,000 in marginable stock:

Cash core	$ 0	Net worth/Margin equity	$20,000
Margin debit	20,000	Margin market value	40,000
Available to borrow	0	Regulation T (50%)	20,000
Regulation T excess	0	House requirement (30%)	12,000
House surplus	8,000	Buying power	0

The new purchase of $20,000 initiates a fed call for $10,000 ($20,000 × 50%). The computer finds these funds in the available-to-borrow account. After the trade has been made, your account is fully margined, so you can't borrow any more money. Your next step is to confirm that your account equity is sufficient to collateralize your loan. To do this, look at your margin equity amount versus your house maintenance requirement. You have enough; you actually have a house surplus of $8,000 ($20,000 margin equity − $12,000 house requirement = $8,000 house surplus). However, you still cannot borrow additional money. Remember, available to borrow is the lesser of Regulation T excess/SMA or house surplus and here Regulation T excess/SMA is the lesser at $0.

What would happen in the event that your stocks rise in price? Continuing with the example above, let's assume that the market value of your shares has risen from $40,000 to $50,000. What happens?

Cash core	$ 0	Net worth/Margin equity	$30,000
Margin debit	20,000	Margin market value	50,000
Available to borrow	5,000	Regulation T (50%)	25,000
Regulation T excess	5,000	House requirement (30%)	15,000
House surplus	15,000	Buying power	10,000

The computer now recalculates the new balances; the only balance that remains the same is the debit balance. You still owe the firm $20,000. A rise in the market value of the stock doesn't change this fact. However, the rise in market value has created additional available-to-borrow ($5,000) and buying power ($10,000) that you can now use. For instance, suppose you decide to buy $10,000 more in marginable stock increasing your margin market value to $60,000:

Cash core	$ 0	Net worth/Margin equity $30,000
Margin debit	30,000	Margin market value	60,000
Available to borrow	0	Regulation T (50%)	30,000
Regulation T excess	0	House requirement (30%)	18,000
House surplus	12,000	Buying power	0

A fed call is created for $5,000 ($10,000 additional stock purchase × 50% Regulation T), which the computer finds in the available-to-borrow account. The account is again now fully margined, so you can't borrow any more money. Your margin debit has increased to $30,000 ($20,000 + $10,000 = $30,000). You owe your firm this money and it is charging you interest on it. The firm expects you to pay this loan back; if at any time your margin equity falls below the house requirement, you will be subject to a house call violation, and your online broker will demand that you bring in more cash or stock. From this example it's easy to see how in today's rising market, a continual increase in stock prices allows online traders to continually borrow more money. But what happens when stock prices begin falling? Read on.

■ HOUSE MAINTENANCE CALL VIOLATIONS ■

Continuing from our last example, let's assume that the market value of the stocks in the portfolio rise another $15,000 to $75,000 and you use the additional buying power generated from this increase to borrow more money to buy another $15,000 of marginable securities. At this point the account becomes fully margined. The $90,000 market value shown below is a result of the $60,000 original margin market value + $15,000 rise in market value + $15,000 additional stock purchase = $90,000. The $45,000 debit equals the original debit of $30,000 plus the new $15,000 purchase. The account now looks like this:

Cash core	$ 0	Net worth/Margin equity $45,000
Margin debit	45,000	Margin market value	90,000
Available to borrow	0	Regulation T (50%)	45,000
Regulation T excess	0	House requirement (30%)	27,000
House surplus	18,000	Buying power	0

Everything runs smoothly unless there is a major correction in the market. Let's look at a possible drop in stock value when all stocks in the portfolio are held at a 30 percent house maintenance requirement. How far can your margin market value drop before a house call violation occurs? The quickest way to calculate this level is to take the reciprocal of the house maintenance requirement percentage (if 30 percent, then the reciprocal is 70 percent) and divide that number into the debit balance ($45,000 ÷ 70% = $64,285). At the margin market value of $64,285 or a lower one, you will be subject to a house call violation and your firm will demand more funds. For example, let's assume the account drops in market value by $26,000 to a margin market value of $64,000. What happens?

Cash core	$ 0	Net worth/Margin equity	$19,000
Margin debit	45,000	Margin market value	64,000
Available to borrow	0	Regulation T (50%)	32,000
Regulation T excess	0	House requirement (30%)	19,200
House call violation	(200)	Buying power	0

With market value at $64,000, you have committed a house call violation for $200 ($19,000 margin equity − $19,200 house requirement = house call $200). The violation occurred because the margin equity is now only $19,000 ($64,000 margin market value − $45,000 debit balance = $19,000 margin equity), yet the house maintenance requirement is $19,200 ($64,000 margin market value × 30% house requirement percentage = $19,200 house requirement). This violation occurs because your market value has decreased but your debit balance remains the same, and thus your margin equity decreases. Remember you are not bound by Regulation T violation (fed call) because that type of requirement is applied only to initial transactions.

With the market dropping, your online broker starts to get nervous about all the loans outstanding on its books and decides it wants customers to maintain higher margin equity to secure broker loans. Therefore, the firm raises its house maintenance requirements across the board from 30 percent to 45 percent (yes, firms really do this). Borrowing money when the market was going up seemed easy, but now with the market dropping and your online broker raising margin requirement percentages, your account situation goes from bad to worse. After raising the house requirements to 45 percent, your house call violation increases to $9,800 ($19,000 margin equity – $28,800 margin requirement = $9,800 house call). Take a look:

Cash core	$ 0	Net worth/Margin equity	$19,000	
Margin debit	45,000	Margin market value	64,000	
Available to borrow	0	Regulation T (50%)	32,000	
Regulation T excess	0	House requirement (45%)	28,800	
House call violation	(9,800)	Buying power	0	

This house call violation must be met *promptly!* There are three ways to do this: (1) deposit cash in the amount of the call; (2) sell an amount of stock so the total value times the requirement (45% in this case) equals the call amount; or (3) deposit an amount of stock whose total value times the requirement's reciprocal (55% in this case) equals the call amount.

1. DEPOSITING $9,800 CASH. This will reduce your debit balance ($45,000 – $9,800 = $35,200) and increase your equity ($64,000 margin market value – $35,200 debit = $28,800 margin equity). The result is as follows:

Cash core	$ 0	Net worth/Margin equity	$28,800	
Margin debit	35,200	Margin market value	64,000	
Available to borrow	0	Regulation T (50%)	32,000	
Regulation T excess	0	House requirement (45%)	28,800	
House call violation	(0)	Buying power	10,000	

2. SELLING $21,800 IN STOCK ($9,800 ÷ 45% = $21,800 ROUNDED). This will reduce your debit ($45,000 – $21,800 = $23,200) and will reduce your margin market value ($64,000 original market value – $21,800 shares sold = $42,200 new market value). Your equity remains at $19,000. This works because now you have lowered both your debit balance and the house margin requirement is based on the new market value of $42,200 as follows:

Cash core	$ 0	Net worth/Margin equity	$19,000	
Margin debit	23,200	Margin market value	42,200	
Available to borrow	10	Regulation T (50%)	21,100	
Regulation T excess	2,100	House requirement (45%)	18,990	
House surplus	10	Buying power	0	

3. DEPOSITING $17,900 IN STOCK ($9,800 ÷ 55% = $17,900).
Your debit balance will not be affected, but your margin market
value will rise ($64,000 original market value + $17,900 shares
deposited = $81,900 new market value) as will your equity
($81,900 new market value − $45,000 debit = $36,900 new mar-
gin equity). This works because the total amount of the stock deposit will cause equity to rise more than enough to meet the
recalculated house requirement at $36,855 ($81,900 new market
value × 45% = $36,855) as follows:

Cash core	$ 0	Net worth/Margin equity	$36,900
Margin debit	45,000	Margin market value	81,900
Available to borrow	0	Regulation T (50%)	40,950
Regulation T excess	0	House requirement (45%)	36,855
House surplus	45	Buying power	0

To demonstrate the concept of margin more easily, all of our
earlier examples took for granted that all stock positions had the
same house maintenance requirements. In the real world, this is
not true. A diversified portfolio of stocks may have different house
requirement percentages on each stock position. For example, say
you had four stocks in your portfolio with market values and
house maintenance requirements as follows: $10,000 (30%);
$20,000 (35%); $10,000 (40%); and $50,000 (80%) adding up
to total margin market value of $90,000 and a total house re-
quirement of $54,000. Let's look at the example below and we'll
assume that this account already is running a debit balance of
$15,000:

Cash core	$ 0	Net worth/Margin equity	$75,000
Margin debit	15,000	Margin market value	90,000
Available to borrow	21,000	Regulation T (50%)	45,000
Regulation T excess	30,000	House requirement (all)	54,000
House surplus	21,000	Buying power	60,000

Here, the house requirement of $54,000 is equal to the sum
total of all individual stock position house maintenance requirements calculated by multiplying each position's market value
by its specific house requirement: $10,000 × 30% = $3,000 requirement; $20,000 × 35% = $7,000; and so on for each position.

You must perform this type of calculation whenever you have securities positions that maintain different house requirement percentages.

Be on the Lookout for Stocks with High House Maintenance Requirements!

Trading high-flying technology stocks (you know—the dot-com companies) can often get you into margin trouble. Because of their price volatility, many online brokers tend to require higher house maintenance requirements, often even higher than the initial Regulation T 50 percent requirement. You may enter into a trade that you believe is within your margin buying power limits, only to discover that you immediately traded into a house call.

Let's assume you deposit $20,000 in cash and would like to buy a dot-com company on margin. You believe that you only need to meet the 50 percent Regulation T initial requirement, so you fully margin the account and purchase $40,000 of the stock. The only problem is your online firm requires an 80 percent house requirement, or $32,000 ($40,000 margin market value × 80% house requirement percentage = $32,000 house requirement). Remember that house maintenance requirements double as initial requirements when they exceed the Regulation T's 50 percent requirement. This trade results in a house call of $12,000 ($20,000 margin equity − $32,000 house requirement). The table below shows how your account looks after the trade with the house call. Before you have even gotten your feet wet in the market, your online broker is demanding that you meet this call promptly!

Cash core	$ 0	Net worth/Margin equity	$20,000
Margin debit	20,000	Margin market value	40,000
Available to borrow	0	Regulation T (50%)	20,000
Regulation T excess	0	House requirement (80%)	32,000
House call violation	(12,000)	Buying power	0

▪ WHY INVESTORS USE MARGIN ▪

Now that you know more about what can go wrong when borrowing money from your online broker, you may ask yourself, why would any investor use margin? Two very good arguments for implementing margin strategies in your online brokerage account are discussed below.

1. LEVERAGE. Borrowing money from your online broker enables you to use leverage to buy more stock and increase your investment return. Take two scenarios. Customer A deposits $10,000 and buys $10,000 worth of stock. Customer B deposits $10,000 and buys $20,000 worth of the identical stock on margin (borrowing $10,000 from the online broker). The stock rises in price by 50 percent. Customer A's stock is now worth $15,000, and Customer B's stock is worth $30,000. Both customers decide to sell. Customer A makes $5,000 on the sale for a return of 50 percent on the $10,000 original investment. After paying back the broker's loan of $10,000, Customer B makes $10,000 on the trade (the $30,000 sale proceeds less the $10,000 loan less the $10,000 original investment). Customer B's return on the original $10,000 deposit is 100 percent. As good as this sounds, leverage also works the other way. Because Customer B owns more shares, the negative impact on the account will be much greater if the stock declines in price.

2. EASY ACCESS LOAN. Borrowing cash from your online broker can be as easy as writing a check. As long as you have been approved for margin and have available-to-borrow funds in your account, there is no need to fill out additional loan papers. If you need cash, just write a check. Broker loans are often set at lower rates than traditional debt, such as credit card debt. A broker loan could be used to pay down higher interest-bearing debt. But don't forget that any loan from your broker is a *demand loan* that can be called at any time. Also, it is a loan secured by your stocks and any sharp drop in stock prices could result in your broker's demanding more cash or stock from you.

■ STAY BALANCED ■

We've covered some complicated subject matter in this chapter, yet you should have more confidence in your ability to monitor your account balances. Tracking your account balances does not have to be an insurmountable task. Your balances may be larger or smaller than some of the examples that I have used, but the underlying concepts apply to all accounts. Keep the bigger picture in mind when you approach your account balances. When trying to figure out your total account value, think of positions in terms of ownership (long) and obligations (short).

If you decide to borrow on margin from your online broker, think first about the federal Regulation T initial requirements; then consider the house maintenance requirements. Each margin transaction you enter into, whether a stock, bond, or option trade, has a requirement that must be met. Know the requirement and you'll know what is expected of you. If you are uncertain about your online firm's requirements on a particular trade, ask before you enter it. You want to avoid trading into requirement violations at all costs. However, as you begin placing trades, be cautious but don't be intimidated. If you understand the concepts that I have just discussed, you should avoid trouble.

CHAPTER 6

The Trading Exchanges

■ ONLINE BROKERS AS AGENTS ■

With the previous chapters firmly under your belt, it's time to move on to trading. However, don't underestimate all that you have accomplished up to this point. Countless numbers of investors have failed to reach this stage as seamlessly and quickly as you. You may not realize it now, but you already have saved yourself money and time by completing those first steps successfully (before making your first trade), and isn't that what investing is all about—making money by growing your account? You would never have been able to enter a single trade without having finished those earlier tasks. Remember what I told you earlier: Investing online is not as easy as pointing and clicking your mouse. And this will become more evident as you delve into how markets operate.

Trading can be fun and rewarding if you know what you are doing. Talking with friends and colleagues about potential investments, researching companies, tracking the markets, or celebrating winning stock picks are all moments to savor. However, they will be few and far between if you don't understand how trading markets operate or how certain market conditions affect them. Otherwise, you will wind up confused, frustrated, and angry at the outcome of your trade orders. The most common questions posed by online traders are: Where did my order go? Why wasn't my order filled? Why was I filled at that price?

To answer these questions you need to understand how markets operate and how trades are processed. Not all securities trade alike nor are all market conditions alike. Some securities trade in auction markets like the New York Stock Exchange (NYSE) where buyers and sellers set market prices by competing with each other, whereas other stocks trade in negotiated markets like the National Association of Securities Dealers Automated Quotations (Nasdaq), where buying and selling are done out of dealers' inventories. Still other markets, such as electronic communication networks (ECNs), consist solely of computer hardware and software that merely match anonymous customer orders.

Most of the time, trades processing on exchanges operate smoothly. Extreme market volatility or heavy trading volume, however, can alter the mechanics of how your trade is executed. Recognizing these situations will influence the types of orders you place. For example, buy and sell orders in auction markets may yield results different from identical orders placed in negotiated or ECN markets. Trades executed under fast market conditions, where extremely high volume causes stock quotes to be delayed, can result in orders being executed at prices other than the displayed stock quotes. You will never be able to invest to your utmost advantage unless you understand this.

You are at the controls when it comes to placing your trades. Your online broker merely follows your trade instructions. The process begins when you enter your order online. It is you who decides when to enter the marketplace, how many shares to buy or sell, and the price. You also set the parameters of whether the order will be at market or at a limit price, for the day or good until canceled, or a partial execution or all or nothing. The outcome of any trade starts with your instructions; when the trade execution is not what you had intended, you most likely gave the wrong instructions.

Online brokerage firms do not act as your investment advisor. They are not picking stocks or timing the market for you. Their relationship with you is only as an *agent* in your transaction, which means that they take your order, send it to the appropriate marketplace or exchange for execution in accordance to your instructions, and then report back the results. They do not act as *principals,* who buy and sell from their own inventories and try to collect profits from the markup or spread. In fact, it is illegal for them to act as both an agent collecting a commission and as a principal taking a markup in the same transaction. Your online broker acts only as an agent and collects a commission.

As an agent, your online broker sends your orders to the various markets for execution. Once your order is entered online, it is routed to a market that can fill it at the best execution price available. The broker can send orders to several different places—stock orders to the NYSE, the American Stock Exchange, the Nasdaq, a market maker, a regional exchange like the Philadelphia Exchange, an ECN such as Island, or internally (kept in-house). Option contracts can be directed to such exchanges as the American Exchange, the Pacific Exchange, or the Chicago Board Options Exchange.

There is so much more that goes on in the processing of your trades than you could ever imagine. Visit your local stock exchange if you have any doubts. What you'll see will surprise you. The mechanics in executing a trade are more involved than what you experience sitting at your personal computer. Look at the structure of the following exchanges and do your best to understand them. It may be difficult to absorb it all, but don't worry. There is no need to commit these processes to memory. The point in showing you these exchange operations is to demonstrate that executing your trade orders is not as easy as you may think. There is a lot going on behind the scenes.

■ THE NEW YORK STOCK EXCHANGE ■

The New York Stock Exchange is one of the oldest and most recognized exchanges in the United States. Known as the Big Board, it is located at 11 Wall Street in New York City as a monument to all things capitalistic. Founded in 1792 and registered as an exchange with the SEC in 1934, the NYSE today is a nonprofit corporation boasting 412 member firms. The governing body of the exchange consists of a 25-member board of directors, a chairman and CEO, 12 representatives of the public, and 12 representatives of the securities industry.

The exchange functions as an auction marketplace. Member firms, of which your online broker is one, meet on the exchange floor to buy and sell securities on your behalf. Only exchange members are permitted to trade on the exchange floor. The NYSE has about 3,700 securities listed on the exchange. A listed security is one that is priced and traded on a registered exchange as opposed to an unlisted security traded in the over-the-counter market. Not all companies are eligible to be listed on the NYSE. Companies must have and must maintain minimum capital requirements in order to be listed.

All trading of individual securities takes place at a certain spot on the exchange floor known as the trading post. Brokers needing to buy and sell shares of RJ Reynolds, for example, must go to the trading post where RJR (the stock's symbol) is being traded. Each post may trade several different stocks and it is the responsibility of individuals known as *specialists* to maintain a fair and orderly market in the stocks they are assigned.

The specialist is the backbone of the NYSE's auction market. Although most orders are handled by the NYSE's Super-DOT electronic trading system, it is the role of the specialist that makes the NYSE unique. The rules of supply and demand establish the inside market or best quote for a security, but it is the specialist who stands ready to buy and sell stock for his or her own account in times of market volatility. The inside market quote represents the highest price someone is willing to pay for a stock (its bid price) and the lowest price someone is willing to sell their stock for (its ask price).

At the time of this writing, the majority of stocks traded on the NYSE and other market centers are trading in increments based on fractions, such as $\frac{1}{16}$. However, as of September 25, 2000, 57 stock issues will have switched over to decimalization pricing. For example, today you may notice a number of stocks as bid 20.01 and ask 20.05. A complete change to decimalization is not scheduled to be phased in until April 9, 2001. When this occurs, stocks will trade in increments of 1 cent, and options will trade in increments of 5 cents (option issues quoted under $3) and 10 cents (option issues quoted at $3 or greater). These new trading increments are known as minimum price variations (MPVs). Because most stocks are still quoted in fractions, all pricing examples throughout this text will employ fractions.

Quotes on the NYSE reflect your order to buy or to sell. If the quote on the NYSE is bid 20 and ask 20⅛ and you enter a buy at 20¹⁄₁₆ and your online broker sends the order to the NYSE, the quote would change to bid 20¹⁄₁₆ to ask 20⅛ (see below). Market forces of supply and demand determine prices on the NYSE.

Last trade: 20¹⁄₁₆—Both a buyer and a seller have executed a trade at 20¹⁄₁₆.

Bid: 20¹⁄₁₆—Price that you are willing to pay for the stock.

Spread: —Difference between the bid and ask price, here ⅟₁₆.

Ask: 20⅛—Price for which someone else is willing to sell
             the stock.

Trading on the NYSE

Specialists can trade as dealers, buying and selling stocks for their
own account, or as agents, executing orders that have been left
with them by other brokers. It is unlawful for a specialist to execute orders on behalf of his own account when he is holding an
executable public order. It is normally the commission house broker or the two-dollar broker who receives the order via the broker
booth support system that runs your order out to the trading posts.
Commission house brokers are floor brokers hired by member firms
to execute their own customer orders. When they are busy, orders
are given to two-dollar brokers for execution. Two-dollar brokers
are freelance floor brokers who long ago got their name because
they were paid $2 for executing one round lot of 100 shares.

The specialist does not take part in all trade executions. Yet all
trades must take place in front of the specialist post. Floor brokers
who meet in front of the specialist's trading post form what is
called the "trading crowd." Here floor brokers representing buyers and sellers from all over the world shout out bids and offers in
an attempt to execute customer orders at the best price.

Orders not executed electronically are traded on the exchange
floor in the following manner. You enter an order on your computer to buy 1,000 shares of XYZ Corp. at the market when the
stock quote is bid 25 and ask 25¼, size 10 x 10. The size represents
the number of shares bid and offered and is abbreviated for quot-
ing purposes. The true size is found by adding two zeroes to whatever numbers are printed. Therefore, for XYZ, there are 1,000
shares bid at 25 and 1,000 shares offered for sale at 25¼ (ask).

Bid: 25   Size 10 (Someone wants to buy 1,000 shares at 25.)
Ask: 25¼   Size 10 (Someone wants to sell 1,000 shares at 25¼.)

At the same time your order to buy was being entered, a customer at another firm in Arizona enters an order to sell 1,000 shares
of XYZ Corp. at market. Both orders are routed to the exchange
floor. The floor broker takes your order out to the post, where an
inquiry is made about the market for XYZ. Working to get you a
better price, the floor broker representing your order shouts out,

"25⅛ for 1,000." Hoping to get a better price than the current ask of 25¼, the broker representing the Arizona customer and recognizing the opportunity to get a better price for his customer, shouts, "Sold 1,000 at an ⅛." The trade is completed and a report is sent back to your broker confirming that you have purchased 1,000 shares of XYZ at 25⅛, actually one-eighth better than the inside market quote. (This is known as *price improvement*.) The report is then posted to your online account.

Because volume can get heavy and orders are continuously arriving at the post, the exchange has implemented official procedures for handling orders that arrive simultaneously; specialists and floor brokers in the crowd execute orders according to a procedure known as *priority, precedence,* and *parity.*

PRIORITY. Only one order can have priority and that order is the first order arriving at the post that is at the highest bid and the lowest offer. It is determined by the time of entry. Sometimes priority comes down to mere seconds. The broker who has priority must receive the next execution unless there is a subsequent better bid or offer. The order must be for at least one round lot. (A round lot order refers to a generally accepted unit of trading.) Most exchanges consider a round lot order to consist of 100 shares and multiples of 100—200, 300, 400, 500, and so on. An odd lot is an amount less than the generally accepted unit of trading. A trading unit of 1 to 99 shares would be considered an odd lot. The order will still maintain priority even if it is left with another broker to be executed. Customer orders, or "off-floor" orders, have priority over orders initiated on the floor.

PRECEDENCE. Precedence is considered only after priority. The broker that can best fill the order or who can fill the order completely has precedence. In the event that priority cannot be established, then larger orders take precedence over smaller orders.

PARITY. Parity is used when priority and precedence can't be determined. If two brokers enter orders at the same time and at the same bid or offer and for the same number of shares, they must come to an equitable decision on their own or settle the impasse by a coin toss. Yes, a coin toss. With all the technology available, there is a small chance, rare but possible, that your execution could be based on the flip of a coin.

FIGURE 6.1 // A Stock Trade on the NYSE

| Online customer A enters an order to buy 100 shares of IBM. | Online customer B enters an order to sell 100 shares of IBM. |

The two orders are routed by the online brokers' order-routing system to the NYSE. Orders can be sent to the floor in two ways. If they go through the broker booth support system, the orders are received by each brokerage firm's clerks. The clerks then pass orders on to the firm's floor brokers, who take them to the trading post for execution. If the electronic SuperDot system is used, orders are sent directly to the specialist's workstation.

At the post, the specialist who handles IBM makes sure the transactions are executed fairly and in an orderly manner.

The two floor brokers compete with other brokers on the trading floor to get the best price for their customers. The brokers representing customer A and customer B agree on a price.

After the transaction is executed, the specialist's workstation sends a notice to the firm originating the orders and to the consolidated tape so that a written record is made of every transaction.

The transaction is reported by computer and appears within seconds on the consolidated tape displays across the country and around the world.

The transaction is processed electronically, crediting customer A's brokerage firm and debiting customer B's brokerage firm. Both customers receive a trade confirmation from their respective firms within a few days describing the trade, its terms and conditions, and the exact amount to be tendered or credited.

| Customer A settles his account within three business days after the transaction by submitting payment to his online brokerage firm for the 100 shares of IBM plus any applicable commissions. | Customer B's trade is also settled in three business days. Her account will be credited with the proceeds of the sale of stock minus any applicable commissions. |

Source: NYSE, *You and the Investment World*, NYSE Inc., 1998.

The Specialist's Book

Also referred to as the limit order book, the specialist uses this electronic book to record customer limit orders and stop loss orders that are "away from the market." The book also contains the specialist's inventory of stocks as well as customer market orders to sell short. Orders are recorded in the book chronologically by price and by the sequence in which they were received. The inside quote is taken from the specialist's book and is valid only for the moment it is given. Quotes taken from the book give both the best bid and ask prices along with their size. A quote doesn't reflect any orders that may be held by brokers in the crowd.

Specialists execute orders from their book on a basis of first in, first out. Subsequently, the bid and ask quotes and their sizes are constantly changing. Because of these dynamics, you need to understand that your orders are executed according to the prices reflected on the specialist's book when the order is presented, not at the quoted price that may be displayed on your PC. A sample page from a specialist's limit order book is shown below.

Sample Page from a Specialist's Limit Order Book Trading in the Hypothetical ABC Corp.

BUY	ABC	SELL
Broker A—200	30	
Broker B—100		
Broker K—100	$\frac{1}{16}$	
Broker F—100	$\frac{1}{8}$	
Broker G—300		
	$\frac{3}{16}$	
Broker J—200	$\frac{1}{4}$	
	$\frac{5}{16}$	
	$\frac{3}{8}$	
	$\frac{7}{16}$	
	$\frac{1}{2}$	Broker C—100
		Broker D—200
	$\frac{9}{16}$	Broker L—100
	$\frac{5}{8}$	Broker E—600
	$\frac{11}{16}$	
	$\frac{3}{4}$	Broker H—300
	$\frac{13}{16}$	
	$\frac{7}{8}$	Broker I—100
	$\frac{15}{16}$	

(Callout: "Best bid" pointing to Broker J—200 at $\frac{1}{4}$; Callout: "Best offer" pointing to $\frac{1}{2}$ / Broker C—100)

The quote for ABC stock that would be displayed to the public in the above example would be 30¼ to 30½, size 2 x 3:

Bid: 30¼   Size 2 (Broker J wants to buy 200 shares at 30¼).
Ask: 30½   Size 3 (Brokers C and D want to sell a total of 300 shares at 30½.)

If a broker enters the crowd with a sell order for 400 shares at the market, the specialist would fill the order with broker J's 200 shares at 30¼ and broker G's 200 shares at 30⅛. This would fill the broker's sell order completely and still leave broker G with an outstanding limit order to buy 100 shares at 30⅛. If, on the other hand, an order to buy 300 shares of ABC at the market enters the crowd, the specialist would fill the complete order from broker C and broker D.

Sometimes the specialist will "stop your order out" at a certain price, a technique known as *stopping stock*. For example, a market order to sell 100 shares of ABC can automatically be executed at 30¼ in the above example. The specialist can stop you out at 30¼, thus guaranteeing you that price while still working to get you a better price. If a higher sell price can't be obtained, the order is filled at 30¼, even if the bid price drops to 30⅛. It is the role of the floor brokers and the specialists to fill your orders at the best possible execution price attainable under the prevailing market conditions.

▪ THE AMERICAN STOCK EXCHANGE ▪

The American Stock Exchange (AMEX), like its floor exchange counterpart the NYSE, is a private nonprofit corporation that also trades stock auction style. The AMEX is the second largest floor exchange in the United States and was originally referred to as the Curb Market. In 1998, the AMEX and the National Association of Securities Dealers (NASD) merged to form the Nasdaq-AMEX Market. The AMEX was the first exchange (on May 7, 1997) to trade all stocks in one-sixteenths.

The AMEX has approximately 661 regular members who trade equities and about 203 option principals who execute transactions in option contracts. The AMEX uses a specialist system to facilitate a fair and orderly trading market for its stocks. Unlike the NYSE, AMEX specialists act as a unit of three or more individuals who trade assigned securities at specified posts; but like the NYSE, the vast majority of public orders are executed without the intervention of any specialists. Orders are transmitted to the exchange electronically when member organizations (e.g., your online firm) enter buy and sell orders for the public or when registered floor brokers place orders.

Orders sent to the AMEX are routed to the trading floor by means of the Common Message Switch (CMS). After an order is received, it then passes to the AMEX Order File (AOF). The AOF retains order details and then sends the order to the appropriate AMEX order-processing application. For stock trades, these applications are the AMEX (Equity) Display Book (ADB) and the Equity Odd-lot Auto-Ex. The ADB and the NYSE's limit order book perform similar functions. The Equity Odd-lot Auto-Ex offers automatic execution of eligible customer orders at the national best bid/offer (NBBO).

Orders that are not entered into the AMEX automated order-processing system are executed and reported manually by floor brokers. Floor brokers have the option to enter the order into the AMEX automated order-processing system or not. If they do, the order is handled like any other order that would have originally been entered into the order-processing system by a member firm's order room.

The AMEX describes its typical postopening trade execution process this way:

> After the opening and throughout the trading day, round lot orders are accumulated in the ADB in time sequence by order type and price. Through the ADB, the Specialist can report executions on individual orders or a group of orders. Guaranteed locked-in trade reports are automatically sent to the trading parties and the Market Data System for display on the tape. Odd-lot market orders routed through the AMEX systems after an issue opens are automatically executed and reported on an individual basis, at the current national 'best bid/offer' (BBO). Odd-lot limit orders to buy with limit prices equal to or higher than the offer and sell orders with limit prices equal to or lower than the bid are also automatically executed at the BBO. 'Away from the market' odd-lot limit orders are routed to the Specialist for execution and reporting. (Source: American Stock Exchange <www.amex.com>.)

A flow chart of a trade execution is shown in Figure 6.2.

FIGURE 6.2 // A Stock Trade on the AMEX

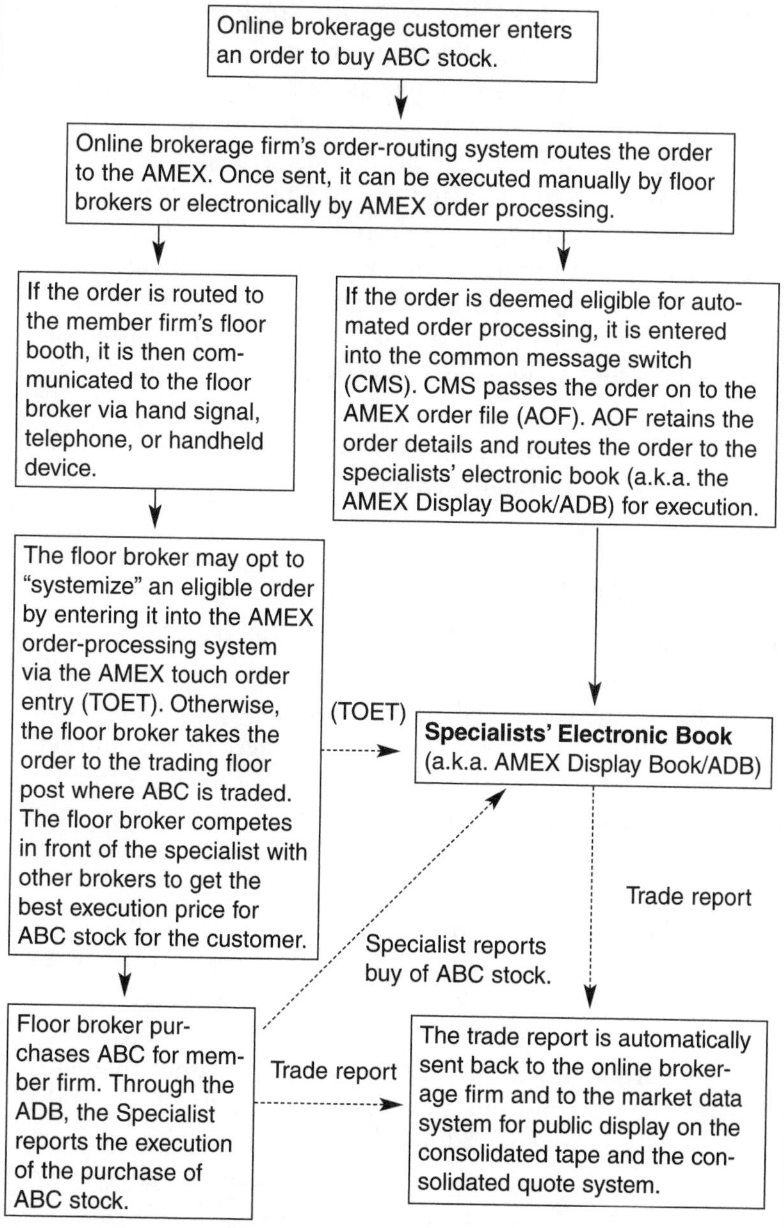

Online brokerage customer enters an order to buy ABC stock.

Online brokerage firm's order-routing system routes the order to the AMEX. Once sent, it can be executed manually by floor brokers or electronically by AMEX order processing.

If the order is routed to the member firm's floor booth, it is then communicated to the floor broker via hand signal, telephone, or handheld device.

If the order is deemed eligible for automated order processing, it is entered into the common message switch (CMS). CMS passes the order on to the AMEX order file (AOF). AOF retains the order details and routes the order to the specialists' electronic book (a.k.a. the AMEX Display Book/ADB) for execution.

The floor broker may opt to "systemize" an eligible order by entering it into the AMEX order-processing system via the AMEX touch order entry (TOET). Otherwise, the floor broker takes the order to the trading floor post where ABC is traded. The floor broker competes in front of the specialist with other brokers to get the best execution price for ABC stock for the customer.

(TOET)

Specialists' Electronic Book (a.k.a. AMEX Display Book/ADB)

Trade report

Specialist reports buy of ABC stock.

Floor broker purchases ABC for member firm. Through the ADB, the Specialist reports the execution of the purchase of ABC stock.

Trade report

The trade report is automatically sent back to the online brokerage firm and to the market data system for public display on the consolidated tape and the consolidated quote system.

■ THE PHILADELPHIA AND OTHER REGIONAL EXCHANGES ■

The Philadelphia Stock Exchange, Boston Stock Exchange, Chicago Stock Exchange, Cincinnati Stock Exchange, and the Pacific Stock Exchange make up what are known as the regional exchanges. They are national security exchanges registered with the SEC that list not only regional company stocks but also stocks from the NYSE and the AMEX. Securities listed on regional exchanges and major exchanges simultaneously are referred to as *dually listed stocks.*

The listing requirements of the regional exchanges are less stringent than those of the larger national exchanges. Because of this, you may find names of smaller local companies listed on the regionals. Trading volume on regionals amounts to only a fraction of that which takes place on the Big Board (i.e., the NYSE). Yet more than 50 percent of the companies listed on the NYSE are also listed on the regional exchanges.

The Philadelphia Stock Exchange

The Philadelphia Stock Exchange (PHLX) is the oldest stock exchange in the United States. It was founded in 1790 to facilitate the trading of newly issued bank stocks and government bonds. Where once traders gathered on street corners to buy and sell securities with slips of paper, today the PHLX can boast that it was the first exchange to enter the world of the Internet. The PHLX trades over 2,600 listed stocks, over 800 equity options, 14 sector index funds, and 100 "currency pairs."

The PHLX strives to fulfill its self-regulatory obligations as well as the SEC's mandate to fill customer orders at the best execution quality possible. Like so many other exchanges today, the PHLX has invested heavily in technology to meet this challenge. Customer orders on the PHLX are executed either manually by specialists or electronically by a system called PACE or by the recently installed Advanced Price Improvement (API) mechanism. Both electronic systems are in place to execute eligible trades at prices better than the national best bid/offer (NBBO).

In 1998, the API mechanism was put in place to complement the PACE system, which includes the Public Order Exposure System (POES). The POES gives the specialists a 30-second window to improve the execution price of certain orders. Eligible orders processed by the API mechanism take priority over the POES and thus ensure an immediate turnaround of orders at improved pricing. According to the PHLX, "The API Mechanism instantly evaluates the NBBO at the time of order entry, and if the order is deemed eligible . . . the order will automatically be executed at a price that is $\frac{1}{16}$ better than the NBBO—no manual intervention by a specialist is necessary." The PHLX's PACE system with API mechanism capabilities, as well as the Boston Exchange's Boston Exchange Automated Communications and Order Routing Network (BEACON), and the Pacific Coast Exchange's P/COAST's system are all electronic mechanisms put in place to ensure that your order receives the best execution price possible.

▪ ELECTRONIC COMMUNICATION NETWORKS ▪

Electronic communication networks (ECNs) are the new kids on the block for retail order execution. ECNs, or alternative trading systems (ATS) as they are called, are not stock exchanges, however, they do register with the SEC as an ATS under Rule 17a-23. Most often, ECNs are also members of the NASD and the Security Investor Protection Corporation (SIPC). In April 1999, Island ECN became the first ECN to approach the SEC with its intention to file to become a registered stock exchange. Other ECNs in the marketplace include Instinet, Archipelago, NexTrade, Spear, Leeds & Kellogg, and Redibook.

ECNs are pure electronic trading systems that consist only of computer networks. There are no exchange floors or people involved in the execution of your order. These computer systems gather, organize, and match customer orders without the assistance of a specialist or market maker. Market makers are dealers who buy and sell securities from their own inventory, acting as principal and profiting from the spread (a further discussion of market makers is found in the following section on the Nasdaq market). In the ECN marketplace, buyers and sellers bypass specialists and market makers and meet directly to represent their own trades in the marketplace. If you entered an order to sell a stock at $15, the computer matches your order with another customer who wants to buy the stock at the market or at the price of $15. If a match is found, your order is executed. Currently, ECNs process mostly Nasdaq securities only and, according to the SEC, account for 22 percent of all trading in Nasdaq stock. Island ECN, for instance, trades such well-known stocks as Dell, Microsoft, Intel, Yahoo!, and Amazon.com. It processes from 80 million to 100 million shares daily and transacts over $5 billion in volume each day.

Although ATSs may establish their own computerized rules and procedures, the mechanics of order processing on ECNs are basic. (See Figure 6.3.) An online broker choosing to participate in an ECN market would route your buy or sell order to an ECN's computer. If the order is matched with another investor's order, an instantaneous execution occurs. If there is not a match, the system could send unmatched orders to the Nasdaq or display the order until a match is found and the order can be executed.

The simplicity of processing trades on ECNs reduces trading costs and therefore makes them attractive for both brokerage firms and customers alike. An additional advantage of ECN trading is that it offers extended trading hours. Unlike the current operating hours of

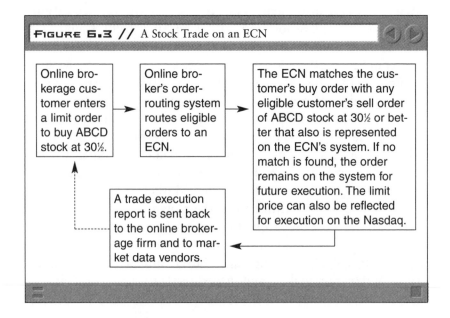

FIGURE 6.3 // A Stock Trade on an ECN

Online brokerage customer enters a limit order to buy ABCD stock at 30½.

Online broker's order-routing system routes eligible orders to an ECN.

The ECN matches the customer's buy order with any eligible customer's sell order of ABCD stock at 30½ or better that also is represented on the ECN's system. If no match is found, the order remains on the system for future execution. The limit price can also be reflected for execution on the Nasdaq.

A trade execution report is sent back to the online brokerage firm and to market data vendors.

the NYSE and over-the-counter markets that primarily trade from 9:30 AM EST to 4 PM EST, some ECNs trade from 8 AM to 8 PM. Some are suggesting that these hours may be extended to 24-hour trading.

■ THE NASDAQ STOCK MARKET ■

Securities that do not trade in the auction markets or on traditional exchange floors trade in what are known as negotiated markets. These types of markets are made up of a network of broker-dealers or market makers who communicate electronically. These market makers stand ready to buy and sell securities to and from institutional and public investors for their own accounts. They risk their own capital in order to supply liquidity to the markets. The biggest of this type of market is the Nasdaq Stock Market.

The Nasdaq Stock Market began operations in February of 1971 as the world's first electronic stock market. It's currently the fastest growing stock market in the United States and ranks second among the world securities markets in terms of dollar volume. In 1994, it surpassed the NYSE in annual share volume. The Nasdaq has two tiers of listed companies: The Nasdaq National Market, which comprises the top 4,000 Nasdaq companies that have met higher listing requirements, and the Nasdaq Small-Cap Market, which is made up of over 1,000 small emerging-growth companies. The Nasdaq also created the OTC Bulletin Board (OTCBB) to give investors information on and access to securities not listed on the Nasdaq. Ever evolving, the NASD and the AMEX merged in 1998 to form The Nasdaq-AMEX Market Group.

The Nasdaq is a negotiated market where market makers and ECNs compete for customers' buy and sell orders. Unlike the NYSE, the Nasdaq has no central trading location; instead, the approximately 1,000 participants (market making firms, order entry firms, and ECNs) communicate electronically by computer networks or telephone. Both the SEC and the NASD regulate the market. The NASD is the self-regulatory body that governs and enforces regulations pertaining to trading and market making activities. NASD member firms are permitted only to do business with other NASD member firms.

Market makers who wish to trade on the Nasdaq must not only be NASD members but must also meet certain minimum net capital requirements. NASD members must also adhere to the Rules of Fair Practice governing broker-customer procedures; the Uniform Practice Code, covering broker to broker-dealer relationships; and the Business Conduct Committee, which handles grievances. There are more than 4,800 companies listed on the Nasdaq, with a total market value of $5.2 trillion. Some of the more well-known companies are 3Com, Oracle, Microsoft, Intel, WorldCom Inc., Dell Computer, Amgen Inc., Amazon.com, eBay, Starbucks, and Yahoo!

Market Makers on the Nasdaq

Although there are countless computer systems and telecommunications networks that support Nasdaq trading, the backbone of the system is the market maker. These independent dealers act as distributors for Nasdaq-listed stocks. They invest their own capital at their own risk to build an inventory of stocks, which they hope to trade actively for a profit. Their goal, like that of most investors, is to buy low and sell high. Market makers display quotes to the public that reflect their buy and sell interest. Each market maker has access to Nasdaq's trading and quote system, and once a quote is posted, it is displayed for all market participants to see. It is important to understand that when you trade on the Nasdaq, you are trading with market makers, order entry firms, and ECNs in a negotiated market, not necessarily with other public investors in an auction market. Therefore, many times you are buying and selling at market maker prices. To keep Nasdaq markets fair and orderly, and maintain liquidity, market makers are required to do the following:

- Disclose their buy and sell interest by displaying two-sided quotes for all stocks in which they choose to make a market (buy and sell stock out of inventory).
- Display both quotes and orders in the Nasdaq in compliance with the Securities and Exchange Commission's order-handling rules.
- Honor their quoted prices and report trading in a timely manner.

In January 1997, the SEC imposed new order-handling rules on the NASD to allow ECNs access to the Nasdaq trading and quotation system. It also mandated that eligible customer limit orders between 100 and 10,000 shares that are priced better than a dealer's own quote be reflected in the displayed quote or forwarded to an ECN for display. These rule enhancements have reduced the average spread size on a stock quote by 40 percent and has resulted in increased liquidity and cost savings to all online traders.

Quoting and Executing Trades on the Nasdaq

The most confusing aspect of trading in the Nasdaq market for online investors is how to read the Nasdaq quotes. Even though the 1997 SEC order-handling rules made it possible for certain customer bids and offers to be displayed, the inside market quotations are generally market maker quotes. The inside market quotation, or "inside market," shows the highest price that a market maker is willing to pay you for your stock—the bid—while the ask price is the lowest price at which a dealer is willing to sell stock to you. In the Nasdaq market the bid and ask represent two different trades. The difference between the bid and ask price is known as the spread and represents the market maker's profit. Quotes are normally good for at least 100 shares or one round lot.

Executing a trade on the Nasdaq first begins with the quote. A Nasdaq stock quote could display a price of 30 to 30¼, which means that the best price at which you can sell your stock to a market maker is 30—the bid—and the lowest price at which you can buy stock from a market maker is 30¼—the ask. Now, if you have an order in to sell 100 shares at 30⅛, and you see trades on the tape being executed at 30¼, your stock may not have been sold (even though your offer to sell at 30⅛ is lower than the last trade at 30¼).

Last Trade: 30¼—Price at which someone purchased stock from the market maker.

Bid: 30—Price at which a market maker is willing to buy stock from you.

Spread: —Difference between bid and ask and is the market maker's profit.

Ask: 30¼—Price at which a market maker is willing to sell stock to you.

Unlike the NYSE, where the last trade represents both a buy and a sell, a trade executed at 30¼ on the Nasdaq, when the stock is quoted 30¼, most likely reflects only buy trades. Remember, you are trying to sell stock to the market maker and he or she is only willing to pay you 30 for your stock when the inside market is bid 30–ask 30¼. Therefore, your online broker may not owe you a trade report. To get an execution on your sell order at 30¼, the quote would need to move up to bid 30¼–ask 30½, or another public order to sell at a better limit or at market would need to be entered. Quotes on Nasdaq work as follows:

Quote	Market Maker	Customer
BID	Buying	Selling
ASK	Selling	Buying

You will come across two levels of quotes on the Nasdaq. The standard publicly displayed quote that I have been discussing is referred to as the inside market quote, the best quote, or a Level 1 quote. It shows the highest price attainable when you sell your stock and the lowest price available when you buy stock. The second type of quote is a Level 2 quote, which was discussed in Chapter 2. As a reminder, a Level 2 quote displays each individual market maker's or ECNs bid/ask and size. Level 2 quotes show all of the market makers and ECNs participating in the stock and therefore gives you a better indication of how the stock is truly trading.

Small Order Execution System (SOES)

The SOES is an automatic execution system used to execute stock orders up to 1,000 shares. Participation in the SOES is mandatory for all market makers in Nasdaq national market securities. Orders entered into the SOES by your online broker are sent to a market maker with the best bid or ask. The SOES ensures that the order is filled automatically at the best price. You, as a retail client, cannot send orders directly to the SOES. It is an internal system used at times by your online firm to get the best fill possible and was meant to help small investors by providing liquidity on smaller orders. Although your online broker is highly regulated, as a retail customer, you are not and abuses of the SOES have occurred by individuals known as "SOES bandits." For example, an SOES bandit intending to sell 20,000 shares of a Nasdaq stock would enter 20 continuous orders to sell 1,000 or fewer shares at the market, knowing that the trades could be executed automatically by the SOES. This splitting of an order to intentionally manipulate the SOES system is considered a violation and could be met with a reprimand or worse from your online broker.

Today, the new order-handling rules give you greater access to the Nasdaq market. However, although Nasdaq has leveled its playing field for retail investors and is no longer 100 percent market maker–quote driven, it still is, at its core, a negotiated market where market makers buy stock from you and sell stocks to others in search of profits.

A flow chart showing a typical trade execution on the Nasdaq is shown in Figure 6.4.

■ OPTIONS TRADING AND THE CHICAGO BOARD OPTIONS EXCHANGE ■

Option contracts trade on several exchanges. Unlike stock exchanges, options exchanges do not have a multitiered market structure. They do not differentiate themselves by being either a major or a regional exchange. There is no real primary market for option trading. The Chicago Board Options Exchange, the Philadelphia Stock Exchange, the American Stock Exchange, and the Pacific Stock Exchange all trade option contracts and can compete for the same customer orders. Option contracts trade in an auction style market where option investors come together with market makers to buy and sell.

The Options Clearing Corporation (OCC) is the issuer of all option contracts on the CBOE, the PHLX, the AMEX, and the PCOS. As the issuer, the OCC guarantees that both parties fulfill their trade obligations. This essentially means that the OCC takes the opposite side of every option contract that is traded, becoming the seller for every buyer and the buyer for every seller. As its name suggests, the Options Clearing Corporation's main function is to clear option trades. This allows option traders to buy and sell without having to track down the other party in the transaction. It is the OCC that processes the exchange of money and maintains option trade records. It also sets the ethical standards under which all option traders operate.

The largest options marketplace in the world is the Chicago Board Options Exchange (CBOE). Today, the CBOE accounts for

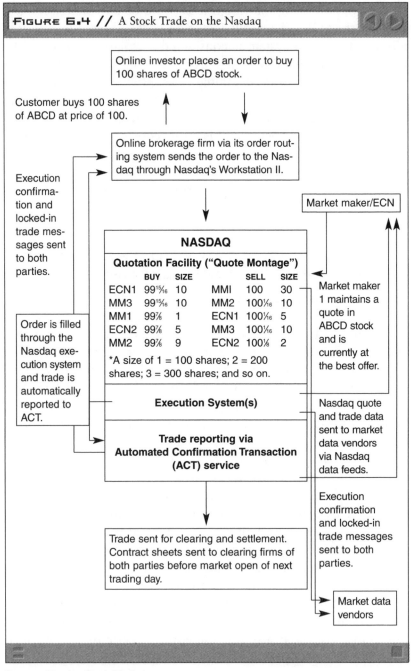

Figure 6.4 // A Stock Trade on the Nasdaq

Source: Nasdaq Stock Market.

more than 51 percent of all U.S. options trading and 91 percent of all index options trading. In 1999 alone, it handled 221,256,576 option contracts. It was founded in April 1973 and is located in downtown Chicago. The CBOE conducts trading business on a 45,000-square-foot trading floor with 50,000 miles of electrical wires. It is said that the exchange floor is wired with enough phone cable to service a city of 200,000 and contains more information display screens under one roof than any other building in the world.

Because it is likely that your option order will wind up on the CBOE, let's look at the exchange more closely.

ORDER ROUTING SYSTEM. The order routing system (ORS) is the network of communication lines from retail member firms' computers that collect, route, store, and execute public customer options orders. Options orders placed on your computer and routed to the CBOE would be sent to the ORS. The ORS automatically routes orders up to 2,000 contracts to one of four locations at the exchange. These orders can go to a CBOE's member firm's floor booth, a floor broker in the trading crowd, a CBOE's order book official's electronic book (E-book), or the retail automatic execution system (RAES). Your order's final destination is based on price and volume parameters, which are set by the CBOE and each member firm.

MARKET MAKERS. Market makers on the CBOE are entrepreneurs who compete with each other for option orders. They compete to trade against your order in an open outcry auction market. Recently, almost all listed options have been assigned to a designated primary market maker (DPM) system. A DPM is an exchange-appointed organization that can act as a market maker, floor broker, and in place of the order book official. When acting as a market maker, a DPM must give priority to orders he or she represents as a floor broker similarly to the specialist on the NYSE where public orders maintain priority.

ORDER BOOK OFFICIALS. These officials (OBOs) are salaried employees of the CBOE or DPM who maintain the E-book or the public customer limit book. OBOs do not trade on their own accounts and have no vested financial interest in any trades that occur.

FLOOR BROKERS. These brokers perform as agents and execute orders on behalf of public customers and firms only. Floor brokers are equipped with a PC-based touch screen known as the public automated routing (PAR) system that quickly and efficiently represents customer orders to the trading crowd.

RETAIL AUTOMATIC EXECUTION SYSTEM. This system (RAES) is part of CBOE's ORS system. Public customers' market orders and marketable limit orders of 20 contracts (the number of contracts eligible may be greater in some cases) or less that are sent to the RAES receive instantaneous execution. Only customer orders that fall within certain premium levels, contract size, and series parameters are guaranteed an immediate execution at the current inside market. In most cases, buy and sell orders submitted for 20 contracts or less and trading at a premium of less than $10 are eligible for the RAES. The RAES provides public customers with a guaranteed firm quote and a quicker turnaround time on executed orders.

Many technological innovations that assist in achieving quality executions and timely reporting have been advanced on the floor of the CBOE. In addition to the RAES, PAR, and E-book, the CBOE also implements technologies such as Mobile Par, which is a hand-held unit for floor brokers to better communicate with the trading crowd; booth automated routing terminal (BART), or "electronic runner," which helps member firms better manage order flow; and market maker handheld terminals (MMT) that bring personalized computer trading support to market makers. The CBOE also plans to debut in 2000 a screen-based trading system named CBOE Direct, which in addition to other floor enhancements will allow the exchange to participate in after-hours trading markets.

Figure 6.5 is a flow chart showing the execution of an options trade on the CBOE.

■ Stock Exchange Trading Halts ■

At times the stock market becomes so volatile that exchanges may halt trading. This rarely occurs, but it is something to consider. During a halt in trading, you can attempt to cancel any of your open orders that may be on the system during the stoppage. The

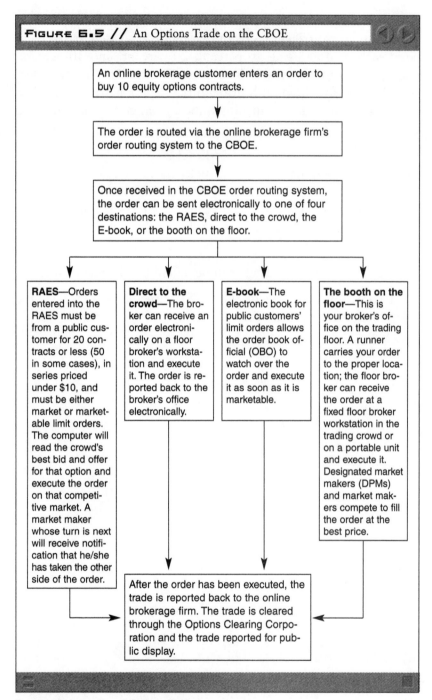

FIGURE 6.5 // An Options Trade on the CBOE

An online brokerage customer enters an order to buy 10 equity options contracts.

The order is routed via the online brokerage firm's order routing system to the CBOE.

Once received in the CBOE order routing system, the order can be sent electronically to one of four destinations: the RAES, direct to the crowd, the E-book, or the booth on the floor.

RAES—Orders entered into the RAES must be from a public customer for 20 contracts or less (50 in some cases), in series priced under $10, and must be either market or marketable limit orders. The computer will read the crowd's best bid and offer for that option and execute the order on that competitive market. A market maker whose turn is next will receive notification that he/she has taken the other side of the order.

Direct to the crowd—The broker can receive an order electronically on a floor broker's workstation and execute it. The order is reported back to the broker's office electronically.

E-book—The electronic book for public customers' limit orders allows the order book official (OBO) to watch over the order and execute it as soon as it is marketable.

The booth on the floor—This is your broker's office on the trading floor. A runner carries your order to the proper location; the floor broker can receive the order at a fixed floor broker workstation in the trading crowd or on a portable unit and execute it. Designated market makers (DPMs) and market makers compete to fill the order at the best price.

After the order has been executed, the trade is reported back to the online brokerage firm. The trade is cleared through the Options Clearing Corporation and the trade reported for public display.

Source: Chicago Board Options Exchange.

rule that governs trading halts on the NYSE is NYSE Rule 80b. It is based on three trigger levels of market declines that are recalculated each quarter using 10 percent, 20 percent, and 30 percent, respectively, of the average closing value of the Dow Jones Industrial Average for the month prior to the beginning of the quarter. Each trading level halt shuts down the exchange for the following time periods:

Level 1
Before 2 PM—1 hour
2 PM to 2:29 PM—30 minutes
2:30 PM or later—Trading
   continues unless a Level 2
   halt exists.

Level 2
Before 1 PM—2 hours
1 PM to 1:59 PM—1 HOUR
2 PM or later—Trading halted
   for the rest of the day.

Level 3—any time—Trading shall be halted for the rest of the day.

(Call your online broker or the NYSE directly to find what the current trigger halt levels are.)

CHAPTER 7

Getting Started:
It's Time to Trade

BEWARE INTERNET SCAMS

- "In First Case of Its Kind, Commission Sues Three Individuals for Illegally Offering Securities over Internet Auction Site"
- "SEC Charges 82 Individuals and Companies in Second Nationwide Microcap Fraud Sweep"
- "SEC Steps Up Nationwide Crackdown Against Internet Fraud, Charging 26 Companies and Individuals for Bogus Securities Offerings"
- "Agency Files Four More Cases Against Purveyors of Fraudulent Spam, Online Newsletters, Message Board Postings, and Websites in Its Ongoing Effort to Clean Up the Internet"

These are just a few of the Internet-related announcements that recently appeared on the Securities and Exchange Commission's Web site <www.sec.gov>. If they make you uneasy, they should. Simply because something is posted on the Internet and sounds official doesn't mean that it is. Securities con artists are migrating from the old telephone scams to the Internet. Rumors and fraudulent misrepresentations abound in cyberspace. Unfortunately for all of us, the anonymity of the Internet permits unscrupulous persons to profit by posting misinformation in online chat rooms, on bulletin boards, and in discussion forums without serious threat of legal action. The SEC does a tremendous job in uncovering fraud, but with more people accessing the Internet, its task becomes increasingly more difficult.

The SEC has identified two prominent scams: (1) pump and dump and (2) illegal touting. In a pump and dump scam, an individual or company touts online the virtues of a worthless security in the hope of luring the public into buying the shares and thus running up the stock price. Often these hoaxers compensate a third party to post an official looking publication on the Internet recommending the stock. The third parties usually own shares of the worthless securities and subsequently dump the stock after the public has driven the price up, leaving public investors holding valueless securities. In illegal touting, persons, usually brokers or company insiders, make stock recommendations or misrepresentations on Internet sites without disclosing that they are receiving compensation for doing so. These people get paid handsomely in cash or stock for their efforts while you wind up with a poor investment.

Many Web sites today, such as America Online, Yahoo! Finance, and The Motley Fool offer discussion forums. These forums are generally composed of anonymous investors located in all parts of the country who post opinions on such topics as general investing or specific stock selecting. Honest and trustworthy people engage in these discussions the majority of the time. However, some sites may not monitor users' participation, others may charge a fee for posting information, and some may not allow discussion on certain security topics, but the SEC in its report, "Online Brokerage: Keeping Apace of Cyberspace" (November 1999), notes that there is anecdotal evidence that postings in online discussion forums have caused volatility in some stocks. It points out that "readers may find it difficult to differentiate among accurate information, 'noise' (e.g., unsubstantiated opinions or rumors), or fraudulent misstatements."

In April 1999, a PairGain Technology (a small technology company) employee posted a false message on a Yahoo! Finance message board proclaiming that PairGain was in the process of being acquired by an Israeli company. The posting in turn was linked to a forged Bloomberg financial news service page that also reported the takeover. The share price of PairGain's stock subsequently rose by 31 percent. The scam was eventually exposed and the stock plummeted.

The sophistication and the extent of the efforts that individuals are making in an attempt to cheat you out of your money are astounding. Don't let investment fraud happen to you. If something sounds too good to be true, it probably is. Valid information will be disseminated through official sources. The NYSE Listed Company Manual notes that a NYSE-listed company is "expected to release quickly to the public any news or information which might reasonably be expected to materially affect the market for its securities." The NASD Manual requires Nasdaq-listed companies to promptly disclose any material developments through the news media.

Help is always out there to navigate safely through this menagerie of stock information. The first place to look for assistance is your online broker. Call your representative or send an e-mail to confirm any information that you may have picked up from a chat room or discussion forum on the Internet. If it's legitimate, your online broker will be able to retrieve it. If the broker can't, what you have is nonpublic information that is considered a rumor. Second, you can log on to <www.sec.gov> or <www.fraud.org>. Fraud.org is the National Fraud Information Center's Web site, which covers Internet fraud. The SEC's Web site is particularly useful and has specific announcements pertaining to security cyberfraud alerts. Investors are advised to read the SEC's Cyberspace Alert before purchasing any investments promoted on the Internet. You can also do your part by reporting suspicious Internet offerings via e-mail to <www.enforcement@sec.gov>.

▪ HAVE CONFIDENCE IN THE TRADE EXECUTION PROCESS ▪

The moment you enter an order on your PC, it is transmitted to your online broker, where it is then forwarded to one of the many markets that conduct trading in your particular security. Your online firm sends your trade down one of these paths in an attempt to get you the best execution price possible. This choice is based on which market can best fill your order at the lowest relative cost under the prevailing market conditions and, yes, sometimes it is based on "payment for order flow." Payment for order flow means that certain markets, primarily market makers, pay online firms cash for sending them orders.

It has yet to be proved whether payment for order flow causes inferior execution prices for public customer orders, but it is widely accepted that without such payment the discount brokerage industry and its dirt cheap commissions would not be where it is today. Do you need to worry about this issue? No. Let the SEC and the other governing bodies study and debate it. There's not a lot you can do about it anyway. Look at it this way: Cheaper commissions are something tangible. A $5 commission on a trade that once cost $100 guarantees you a $95 saving on each trade you make. Price improvement on the other hand is more illusive and may not occur on every trade. Although it is sought after, it is not guaranteed. Deep discounted commissions on the other hand occur on every trade.

You will begin to notice as you trade online that many of your orders don't go to the NYSE. Instead, they may go to regional exchanges, ECNs, or market makers. When you consider such factors as securities regulations governed by the SEC and NASD, the competition between exchanges, and your online broker's own self-interest, the question arises, Do you really need be concerned about where your order is being sent? The answer is no and here is why.

The many self-regulatory organizations, the SEC, and the NASD diligently govern and monitor the securities markets to ensure that they maintain open and orderly markets that deal fairly with the public. These regulatory bodies have instituted many policies and procedures to ensure greater public representation in the marketplace. I spoke earlier about the SEC's new order-handling rules and the new limit order protection rules that have already helped reduce spreads in Nasdaq trading by 40 percent. In cases where the SEC has discovered evidence of collusion by market makers to keep spreads high, it has issued steep fines. In fact, in 1997 dealers paid $910 million to settle private lawsuits, and in early 1999 they agreed to pay investors an additional $791,000 plus $26 million in fines. These regulatory agencies are continually watchdogging the markets to ensure that you are getting the best execution possible.

Competition between exchanges, ECNs, and market makers has also led to fairer and more efficient markets. Keep in mind, your online brokerage firm is a customer of the NYSE, the AMEX, the regionals, the Nasdaq market makers, and the new ECNs. The product that your online brokerage firm expects from these markets is best execution on your trades. Each individual market realizes that online firms have the option and the responsibility to send orders to the markets that result in best execution for the customer—that's you. If a particular market does not provide the highest execution quality possible on your order, that particular market is in jeopardy of losing your online firm's business. Even if your online broker is sending orders to a market maker in exchange for payment for order flow, that market maker would still be bound by the SEC and NASD regulations to give you the best possible execution. The exchanges recognize this competitive battle and have responded by implementing new technologies, while also reducing trading increments on stocks from eighths to sixteenths. These changes have already caused price improvement to rise 58 percent on the PHLX alone; and by the time this book hits the market, the NYSE will already be trading some stocks in decimals and reducing spreads even further.

Finally, your online firm does not want to lose you as a customer. It wants to keep you happy. Remember, they spent a lot of money trying to get your business. The number one way to keep it is to make sure that your order is executed quickly, accurately, and at the best possible price. The very best online brokerage firms routinely monitor their order flow to ensure that the markets that are executing your orders are doing so at the best execution prices possible. They run what are known as "exception reports" to ensure that markets are executing orders (your orders) according to specific quality execution measures. If they aren't, your online broker will investigate and will switch markets if warranted. In the end, your online brokerage firm realizes that it is your final review that counts. It understands that if you are not happy with your trade executions, you can always move your account to one of its competitors.

■ WARNING! HOT STOCK
MARKET AHEAD ■

Wouldn't it be nice if this heading flashed across your computer screen every time the market became overheated? Unfortunately, it doesn't and that is why, as you get poised to enter your trade, it is up to you to be alert to the prevailing market conditions. As you have seen, technology plays an integral role in processing and executing your trades. Your online firm relies heavily on computer networks to distribute your orders to the various marketplaces, but as efficient as these computer systems are, they do have their limitations.

The electronic back and forth between online brokers and the executing marketplaces functions smoothly most of the time. When you're trading at your computer, this interplay goes on totally unnoticed. An execution report on an order can seem to come back to you in less time than it took for you to enter the order. The truth is that some online traders have become too dependent on this instantaneous feedback, which in turn has caused many of them to become complacent when entering their trades. Never assume that because you received an immediate execution on a trade today, you will receive the same result tomorrow. Market conditions change!

Online firms and market exchanges allow some trades, generally small customer orders of 3,000 shares or less, to bypass human touch and be processed solely by computers. For example, an order to buy 1,000 shares of XYZ Corp. at the market could be filled and reported back within seconds and is known as an autoexecution. However, during turbulent market conditions when there is significant price volatility and heavy trading volume, some firms, in an attempt to reduce their exposure to market risk, will lower the number of shares they permit to be traded automatically or will switch entirely from an automatic execution system to a manual system. Under these changes, the same market order for XYZ above could take several minutes to execute and be reported back to you at a price different from the quoted price. This change in procedure is permissible by the NASD as long as it is consistent with best execution practices, is not excessive, and is warranted by market conditions.

Online brokerage firms' automatic execution procedures are not disclosed to the trading public. Each online brokerage firm and executing marketplace implement their own policies and parameters for autoexecution. Because you will never know exactly how many shares are eligible for autoexecution, or if autoexecution is "on" at all, a good rule of thumb to follow is this: The number of shares eligible for autoexecutions is usually reduced or switched to manual whenever a stock is deemed to be hot. You will recognize a hot stock because its volume will be excessive, its displayed quote will be volatile, and its name will most likely be plastered all over the financial news networks. Hot initial public offerings trading in the secondary market would also fall into this category.

■ WHAT TYPE OF ORDER SHOULD YOU PLACE? ■

Don't become the type of customer who enters orders blindly. As you have seen, trades can be affected dramatically by prevailing market conditions. Your defense is the types of orders you place. Because the language of trading is very specific, your orders tell the broker exactly how they should be handled. Traders are not clairvoyant; they can't read your mind. They execute orders only according to instructions inherent in each order. Some orders are more appropriate for certain market conditions than others. Therefore, before you place an order, including option trades, you should be aware of all the possible outcomes and, most important, be able to live with the results.

Market Orders

Market orders tell the broker that you wish to buy or sell a security now. You don't care what the price is; you're saying just buy it or sell it. Market orders are executed at the current market price when the order is represented at the exchange, not at the quoted market that may be displayed on your computer. Market orders guarantee quantity, not price. Most market orders to buy will execute at the quoted ask and most market orders to sell will fill at the quoted bid, but be aware that markets move quickly and can result in your final execution price being different from the quoted price. For example, a market order to buy ABC Corp. when the bid is 20 and the ask is 20⅛ could fill at 20¼ or higher if the stock price is moving quickly.

Be aware of *fast markets*. Fast markets occur when there is tremendous volatility, volume, or breaking news in a particular stock. During fast markets the displayed quotes don't reflect the current market price of a stock or option. Under these conditions, updating quotes by the exchanges on the system simply becomes impossible. A market order placed on a hot stock trading in a fast market could be filled *many points* away from the last printed quote. Stocks trading in fast markets exhibit unusual volume and are often associated with hot initial public offerings or stocks with breaking news releases over the Internet or television. If a particular television analyst recommends a stock, chances are very good that millions of other investors have heard the same news, causing a rush to the stock and thus a fast market in the stock. You should not place market orders on stocks in fast markets unless you are willing to accept a price that might be quite different than the last printed quote.

Limit Orders

Limit orders can help you avoid price execution surprises. Limit orders set the maximum price that you are willing to pay for a stock and the minimum price that you are willing to accept for the sale of your stock. However, unlike market orders, limit orders do not guarantee an execution. If filled, they guarantee only your limit price or better. If you decide that ABC Corp. is a good buy at 31 but not at a higher price, you could place a buy limit order at 31. "Buy 1,000 shares ABC at 31" tells the trader that you only want ABC at a price of 31 or less; if the trader can't buy at 31, he or she is not to fill the order.

Limit orders fall behind other limit orders. If ABC is quoted on the NYSE at bid 31 and ask 31¼, size 100 x 50, this means there are 10,000 shares ahead of your order that must be filled before your order can be executed and is known as "stock ahead." If a stock is moving quickly, quoted at 10, 10¼, 10½, 10⅞, 11 . . . all in a matter of seconds and you believe it is still a good buy at 12⅛ or less, a limit order to buy at 12⅛ should be placed. Although 12⅛ is slightly above the market at the time of entry, a trader receiving this order would try to execute it at 12⅛ or better. If the stock happens to be at 12½ at the time your order gets represented in the market, it will not be filled, but that's OK because you only wanted the stock at 12⅛ or less.

Unless specified as a stop order (see below), limit orders to buy that are entered reasonably (about 30 percent) above the current ask price and limit orders to sell entered reasonably (30 percent) below the current bid price assume you want the price you indicated *or better* and are executed instantaneously.

Day Orders

Day orders set the time frame of your order to one trading session only. All orders placed online are assumed to be day orders unless you indicate otherwise. Be extremely careful when placing orders near the close of the market. A stock order that you begin placing online for the day at 3:58 PM EST could actually be entered after the close at 4:00.56 PM. This order would then be a day order for the following trading session the next day. Many customers have unwittingly duplicated orders because of this oversight.

Good until Canceled (GTC)

Good until canceled orders at most online brokerage firms stay on the system for 90 days. Stay on top of GTC orders; they should appear on your monthly or quarterly statements. A forgotten GTC order placed two months ago could easily be triggered today.

Stop Orders

Stop orders are used to lock in trading profits or stem trading losses. They consist of a stop price, which, when reached, triggers a market order to either buy or sell. For example, a stop order to sell would read, "Sell 1,000 ABC at 35 STOP." The stop price is $35. This order would become a market order to sell when the last stock price touches $35. Your online broker may not accept stop orders on option trades. You will need to check with your online firm to review their option-trading policies.

BUY STOPS. These are entered above the current market's ask price and can be used to lock in profits on short sales. If you shorted a stock at $40 and it is currently trading at $30, you have a paper profit of $10. To lock in some of this profit, you could enter a buy stop order at $36 (Buy 1,000 XYZ at 36 STOP), which is above the current market price of $30. This tells the trader that if the stock moves up to $36, you want to buy it back at the market. Once the stock hits the stop price of $36, a market order to buy is triggered.

SELL STOPS. These are entered below the current bid price. If you own a stock at $50 when the current market is $60, you have a paper profit of $10. You could place a sell stop at $55 to lock in some of that profit (Sell 1,000 XYZ at 55 STOP). If you were to go away on vacation and not have access to a computer, this would safeguard your profit in the event that the stock started to move down while you were away and unable to place a trade. Sell stops, like buy stop orders, become market orders to sell when the sell stop price is hit.

STOP LIMIT ORDERS. These are stop orders that become limit orders when the stop price is hit. A stop limit order to sell would read, "Sell 1,000 ABC at 35 STOP 35 Limit." This avoids a stop order from being executed far away from the stop price. For example, if you owned a stock at $30 and placed a GTC sell stop order, "Sell 1,000 ABC at 35 STOP GTC," when the price of ABC closed at $45, and bad news came out overnight that caused the stock to drop and open the next day at $25, your sell stop order would execute at $25. Clearly not what you had intended. The stop limit order to "Sell 1,000 ABC 35 STOP, 35 Limit" would have told the broker, "Yes get me out, but only if you can get me out at $35 or more. If not, don't sell it." This stop limit order would have become a limit order as soon as the stock price touched $35.

The good news about a stop limit order is that you would not have sold your stock at $25 and ABC could potentially go back up. The bad news is that you would not have sold your stock at $25, and ABC could continue to fall, increasing your losses. Begging the question, Should you place a stop order or a stop limit order? There is unfortunately no pat answer. Knowing that stop orders turn into market orders and are guaranteed to fill, while stop limit orders turn into limit orders and are not guaranteed to fill, the decision depends on what makes you more comfortable.

All or None [AON]

All or none added to an order stipulates that you want your order filled entirely or not at all. Limit orders without an AON contingency can be filled in whole or in part. An AON order would read, "Buy 2,000 ABC at 30 AON DAY," which notifies the trader that you only want ABC at 30 or less if you can get all 2,000 shares. AON orders can be executed anytime during the trading session. They are not displayed in the current quote, however. Adding an AON contingency to small orders of 1,000 shares or less on stocks that exhibit heavy volume is not necessary. Adding an AON contingency to an order may actually delay an otherwise immediate execution.

Fill or kill tells the broker to execute the order immediately in its entirety, but if not, then cancel it now.

There are other types of orders that you may come across as you get more involved with trading. However, the order types covered above are the most common and should be sufficient in helping you execute trades under any market conditions.

■ THE UNEMOTIONAL INVESTOR ■

Is there such a person as the unemotional investor? Quite frankly, I doubt it. There aren't many online traders or any other types of investors for that matter participating in the markets today who don't allow emotions to play a part in their trading decisions. It is only human nature. There has always been a lot of talk about the psychology of the markets. What moves markets? Is it the technical fundamentals that gyrate market indexes from great highs to devastating lows? Or are these movements tied to a more subjective influence where investors' anticipated fears or optimism initiate broad sell-offs and run-ups? The answer is debated heavily, but one aspect is not in question: Investors' emotions influence their trading.

It is impossible to trade as if you were a robot. In fact, many great portfolio managers who pride themselves on beating the S&P 500 Index by using technical analysis also maintain that you need to possess a "feel" for the market. There seems to exist an intangible something that leads some professionals to a successful stock pick, while others just don't seem to have the knack. I guess if you are a professional money manager, developing that intuition may become possible, but my advice to you is, Don't attempt to feel your way around the Dow Jones Industrial Average with your emotions. Forget about developing a knack for trading. Make your decisions based on sound analysis. Don't allow your emotions to take charge of your investment decisions.

Attempting to time the markets—guessing when the market is at its lowest or highest—by feel is virtually impossible. Avoid buying and selling into the daily market cycles on enthusiasm alone. It's easy to get swept up in the moment. Invest in companies not in market swings. Good companies exhibit steady characteristics, such as good management, a desirable product, a competitive advantage, a strong growth potential, and strong earnings. These companies tend to perform better over the long run, whereas market cycle spikes are fleeting, merely isolated points on a chart. Emotional investing can rear its ugly head in many ways.

■ THE STUBBORN INVESTOR ■

It's bad enough to make a losing stock pick, but don't perpetuate your losses by sticking with a bad investment. If all the signs point to permanent losses, and it's clear that the stock's future doesn't look bright, don't let your pride stand in the way—dump your investment. It may be time to reevaluate your strategy, learn from the experience, and move on to your next trade. No investor is perfect and there are going to be times when you choose the wrong stock.

Several years ago I handled margin duties for a client whose portfolio holdings were in the high millions. His account was made up primarily of stocks that he had sold short, betting that the market would decline. The market, however, did not cooperate; it continued to rise. Even as the losses mounted, this customer was convinced that the decline in his portfolio value and resulting margin troubles stemmed not from his own investment strategy but from isolated anomalies in the market. He held tightly to this belief for well over a year as the market continued its steady rise.

Each morning I would call to inform him that his net worth had again decreased. Our firm even went so far as to suggest that he reevaluate his strategy, but he was resolute. He always simply responded that the crazies would soon be out of the market and he would soon be back in the black. In his mind everyone else was doomed to fail except him. He considered himself the only sane investor. He was convinced the market would soon turn bearish and his investments would finally pay off. This in the face of all signs pointing to a prolonged bull market. Unfortunately for him, his forecast never came true. He lost a tremendous amount of money.

It's easy to look back in hindsight and fault this customer. No one at that time had a crystal ball to look into the future. He had every right to stick to his strategy, and as an online brokerage firm, we could only monitor his account and offer our objective thoughts about his situation. We could not force him to change. Yet if he had stepped back and looked at the market objectively without emotion, he may have seen things for what they were and possibly changed his strategy. Unfortunately, he couldn't accept evidence that his strategy was faulty. In the end, he did not change his investment course.

■ THE PANICKED INVESTOR ■

"Oh no, I just bought a stock two hours ago and it's already down one point [$1]; what should I do? I have to cut my losses and sell." This scenario plays out a thousand times a day for online traders. It's tough to sit back and watch as an overall market decline beats down your stock. However, too many investors succumb to their fears and act on them. They forget the reason why they purchased the stock in the first place and wind up selling. If the fundamentals of the stock have not changed and there's been no major downshift in the overall economy, why sell your stock? (And if you're not buying on sound fundamentals, what are you basing your buying decisions on?)

Everyone has heard the saying Buy Low, Sell High. Unfortunately, far too many online traders are buying high and selling low. They disregard all of their hard work in researching their stock picks and simply follow the herd. It sounds like a cliché, but the underlying fact remains, "The market will go up, and the market will go down!" It's risky to trade in the stock market—no doubt about it—and if you can't handle the risk, then you're going to have difficulty investing. Yet by doing the work necessary to make informed investment decisions, you *can* minimize your risk.

If you happen to buy a stock that goes down because of a broad market decline within the first few hours or days of your trade, don't panic. Think: What attracted you to the stock in the first place? Was it a long-term investment or did you plan on taking short-term profits? If the answer is a long-term investment, go back and look at the company. Has anything changed? Does it still have sound fundamentals such as strong earnings growth, competitive products, and a bright future? If the answer is still yes, why sell? In fact, some investors would see a temporary decline in a stock's price as an opportunity to buy more shares at a cheaper price.

■ UNEMOTIONAL NUMBERS THAT YOU CAN BECOME ATTACHED TO ■

What type of investor will you be? Are you going to do your homework and look at the numbers, reviewing company annual reports, sector trends, and general economic growth trends? Or are you simply going to pick stocks based on armchair investing, hot tips from friends, or advice from the hundreds of talking heads on financial news networks? I'm not saying that recommendations from a friend or television financial commentator aren't valid; it's just that if someone advises you to buy or sell a stock, you should at least have some idea of why they're advising you to buy or sell.

The more investment decisions you can make based on solid financial information, the better off you'll be. You don't need to become a technical stock analyst to follow the markets. What can you do if you don't have time to peruse all the market data out there? A basic understanding of a few tools for analyzing companies and an understanding of economic indicators are a good way to get started. Familiarize yourself with the terms explained in the following two sections. The next time someone says, "Hey, I have a great stock pick for you," you can impress the friend by replying, "Well, I'm not so sure about that company. Its P/E ratio seems high and the FOMC is meeting today, so I'm waiting to see what will happen to interest rates."

■ INFORMATION ABOUT STOCKS YOU SHOULD KNOW ■

EARNINGS PER SHARE. These are derived from a company's net profit after payment of debt interest, taxes, and preferred shareholder dividends. Earnings per share (EPS) are the company's profit that would be available for dividend payments to common shareholders and are calculated by dividing the company's net profit by the number of shares of common stock outstanding. For example, a company that earned $20 million last year and has 10 million common shares outstanding would report earnings per share of $2. Increases in the EPS number is a positive sign and indicates that the company is growing.

Earnings surprises can be devastating to a stock's current market price. If analysts forecast earnings of $2.00, but actual earnings come in at $1.50, the stock could tumble. On the other hand, if earnings are better than expected a stock can run up sharply. There is a way to avoid trading into any major earnings surprises. "Whisper" forecasts are unofficial earnings forecasts circulated before official earnings announcements. A 1999 SEC Executive Summary on the Online Brokerage Industry points out that a recent study comparing "whisper" forecasts to EPS forecasts from First Call, a commercial source of earnings forecasts, found that whisper forecasts were on average more accurate. There are specific companies who now disseminate whisper forecasts on the Internet. One such company is WhisperNumber.com.

PRICE-EARNINGS RATIO. The price-earnings ratio (PE), also referred to as a stock's *multiple,* is one of the most widely followed ratios in the industry. It's calculated by dividing the current market price of a company's stock by the company's earnings per share. For instance, a stock selling for $50 a share that had earnings per share of $2 would have a PE ratio of 25—that is, said to be trading at a multiple of 25. The PE ratio shows the relationship of a stock's price to its earnings.

Because we invest in companies for their earnings growth, the PE ratio indicates the relationship between how much we are paying for a company's stock relative to its earnings. It also allows you to compare the PE of other companies within the same industry. One problem with the PE ratio: it is derived from past rather than future earnings. Two stocks with the same PE ratio may have totally different prospects for the future. Generally speaking, the higher the PE, the more you will pay for the stock and the more you will expect the company's earnings growth to be. High PE stocks tend to be newer, fast-growing companies; they usually carry more risk than stocks with lower PEs. Tracking PE is not a perfect science. For instance, a newer, fast-growing company with a high PE and higher risk could actually be a better investment than a slow or no-growth company with a lower PE.

BOOK VALUE. This can be derived from a company's consolidated financial statements. It is simply the difference between the company's assets and its liabilities. As an investor, you want to compare the value of a company's assets to the size of its debt and equity. A company that carries a lot of debt on its books will have a low book value. This excessive debt may limit its profitability and could make the company a poor investment. On the other hand, a low book value could mean that assets are being undervalued and therefore the stock could be underpriced and a good bargain. Ultimately, book value is an indication of the value of a company's securities in liquidation after it pays off creditors and preferred shareholders.

RETURN ON EQUITY. Return on equity (ROE) is expressed as a percentage and is the amount earned on a company's common stock investment for a particular period. It indicates just how well the company is managing its profits. Remember that profits not paid out in the form of dividends are reinvested and employed back into the company. You can calculate ROE by dividing net income by common stock equity (shareholder's equity on the financial statement). This percentage can be compared to past ROE numbers to see how the company has been doing over time or how it has stacked up against industry composites to compare how the company is doing vis-à-vis its competitors.

■ ECONOMIC INDICATORS YOU SHOULD UNDERSTAND* ■

The *consumer price index (CPI)* is a measure of the average level of prices of a fixed market basket of goods and services purchased by consumers. Monthly percentage changes in the index reflect the rate of change in such prices. Changes in the CPI are widely fol-

*Source: *Econoday Calendar 2000*, Econoday Inc. <www.econoday.com> 800-988-3332.

lowed as a primary indicator of inflation because consumer spending accounts for a large percentage of economic activity.

Durable goods orders are a measure of new orders placed with domestic manufacturers for immediate and future delivery of factory hard goods. Durable goods orders are a leading indicator of industrial production and capital spending. Levels of, and changes in, durable goods orders are widely followed as an indicator of factory sector momentum. Durable goods orders are a major indicator of manufacturing sector trends because most industrial production is done to order.

The *Federal Open Market Committee (FOMC)* meeting is the meeting at which the near-term direction of monetary policy is set. The decision to raise or lower interest rates is decided at these meetings. The FOMC meets eight times per year. Most changes in monetary policy are announced after FOMC meetings.

Gross Domestic Product (GDP) is the broadest measure of aggregate economic activity available, encompassing every sector of the economy. The GDP represents the total value of the country's production during the period indicated (a quarter) and consists of the purchases of domestically produced goods and services by individuals, businesses, foreigners, and government entities. Quarterly percent changes (at an annualized rate) in the GDP reflect the growth rate of total economic output. GDP growth is widely followed as the primary indicator of the strength of economic activity.

Housing starts are a measure of the number of residential units on which construction is begun each month. Monthly percent changes reflect the rate of change of such activity. The level of housing starts is widely followed as a major indicator of residential construction trends because it reflects the commitment of builders to new construction activity. Purchases of household furnishings and appliances quickly follow.

International trade is a measure of the difference between imports and exports of both tangible goods and services. The level of the international trade balance and changes in exports and imports are widely followed as indicators of trends in foreign trade. Although the trade balance is small relative to the size of the economy, changes in the trade balance can be quite substantial relative to changes in economic output. Measured separately, imports and exports are important components of aggregate economic activity, representing approximately 15.5 and 13.0 percent of the GDP, respectively.

The *National Association of Purchasing Managers (NAPM) Survey* is a composite diffusion index of national manufacturing conditions. Readings above 50 percent indicate an expanding factory sector. The NAPM Survey is closely followed as an indicator of strength in the manufacturing sector.

Payroll employment is a measure of the number of people being paid as employees by nonfarm business establishments and units of government. Changes in payroll employment are widely followed as an indicator of economic activity because payroll employment encompasses every major sector of the economy. Many other important economic indicators are dependent on its information.

The *producer price index (PPI)* is a measure of the average level of prices of a fixed basket of capital and consumer goods paid by producers. Monthly percent changes reflect the rate of change in such prices. Changes in the PPI for finished goods are widely followed as an indicator of commodity inflation. The PPI is available nationally by stage of production, industry, and commodity. The PPI for finished goods is the most widely quoted because it accounts for price changes throughout the manufacturing sector.

Retail sales are a measure of total receipts of retail stores that sell durable and nondurable goods. Monthly percent changes reflect the rate of change of such sales. Changes in retail sales are widely followed as an indicator of consumer spending because they account for nearly one-half of total consumer spending and approximately one-third of aggregate economic activity.

CHAPTER 8

Working with Your Online Broker

■ Online Trading Is Not Always Online ■

I know what you're thinking, "What is this guy talking about? I'll never speak to my online broker. I'm always going to be trading online." Well, like it or not, there are going to be times when talking and dealing with your online broker is unavoidable. If I had a nickel for every customer who called my office proclaiming he never spoke to his online representative, I'd be sitting on a beach sipping a cold drink. It always boggled my mind that I could be conversing with someone who insisted he never spoke to a live person. What was I—chopped liver? Didn't I count?

Granted, almost all interactions with your online firm will be online. You will retrieve research, get quotes, scan news, place trades, and monitor balances directly from your PC without ever speaking to anyone. Yet there are times when you absolutely must call your online broker, and, chances are, those will be the most critical of all—a system crash that disrupts online access to your account; your entering the wrong trade; an execution report being questioned; your needing to verify information; or your simply wanting to ask a question.

Even if you are knowledgeable and transact business diligently, the simple truth is that online investing is not always done online.

If you expect to achieve a satisfactory result from your verbal encounters, you must understand how your online firm operates. How does it approach your call and how does it resolve your problems? Working with your firm is a two-way street. Just as you come to expect certain things from your online brokerage firm, it too expects certain things from you. If you have never worked with an online broker before, you may be in for some surprises.

The first thing that you'll notice is how difficult it can be to actually get a representative on the line. Horror stories abound about customers being put on hold for 15 minutes to one hour or longer. Some firms communicate solely through e-mail, whereas others manage your calls electronically by a Touch-Tone or voice-activated service. Either way, the outcome is the same; generally speaking, it will take you longer to get through to someone than you might like. Second, once you do engage in a conversation with a live representative, you may be taken aback by the fast pace at which the conversation takes place. Your online firm will not embrace nor encourage the conversational style that you once experienced at your bank, full-service brokerage firm, or mutual fund company. Do not misinterpret this treatment; online firms want to nurture customer relationships, but because they operate under a unique business model, they go about it differently.

Online brokerage firms are high-transaction, low-cost trade facilitators. They offer ease of trading, free research, free real-time quotes, 24-hour account access, and sometimes even free analyst recommendations, all for as low as a $5 commission. Did you ever stop to think how they could possibly do all of this? Well, a big reason is that they transact business fast—volume is key. Electronically or with the spoken word, customer interactions are serviced in rapid-fire succession. The name of the game is to move customers along. You may consider this abrupt, but your online firm considers it efficient.

The stock market by its nature demands speed. Each second that transpires represents price movements in the markets, each tick of the clock translating into hundreds of thousands of dollars of potential gains or losses for online customers. You, as one of these customers, have come to expect the timely service, and your online firm does everything possible to deliver it. It is critical that you understand how to work within the confines of this fast-paced environment.

▪ SERVICE CALLS VERSUS TRADING CALLS ▪

Why have you decided to call your broker today? Did the system go down and thus make it necessary to place a trade with a representative, or did you notice that something was off on your account balance and you needed to get it resolved? In your eyes, I'm certain that both calls are equally important and should be handled in the same manner. However, to your online broker these two reasons for calling don't carry the same weight. Customers who call to place trades have priority over customers who call to take care of customer service issues.

I know my old customer service manager would admonish me for making that statement, but don't shoot the messenger here; I'm only telling you the way it is. In customers' eyes, problems affecting their account always seem to be the most important. Whatever it may be, whether they never received their monthly statement, whether they think their account balance is off, or whether they're tracking down a dividend, in their minds their problem should come first. After all, they are the customer. And don't customers always come first?

Well, the answer to that question is yes and no. Yes, you come first if you have a time-sensitive trading issue, but no, you may wait if you have a service issue that can be addressed after market hours or during less busy times during the day. Look at the situation objectively. The markets are open only for a set number of trading hours each day, and each online firm has only a set number of phone representatives available to answer your phone calls. Trading is extremely time sensitive and customers can loose a great deal of money if they can't get in touch with their phone representatives to place a trade. On the other hand, service issues are not time sensitive. Rarely do customers lose money because they couldn't request duplicate statements or review their trading history in a timely manner.

Therefore, if you bring up a service issue, a representative may seem to rush you off the phone or may even ask you to call back after market hours. It's not as if the rep doesn't want to help you, it is that the rep is just trying to prioritize the firm's phone volume. This situation becomes more pronounced right after the market opening at 9:30 AM and just before the market close at 4:00 PM. These two time periods exhibit tremendous telephone volume. You will receive better service and will help your broker tremendously if you avoid calling with service issues during these times.

Now, you may say that this is not your problem and that the firm should hire more phone representatives. Two points about that. One, many firms *are* hiring more phone representatives. But the more online firms move away from the "click and mortar" model to the old "brick and mortal" model (hiring telephone reps and building phone infrastructures and facilities to house them), the more their business costs rise. Online firms need to pay and train the new representatives to answer your calls and these extra costs could show up in higher trading commission charges.

Second, online firms are not asking much from you. Only that you contact them with service issues during off-peak trading hours, when they are able to give you their full attention without seeming to rush you off the phone. You will be much happier with this type of approach. Managing phone volume under extraordinary conditions is a delicate business, and online firms are doing the best they can. The more understanding you are, the more pleasant your interactions with your online firm will be. Representatives remember both the accommodating customers and the unyielding customers. Who do you think they'll work harder for?

■ YOUR ONLINE BROKER'S TOOLS ■

Recorder Telephone Lines

Each call made to your online brokerage's trading representative is recorded. Taping conversations in the investment industry is common practice. These recorded telephone calls protect your interests as well as your online brokerage firm's. Any questions arising out of inconsistencies between what you thought you said and what you thought a representative said can easily be resolved by "pulling the tape."

A call into a recorded phone line normally is preceded by a message indicating that the call is recorded. "All calls are being monitored for quality assurance" is the most common message. However, "We are recording this conversation to protect both your butt and ours" would be more accurate. If you happen to miss the preliminary message, a constant beep in the background stands as a constant reminder that the call is recorded. I recall incidences when customers were actually recording me, and between my beeping and their beeping, it's any wonder we were able to have a conversation at all.

New technology enables firms to keep a greater inventory of recorded phone conversations. This inventory is useless to you unless the specific conversation that you are looking for can be retrieved. Requests to pull a tape given in this manner, "I think I spoke to some man last week sometime during the day," is not adequate. If you want your problem to be resolved, you need to give your firm the exact day, time, and name of the representative. For this reason, keep a written record of all important phone conversations related to trade execution reports, trade cancellation reports, or other important service issues. A more timely and objective resolution to your inquiries will be forthcoming if you approach your firm this way: "I know this to be so because I spoke to your representative John Smith on Monday the 24th at 2:30 PM." Nothing is left to chance. The tape of this conversation can be pulled easily and the issue in question can be resolved immediately. Otherwise, finding a vital conversation is like trying to find a needle in a haystack.

When discrepancies arise, online brokerage customers bear the burden of proving their argument. You must prove your case. For instance, many clients—adult professional businesspeople included—have called in claiming that "so and so" told them that a certain stock was purchased in their account, but the customers couldn't specify the time, day, or representative who gave them the trade execution report. As a firm, we could only press clients for more details, and if none are forthcoming, there is unfortunately not a lot we could do. We could not just give the trade to them. Sure, we try to find the tape, but with thousands of hours of recorded conversations to sift through, the results were never positive. What's more, these "phantom executions" always seem to be in the customer's favor; coincidence? I doubt it.

Whether these claims were true did not matter. Without verification, a trade report could not be honored. We couldn't just give the customer the trade. How could we give a trade to a customer based solely on a conversation that could not be substantiated? How do we know the conversation ever took place? The harsh reality is that some customers do attempt to commit fraud. They make claims that are simply untrue. They try to deceive their broker in hopes of financial gain. For this reason, your online firm discriminates against no one—they mistrust everyone equally! *Mistrust* may be too strong a word, but you get the idea. Don't depend on your memory alone; write down the details of important phone conversations. Avoid missing out on important transactions or having resolutions to your inquires delayed or unresolved because you suddenly have come down with a case of amnesia.

Time and Sales Report

This is an electronic trade execution reporting system subscribed to by, and available only to, your online broker. You can not retrieve time and sales (T&S) information on your PC, although you can request that a T&S report be sent to you. A T&S report displays detailed trade execution information pertaining to listed and Nasdaq national market securities. The system allows your online broker to immediately verify historical trade data on a specific stock. A T&S report shows a stock's quote and size at a specified time; its time sequence of execution in hours, minutes, and seconds; its individual trade volume; and its place of execution (exchange).

A broker can access this information during the trading session to investigate why your limit order was not filled or why your market order was executed at a certain price. To discern if there is a legitimate order challenge, your online brokerage representative can quickly consult T&S to compare line by line details of actual trade activity with your specific trade information. In the majority of cases, factors such as your order's time of entry, stock ahead, or a simple change in the market quote turn out to be the legitimate culprits to explain the reasons why an order was not filled or why it received a certain execution price.

T&S information is a terrific tool that helps representatives better answer specific questions regarding the execution of an order; you should not, however, abuse this service or request it haphazardly. There is no reason to cross-check all of your trades with T&S reports. A less specific but adequate way to track trade prices is to log on to stock-charting Web sites such as <www.Bigcharts.com>. These charts will give you overall stock prices for the time frame that may be in question on a trade. Pulling up a quick chart from such a Web site can generally show you where a stock traded at a particular moment in time.

Don't expect or attempt to force your representative into giving you a verbal execution report from T&S. The rep will not give you one for a very good reason—he or she can't. Only the individual exchanges can issue a legitimate execution or trade cancellation report. T&S reports are extremely detailed, yet they cannot specify whether a displayed trade is in fact your executed trade. Therefore, if a trade report is given from T&S, it is only an educated guess and not a legitimate trade execution report. A sample of an actual T&S report is presented in Figure 8.1.

■ THE THREE Ps: PROFESSIONAL, PREPARED, PROMPT ■

Approach each call to your online brokerage firm as you would any other business call. Be professional, prepared, and prompt.

Be Professional

Too often people associate price with a certain level of status and unwittingly adjust their behavior accordingly. Discounters are perceived differently than premium vendors. At times customers unwittingly permit this bias to creep into their discussions with online trading representatives. They inadvertently harbor a general lack of respect for their online brokerage firm and for the representatives who man the telephones simply because their product—trade execution—is cheap. Some customers chomp on food in midconversation, whereas others ignore the trading representative altogether while they intermittently conduct another conversation simultaneously with other people in the background. How would you react if someone conducted business in this manner with you?

Often, customers perceive the representatives as a generic person at the other end of the phone line and not as a business pro-

FIGURE 8.1 // An Example of a Time and Sales Report

IBM US $ ↓ 108 3/16 − 1 1/16 T N108 3/16/108 3/8 N 110x15 Equity QRM
At 13:19 Vol 3,538,300 Op 109 N Hi 110 N Lo 108 C ValTrd 385.602m

MARKET/TRADE RECAP

Page 1

Volumes scaled by 100

Time : Min Vol 100 USD
Date 5/23 Price Range To
INTL BUSINESS MACHINES C (IBM US) PRICE 108 3/16 T $

Time	E	Bid/Trd/Ask	E	Size	Cond	Time	E	Bid/Trd/Ask	E	Size	Cond
13:19	N	108 3/16 /108 3/8	N	110x15		13:18	N	108 3/8		10	
13:19	N	108 3/16 /108 7/16	N	110x20		13:18	T	108 3/8		1	
13:19	N	108 3/16 /108 5/16	N	110x10		13:18	N	↑108 3/8		9	
13:19	T	↓108 3/16		2		13:18	N	108 5/16 /108 7/16	N	10x10	
13:19	N	108 3/16 /108 7/16	N	110x20		13:18	N	108 1/4 /108 7/16	N	100x10	
13:19	N	108 3/16 /108 5/16	N	110x10		13:18	N	108 1/4 /108 7/16	N	100x10	
13:19	N	108 3/16 /108 3/8	N	110x10		13:18	N	108 1/4 /108 7/16	N	100x10	
13:19	N	108 3/16 /108 5/16	N	110x10		13:18	N	108 1/4 /108 3/8	N	100x10	
13:19	N	108 3/16 /108 5/16	N	110x10		13:18	T	↓108 5/16		1	
13:19	N	108 3/16 /108 7/16	N	110x10		13:18	N	108 3/8		1	
13:19	N	108 3/16 /108 7/16	N	110x10		13:17	N	108 1/4 /108 3/8	N	100x10	
13:19	N	108 1/4		70		13:17	N	108 1/4 /108 1/2	N	100x45	
13:19	N	↓108 1/4		61		13:17	N	108 3/8		6	
13:19	N	108 1/8 /108 7/16	N	100x10		13:17	B	108 3/8		1	
13:19	X	108 3/16 /108 7/16	N	1x10		13:17	N	108 3/8 /108 1/2	N	10x45	
13:19	C	108 3/16 /108 7/16	N	1x10		13:17	T	108 3/8		3	
13:18	N	↓108 5/16		10		13:17	N	108 3/8 /108 1/2	N	10x55	
13:18	N	108 5/16 /108 7/16	N	10x10		13:17	N	108 1/4 /108 1/2	N	100x55	

Copyright 2000 BLOOMBERG L.P. Frankfurt:69-920410 Hong Kong:2-977-6000 London:171-330-7500 New York:212-318-2000
Princeton:609-279-3000 Singapore:226-3000 Sydney:2-9777-8686 Tokyo:3-3201-8900 Sao Paulo:11-3048-4500
I921-325-0 23-May-00 13:19:16

Time—The military time showing the exact displayed Bid/Trade/Ask prices and Sizes.

E—Represents the trading exchange that is posting Bid/Ask prices and Size. Also shows exchange where last trade and volume took place. N-NYSE, X-PHLX, C-Cincinnati, B-Boston, T-Third market (off exchange trade). The left side E closest to Time represents the Bid exchange; right side E beside Size reflects Ask exchange.

Bid/Trd/Ask—Shows the Bid, last trade (when price posted individually) and Ask price for the time posted.

Size—Shows the number of shares (x 100) that are at the Bid and Ask prices. Shows volume (x 100) for executed trades.

Cond.—Indicates whether a print is out of sequence.

Copyright © 2000 Bloomberg

fessional. Don't overlook that online trading representatives have passed stringent NASD qualifying exams. In many cases they hold more industry licenses than their full-service firm brethren. True, online representatives do not dispense advice and they are available via 800 numbers around the clock, but this should not make them a customer's whipping post. Don't forget that these representatives stand between you and a quick trade execution or a speedy resolution to your trading problems. They possess the power to help or hurt you.

Basically, approach each interaction with your online trading representative with the same professional courtesy that you would like to receive. These representatives understand that markets are volatile and that tensions can run high, but when dealing with them, avoid using profanity and, above all, never threaten your online representative with physical or financial harm. Remember that calls are being recorded. This type of behavior can cause a customer's immediate expulsion from the firm, and in light of some recent tragedies within the industry, threats in particular are monitored and can result in legal action.

Be Prepared

Calling to trade or to address a service issue? Be prepared. Have your account number, password, or any other vital information that your firm requires at your ready. Scores of customers contact their online firms every day with no information handy. Sometimes they don't even remember why they are calling. It sounds absurd but it's true. At times like these, customers implement what I refer to as the "quote stall," whereby they continue to ask for stock quotes until miraculously the reason for their call pops back into their heads. Stalling is an abuse of a trading representative's time. Keep in mind there are other customers waiting on hold, so respect your representative's time as well as the needs of other customers.

If you are calling to place a trade, have your account number ready and know what trade you want to enter. Many customers lose money because their trades are delayed while a representative searches the computer for their account number or the quantities of long shares in the case of a sell order. If your online system crashes before you are able to enter a trade, don't panic. Call your online representative, be prepared to give her your account number, get an updated quote, and place your order. Good trading representatives can enter verbal orders as quickly as you sometimes can enter them online yourself but only if you have your information prepared and ready.

The same advice holds true for customer service issues. Be prepared to answer pertinent questions from your online representative regarding your problem. Question such as: When did you first notice the discrepancy? What day was the trade in question? How much money do you think you are due? What month did the transaction occur? Have you spoken to anyone about this problem, and, if so, who? Online firms expect you to have a basic understanding or starting point for addressing a problem. "I think I'm missing a few hundred dollars" or "I thought I bought some IBM shares sometime last week" is not enough information to effectively resolve your concern. Firms take the information that you give them and attack the issue from there. The more information made available to the representative, the quicker and more satisfactory the outcome will be. Remember that you are managing your account now, and you are expected to notice any discrepancies. Your online broker may not immediately pick up on accounting errors and therefore will not be able to point them out to you. Make it a habit to check each individual trade confirmation and monthly statement for accuracy. It is critical that you keep thorough records.

Be Prompt

Conduct the business that you need to and move on. This does not necessarily mean that you terminate your conversation with the representative but only that you keep the call moving forward. Stick to the business at hand. As pointed out earlier, telephone trading representatives move conversations along quickly. If you won't, they will because that is part of their responsibilities as traders. If they hear any hesitation in your voice or if there is an inordinately long silent pause, they will prompt you to the next step. They will ask you directly, "Is there anything else I can do for you?" or "Would you like to place another trade?"

When there are system problems endemic to your firm, all customers are affected. Not only must you get in touch with the trading representative, but all online customers need to do the same. Add to this the number of clients who trade orally as part of their normal course of business, and you begin to get a clearer picture of the tremendous spike in telephone volume during these technical outages. If you don't make your call promptly, everyone is subject to undesirable hold times. It only takes a second or two for a stock to move in price. I'm sure you wouldn't like to be put on hold any longer than necessary, particularly when you need to trade in a volatile market, while another customer is dillydallying on the phone.

■ Don't Get Angry— Get It Solved ■

Executing the Wrong Trade

It is 10:30 in the morning and you are about to go into a business meeting. Before you go, you notice that ABC shares are trading at $38. You already own 100 shares and you decide that you would like to buy more. Your plan is to enter a buy 100 shares of ABC stock at 35, so you quickly go online. Rushing to get to your meeting, you hurry through the trade menus and unknowingly enter a sell 100 shares ABC at $35 instead. Thinking only of your meeting, you fail to inspect your order. You hit the confirm order icon on your screen and send the incorrect order to the broker. You toggle to another screen to review your order and are shocked to realize that you made an error. You have sold 100 shares of ABC by mistake. What should you do?

Call your online broker immediately. Your primary concern is to try to rectify the mistake. Sure, you could accept the trading error and move on with your life, but what if you wind up losing money on the incorrect trade or you simply want to own the stock? After all, your original intention was to buy shares, not sell them. Don't wait another minute, hour, or day to reach your representative. Every minute that goes by reduces the chance that you can be helped. There is *no guarantee* that your mistake can be reversed, but if something can be done, you must take action immediately!

If you decide to accept your trading mistake, you own the trade. You can't call your broker a day or two or weeks later when the stock has moved up in price to $40 and make the appeal that you never intended to sell your shares. The first thing that a trading representative will do on a trade inquiry such as this is to look at the current quote of the stock in question. Nine out of ten times it turns out that the customer is losing money on the trade in question. The broker's thoughts revert back to, why did you wait so long to call? Could it be that you are calling now only because the trade has moved against you? Don't play financial roulette with a trading error.

The above scenario presents you with two problems. One, you have mistakenly sold 100 shares of ABC stock, and, two, you no longer have the buy order in for the 100 shares of ABC stock that you had originally intended to place. If ABC's share price is trading flat (the price hasn't changed), you may be in luck. Your online representative can call the market where the trade was executed and request that the trade be "busted" or "taken away." Again, there is *no guarantee* that this can be done, but it sometimes occurs, so it is worth asking. However, it is unlikely that the executed trade will be reversed if the stock price moves far away from the execution price. But, if the trader can accommodate you, your problem is solved. It's as if your trade never happened. You now need only to thank your representative profusely and reenter the original buy order that you originally intended to place.

In the event that the trade can't be busted, you need to decide whether you want to reenter a buy of 200 shares of ABC to account for the 100 shares that you mistakenly sold and the 100 shares that you intended to buy in the first place. The decision falls back in your lap. The online brokerage representative will wait for your instructions. This doesn't mean, however, that your representative drops totally out of the picture. And this is where the three Ps and having a good relationship with your broker pay off.

Trading representatives understand that honest mistakes happen occasionally, and they will do everything they can to assist you. By law they are not permitted to participate in any gains or losses on your account, but with managerial approval they could possibly waive commissions. If the stock has not moved much in price, waiving the commissions on the trades might possibly make the entire headache a financial wash. Granted, waiving commissions on two trades with today's low commission costs is not a lot of money, but it is better than nothing. It certainly is better than getting charged two extra commissions as a result of your original mistake. Saving a few dollars will not always solve your problems, but it will cushion the blow.

The point is that you don't have to face these types of situations alone. Accepting the trading error is not your only solution. Online brokerage representatives can offer invaluable assistance. Brokerage representatives really do want to help you. The results may not always be to your satisfaction, but at least you can take comfort in knowing that you have exhausted all of your possibilities. In the final analysis, make note of your trading error, learn by your mistake, try not to let it happen again, and move on. Everybody makes mistakes.

Challenging an Order

Having read Chapter 6, you should now have a better understanding of how the exchanges process your trades. You realize there is much more going on behind the scenes than what you experience while sitting at your PC. Inevitably, you won't be satisfied with an execution price on a trade. Take it from me, everyone thinks that they should have received a lower price on a buy order and a higher price on a sell order. It makes no difference that a trading representative can demonstrate with hard evidence (like T&S reports) that an execution price was valid. Many customers are still unwilling to accept the legitimacy of some trade reports. They perceive the online broker and the industry in general as scheming in some way to defraud them. If customers don't receive a price they like, they immediately think that an error has occurred.

Don't challenge every order that you place. Simply being unhappy with an execution price is not sufficient grounds for an order challenge. Sometimes a trader on an exchange is caught napping and a trading error occurs, but from my many years of trading experience and having seen firsthand hundreds of thousands of trade executions, I can say with confidence that the vast majority of trade orders are executed properly by the exchanges. Rarely do mistakes happen. And if they do, legitimate order challenges are based on the following questions: What type of order did you enter—market or limit? What was the market quote and size when you entered your order? What were the prevailing market conditions at the time of order entry—was there a fast market? Was the outcome of your order *reasonable,* considering all of these factors? Remember what I said, "Just because you're not happy with a trade report does not mean that you have an order challenge."

MARKET ORDERS. Market orders are guaranteed to fill quantity, not price. The only discrepancy in a market order execution could be the price at which the order was filled. Make note of the quote and size of the market when your order is placed. If the quote on a stock trading under normal market conditions is bid 20 and ask 20⅛, size 10 by 10, market orders to buy 1,000 shares should be executed at the ask 20⅛, and market orders to sell 1,000 shares should be executed at the bid 20. Market orders should be executed at the inside market quote. Any execution prices significantly away from the inside market quote under normal market conditions would be open to an order challenge.

However, if you receive an execution price away from the quoted price when a stock is trading with heavy volume or is under fast market conditions, then an order challenge may not be warranted. For example, earning announcements on stocks or sudden news or an analyst's recommendation can change the complexion of the marketplace. Heavy volume and sudden news will cause stocks to trade much faster, resulting in delayed quotes and fast markets.

For instance, if a pharmaceutical company announces at 2:30 PM that it has discovered a cure for a certain disease, which will lead to increased revenues, be assured that the company's stock price will jump. A quote on this company of bid 35 and ask 35⅛, size 10 by 10 at 2:30 PM is going to move quickly. The quote at 2:34 PM after the news has been announced could easily change to 38¼ to 39 or higher. Placing a market order to buy at 2:31 PM based on the 2:30 PM quote will most likely result in an execution price significantly away from the earlier ask price of 35⅛. As long as the exchange has executed your order in a *reasonable* amount of time under the prevailing market conditions, you would not have grounds for an order challenge.

LIMIT ORDERS. Limit orders guarantee your limit price or better, but they are not guaranteed to execute. Therefore, limit order challenges are not as subjective as market order challenges. The execution price is not an issue. If you want to buy stock at a limit of $30, execution of the order must be done at $30 or less. Taking into consideration the quote, the size, and the last trade price, the only question that remains is whether you are actually due an execution report in the event that you have not received one. Did the stock trade at your limit price or better with enough volume to accommodate your order?

Two scenarios exist: a stock has either traded *at* your limit price or it has traded *through* your limit price. Trading at your limit price occurs when the last trade matches your limit price (listed stocks only; Nasdaq last-trade price could be either a buy or a sell). A buy order trading through your limit price means that the last trade is transacted at a price lower than your limit order price, and for a sell order, the last trade is transacted at a price higher than your limit price. For example, a buy order on a NYSE-listed stock at 29 should be executed when the last trade is 29, assuming that there was not "stock ahead." This same order is guaranteed an execution if the last trade is lower than your buy limit order, for example, a trade reported at 28⅞. To reiterate, on a listed stock a printed trade below your buy order or above your sell order will trigger an execution.

Always consider the size of the market before entering your limit order. A quote of bid 29 and ask 29⅛, size 100 by 100, before you enter a buy order indicates that there are 10,000 shares already ahead of you to buy the stock at 29. Monitoring the quote on your PC and observing a last-trade print at 29 does not guarantee that your order has been filled unless the shares that are ahead of you (10,000 in this case), the "stock ahead," are executed. Your limit order is executed in the sequence it is received. As you may recall from Chapter 6, the specialist enters orders in the limit order book by price and in the order in which they were received.

Limit orders on Nasdaq stocks are executed a little differently. Although the SEC's and NASD's new order-handling rules have given retail customer orders better representation in the marketplace, the Nasdaq is still considered to be primarily a dealers market. As you may recall, a Nasdaq quote displaying bid 35 and ask 35¼ means that you buy stock at 35¼ and you sell stock at 35. In the Nasdaq market it is possible to witness trades taking place below your buy limit order and above your sell limit order without triggering a trade execution. But similarly to auction market stocks, a limit order to buy 1,000 shares of stock at 35¼ when the market is bid 35 and ask 35¼, should be executed at 35¼, again assuming there is enough size to accommodate the order. In this example, if you happened to notice a lot of trades being executed at 35¼ and your order is still not executed, it would be appropriate for you to call your representative to challenge the open order. Here you would ask the broker to "status the order."

Bad Quotes

Some quotes on your PC and on the consolidated tape may be out of sequence. For instance, a stock trade report displayed on your screen or running across the tape at 1:30 PM might actually have been executed at 9:34 AM. As a result, this print, which could be below your buy limit or above your sell limit, does not guarantee that your limit order has been filled. A quick check of T&S by your trading representative will confirm this. The T&S will clearly display that the price print was an out-of-sequence trade. Although this situation can be frustrating and a bone of contention for many customers, the fact remains that there are no grounds for an order challenge under this circumstance.

Contingency Trades

Contingencies such as all or none, fill or kill, or immediate or cancel placed on limit orders also subject a trade to different execution standards. Determining whether an all or none (AON) contingency order is due an execution report is difficult. You can't simply look at the last trade reports. Attempting to buy 3,000 shares of XYZ at 50 AON can't be filled by the exchange unless there is sufficient market volume to fill the entire order in one complete trade. This order cannot be executed in partial increments. For example, XYZ quoted bid 49⅞ and ask 50, size 10 by 10, does not reflect enough market size to execute this buy 3,000 shares XYZ at 50 AON. A report that 3,000 shares have executed at 50 may only indicate that three separate lots of 1,000 shares each have been traded. Contingency orders often reduce the chance that your order will be filled. All or none, fill or kill, and immediate or cancel are difficult orders to challenge.

To review: Before contacting your trading representative to challenge an order, consider all of the facts; the type of order you entered—market or limit—the quote and size of the market, prevailing market conditions, the last trade, and volume. Order challenges are directed to the appropriate exchanges and are reviewed by the executing brokers. Following up on your order challenges consumes valuable time. Don't challenge orders on a whim; challenge your orders judiciously. If it turns out that you are due a report or a better execution price, terrific, your online firm will correct the mistake. If, however, your order challenge is investigated and found unwarranted, don't dwell on it; move on to your next trade.

■ CANCELED, PENDING CANCELED, OR NOTHING DONE? ■

During the trading day you may wish to cancel an existing buy or sell limit order. Market orders, on the other hand, guarantee an execution and can rarely be canceled. For this reason, I'll focus only on canceling limit orders, which you do by following the order cancellation procedures on your online firm's trading menu. The screen should verify, and prompt you to confirm, the exact order that you are attempting to cancel. Once you are satisfied that everything is correct, you go ahead and cancel your order. However, never assume that your order is canceled until you receive a "verified cancel" report either displayed on the screen or given verbally by your trading representative.

Placing a cancellation request on an open order is merely an attempt to cancel and doesn't guarantee that the order will actually be canceled. Executed trade confirmations are relayed back to your online brokerage firm only by the executing exchanges. Certain market conditions can cause delays in the cancellation reporting process. A buy order executed at 2:00 PM could still appear as an unexecuted open buy order on your account as late as 2:10 PM (this would be a good time to status the order). The computer system still allows you to place a cancellation on this order even though it may actually have been executed. A message reading "pending cancel" will result.

Pending cancel informs you that your request to cancel the order has been received. The executing exchange will now attempt to terminate your order. Don't allow an order to remain in pending cancel status for a prolonged period of time. Pending cancel orders are considered open orders and thus can cause problems, particularly if you attempt to reenter a sell order on a stock that earlier in the day you attempted to cancel, yet that still shows as pending cancel. The computer will identify the pending cancel order as an open order and will deny the new sell order, prohibiting you from overselling your stock. Pending cancel orders must be verified canceled before you can enter a similar order.

Implement a cancel only on orders that you no longer want represented on the exchange. Do not use a cancel when changing an order's quantity or limit price. Execute these changes with what is known as a "cancel and replace" or a "go around" order. A cancel and replace or go around order allows you to immediately change an unexecuted open order without having to wait for a verified cancel. Looking to change your existing purchase of 1,000 shares of XYZ Corp. from a limit price of $50 to $49? Simply cancel and replace or go around on the original order. Change the price only; do not straight cancel the entire order and reenter a new one. Doing so can cause delays or, even worse, a duplication of the original order.

As mentioned earlier, execution reports from the exchanges back to your online broker may be delayed. This will most often occur when a security exhibits extraordinary trading volume. Some active trading clients have recognized that by placing a cancel on an open order that may already have been filled but not reported back may sometimes force the exchange to transmit an execution report. You have every right to attempt to cancel any open order, but I firmly caution against using this practice to force the exchange to give you an execution report. Straight canceling an order tells the broker that you do *not* want the trade. An order that may otherwise have been executed could be canceled if you instruct the broker to do so. Bottom line, cancel only orders that you truly want canceled.

Day limit orders that are not executed during that day's trading session will be marked on your computer screen as "nothing done" after the market close. This means that the order is confirmed unexecuted and therefore canceled. On occasion, exchanges are tardy in sending nothing done reports back to your online firm. Any day orders that remain on your open order screen and are not verified as nothing done must be confirmed as nothing done before you reenter the same order. If you just assume nothing done, there is a possibility that you could receive a late report (sometimes as late as the next day) and consequently duplicate your trade.

To solve this dilemma, contact your online trading representative prior to the opening of the market. Although some online brokerage firms operate 24 hours, 7 days a week, you will not be able to confirm a nothing done report until the employees of the trading exchanges start showing up for work in the morning. Don't bother calling your online firm in the evening, as representatives are not equipped to verify that orders showing as open or pending canceled are in fact executed, verified canceled, or nothing done. Call your broker by 9:00 AM EST, which should give you plenty of time to receive an answer back before the market opens at 9:30 AM EST.

▪ ADDRESSING MARGIN HOUSE CALLS AND EXCHANGE CALLS ▪

Receiving a house maintenance or exchange call notification is the most unsavory aspect of trading on margin (borrowing money from your broker) and usually indicates that your account is over-leveraged. As discussed in Chapter 5, house and exchange calls result when a drop in the value of your stock position causes margin equity to fall below the minimum margin maintenance levels. In short, the market value of your securities is no longer enough to collateralize your loan (debit balance). Your online brokerage firm follows strict guidelines when issuing house and exchange calls. When a mailgram is sent or a telephone call is made to inform you that a house or exchange call is due, you must cover the call (deposit cash/stock or sell stock) by its due date. This date is set by your online firm and is neither arbitrary nor negotiable.

Firms contact you when your account comes under a maintenance violation because they are required to. They no more wish to see your account drop into a call than you do. Some firms have recently instituted higher maintenance requirements in an attempt to reduce margin borrowing and thus protect margin traders against the periodic downturns in the market. Online firms have the legal right to take action on your account to meet house or exchange calls. Your securities will be liquidated to meet calls if you are unable to deposit cash or additional marginable securities.

For over a year, I was responsible for calculating margin violations on customer accounts as well as making the final telephone call. Some margin violations were small whereas others were quite large. From day to day, the violations would range anywhere from $1,000 to $500,000. The feelings expressed by these unfortunate clients and me were mutual; they didn't like getting the call and I didn't like making it. It was tough to speak to people who were in the midst of a financial meltdown. Yet the customers who attacked the situation head on and who worked with me got through it more smoothly than others.

Keep in contact with your online firm. Don't avoid calls from it or engage in verbal warfare. It is your responsibility to rectify the violation. Remember, your trading decisions led to the violation; your online broker acted only as agent in your trades. You should do everything possible to settle the call on your own terms; if not, your online firm will settle it on theirs. When a check or stock has not been deposited or when a security sale has not been made by the call's due date, your firm will arbitrarily begin selling off your stock positions.

Take advantage of your margin or trading representative's knowledge in these matters. By working with your online firm, you may discover ways to meet the call that never occurred to you. The representative might review such possibilities as bank wiring funds into the account; closing open options positions; depositing mutual funds that you were not aware were marginable; appreciating out of the call from an increase in stock value; depositing bonds or stock that you may be holding at home or at another account; or by selling specific security positions versus randomly liquidating your portfolio.

Each customer's account is unique and therefore the means by which a house or exchange call can be met will vary. The only certainty is that the house and exchange calls must be met by the date that your online broker tells you! You can choose to face this battle on your own or you can enlist the aid of your online margin or trading representative; the choice is yours.

■ OPTIONS TRADERS! UNDERSTAND YOUR FIRM'S OPTIONS EXERCISE POLICIES ■

Owners of stock option contracts (long options holders) buy the right to either purchase stock or sell stock at the contract's exercise price on any day prior to the contract's expiration date. This right is called exercising the option. An owner of a put option has the right to sell stock whereas a call owner buys stock. Stock options are referred to as physical delivery options. A January 50 put option on XYZ Corp. allows the owner to deliver XYZ stock (sell) at the predetermined strike price of $50. Conversely, exercising a long January 50 call option on XYZ Corp. allows the owner to receive (buy) XYZ Corp. at $50. (For a quick review of options basics, see Chapter 3.)

Another term synonymous with options that can be exercised prior to the expiration date is *American–style*. The option expiration date is the date on which the option expires—on this date the option no longer holds any value and the rights of the contract are terminated. Equity options expire on the third Friday of the month that is fixed by the option contract. For example, an ABC October option will expire on the third Friday in October. The exact expiration dates of various options may vary. There are option contracts known as Leaps that expire several years into the future. It is important to know your option's expiration date.

The policies of exercising option contracts vary across online trading firms. You can instruct your firm to exercise your option contracts yourself or the firm will do it automatically if the options expire "in the money" on the expiration date. In the money means that the stock price on which an option contract was written is above the strike price of the option in the case of a call option and below the strike price for a put option. For example, a call option with a strike price of 50 would be in the money if the underlying stock price was any price above 50. Most firms use three-quarters of a point in the money to determine automatic exercise. You need to confirm this with your online brokerage firm.

For the above example, a call option with an exercise price of 40 would be autoexercised (automatically exercised) on expiration if the stock closes on that Friday at 40⅞. The option would be seven-eighths of a point in the money and the customer would receive (buy) stock at 40. The customer then has the option of keeping the stock or selling it. Be alert; a few firms' autoexercise policy includes automatically entering a corresponding sell order on the shares delivered in for calls and a buyback order on the shares delivered out in the case of puts.

Automatic buy or sell orders are entered as market orders for the opening of the next trading session. You may be unaware of this policy; using the call option example above would mean that instead of owning stock at 40, your online firm would sell the shares at market on the following Monday and would thus preclude you from participating in any gains the stock may have in the future. Firms also establish different cutoff times for exercising option contracts prior to expiration. It could be 30 minutes prior to the close of trading or 30 minutes after the market close. The nearer you get to an option's expiration date, the more important this time curfew becomes.

Index options like the MNX and the SPX are European-style options and are only exercisable on their expiration date. Because there are no physical securities to deliver, it's impossible to deliver an index. These options are known as cash-settled options and give the owner the right to receive a cash payment. The amount of cash is determined by calculating the difference between the index option exercise price (strike price) and a value known as the exercise settlement value. An OEX January 800 call would be in the money if the exercise settlement value was any number greater than 800. The owner of this call option would receive cash in an amount greater than 800. Put options exhibit the opposite characteristics. Caution: The index settlement value is not the index value. The index settlement value is calculated by a specific formula based on the prices of each individual stock composing the index. This settlement value varies with each expiration and can be obtained by contacting your online broker.

■ NEGOTIATING COMMISSIONS ■

Online brokerage firms certainly don't advertise that they negotiate commissions, yet it is a strategy that they engage in frequently to garner the most profitable customers. Not all firms will negotiate, however, and, unfortunately, not all of you will qualify for additional discounts. Some firms don't have any more wiggle room left in their commission schedules or margin interest rates to accommodate further reductions. It is unlikely that firms charging a commission less than $14 per trade or having margin interest rates below brokers' call rates will be able to discount their fees any further. However, online firms that do charge more may be willing to lower their fee schedules in an attempt to acquire or keep your business.

Negotiations are based on the profitability and volume of your trading account. High–net worth traders who trade actively have a higher success rate than smaller investors who trade infrequently. This is not to say that only high–net worth clients receive lower rates. Negotiated rates are proportional to the amount of revenue generated from trade commissions or margin interest charges. As a sales representative, I brokered lower rates for as many clients with accounts worth $50,000 as I did for clients with multi-million-dollar accounts. The reason: The $50,000 clients were trading hundreds of times a year and thus producing thousands of dollars in revenues, whereas the larger clients were not trading at all. Not every multi-million-dollar account on the firm's books is profitable; surprisingly enough, some may actually be a drain on the firm's bottom line.

If you trade on your account over 100 times a year or have a margin debit balance over $200,000, an online firm may discuss possible ways to make you happy. These criteria may sound exorbitant to some of you, but there are a surprising number of online trading accounts that fall under this umbrella. Suffice it to say that cyberspace hosts a heck of a lot of traders with a bundle of money who like to trade. It is these customers who are at the front of the negotiating line.

If you believe that you are one of the customers at the front of the negotiating line and are about to negotiate with an online firm, be prepared to back up your trading claims with hard evidence. Online firms simply won't take your word. They will request statement histories that clearly show a pattern of active trading or the presence of a large debit balance. By asking for your statements, they are not conspiring to get your account number from your current firm; they only wish to confirm the volume of business you are transacting. The more revenue you can show them, the stronger your negotiating stance will be.

Approach these situations devoid of emotion. To put it bluntly, support your case for lower fees with facts, not your ego or emotion. A firm that charges higher fees does so because they firmly believe they have a superior product. Such firms won't compete on price alone, so it is difficult to force their hand. An emotional threat not to do business with a particular firm because it won't meet your price demands may fall on deaf ears. You could wind up doing business with an inferior firm just to save face and prove a point. In the end, it may turn out that the firm with cheaper commissions is not the one that can meet your trading and investing needs.

You're not always going to be completely satisfied with the final negotiated outcome. Neither party wants to think it has given away too much, and only you can determine whether you can live with the results. Although you may have resigned yourself to a large discount, don't disregard the effects that a smaller discount might have on your bottom line. Before you walk away from a smaller discount, do the math. It may turn out to be more lucrative than you had first thought. The object is not to get your broker down to rock-bottom prices. After all, if price were your only concern, you would simply trade at the cheapest online broker. The trick is to negotiate the best brokerage package available at the lowest possible cost.

Don't take it personally if your online firm refuses to negotiate with you. Remember, your online broker is in this to make money too. It would be financial suicide for online firms to apply additional discounts to all customer accounts. Negotiations are reserved for those clients who produce enough revenue that their accounts are profitable even with an additional discount. Negotiating fees is a carrot dangling out there to entice large and active accounts. Still, don't take the position that the industry has forgotten the masses—it hasn't. Commissions across the board are the lowest in history and customers have benefited directly from this reduction. If you're not trading a couple of hundred times a year and can't negotiate additional discounts, don't sweat it. With commissions as low as $5, you're still doing pretty darn well. Remember, not that long ago online brokerage commissions were averaging close to $60.

CHAPTER 9

The Tax Man Cometh

■ DON'T FORGET ABOUT UNCLE SAM ■

You've been having so much fun trading online that you totally forgot about Uncle Sam—completely understandable. For 365 days of the year, the only concerns you had were whether you were making money or beating the S&P 500 Index. It's not until tax season rolls around that it hits you—you have to make an accounting to the IRS! If you're like many investors, you only consider the tax consequences of your trading and what reporting the IRS expects from you as an after-thought. Big mistake! You need to start thinking about taxes now, not later.

There are two major tax considerations. The first is the dollar amount of taxes you will eventually owe on your buying and selling, and second is the documentation required by the IRS. Do you know what the IRS expects from you? Foremost, you must realize that you are on your own when filing your taxes. Online brokers are not tax advisors, and they will be the first to tell you that. The burden of all reporting rests on your shoulders. As we all know, taxes can be extremely complicated and filing incorrectly can cost you. You should always consult a qualified tax advisor if you have questions pertaining to your own tax situation.

I am neither an accountant nor a tax advisor. But online trading and taxes go hand in hand. A lot more is involved with the tax consequences of online trading than what I am able to cover in this book, but I will lay down a few basics to start you on your way to understanding the relationship between taxes and trading. In compiling the following information, I found articles written by Bill Bischoff for <www.smartmoney.com> and Kaye Thomas for <www.fairmark.com> to be two outstanding resources. Both Web sites are filled with comprehensive tax information for the beginner as well as the more sophisticated investor. If you decide to go it alone without help from a tax advisor, you'll find a wealth of tax assistance on the Internet. Two additional sites that you may want to check out are <www.quicken.com> or <www.fool.com>.

■ How Much Do I Owe? ■

Your online brokerage account will generate tax liabilities in the form of interest income, cash dividends, and capital gains. Interest income is the money paid on balances held in your cash core account or in bonds; cash dividends are distributed from company earnings on your stock positions; and capital gains are produced from profitable stock sales. For tax purposes, capital gains are further broken down into short-term capital gains and long-term capital gains. Selling securities held one year or less produce short-term capital gains, whereas liquidating stocks held over one year produce long-term capital gains. For example, selling stock on February 22, 2000, that you originally purchased on February 22, 1999, would result in a short-term capital gain. (You must hold stock for more than a year to have the sale qualify as a long-term capital gain.)

Under the current U.S. tax code, interest income, cash dividends, and short-term capital gains are taxed as ordinary income. Ordinary income is taxed at higher marginal rates than are long-term capital gains; long-term capital gains are taxed at a special capital gains rate. Depending on your current income level, the marginal tax rate on ordinary income, including short-term capital gains, can be as high as 39.6 percent. The maximum tax rate on long-term capital gains is only 20 percent. By comparing the following Marginal Tax Rate Table for Ordinary Income with the Capital Gains Rate Table, it's clear that you can reduce your tax liability by taking long-term capital gains versus short-term capital gains whenever possible. For example, if you are a 36 percent tax filer and report a $600 short-term capital gain on the sale of stock, your tax liability is $216. This same gain held long-term would result in a tax obligation of $120 ($600 × 20%)—a tax savings of $96.

Marginal Tax Rate—Ordinary Taxable Income 1999

Tax Rate	Single	Married/ Filing Jointly	Head of Household	Married/ Filing Separately
15%	Less than $25,750	Less than $43,050	Less than $34,550	Less than $21,525
28%	Over $25,750	Over $43,050	Over $34,550	Over $21,525
31%	Over $62,450	Over $104,050	Over $89,150	Over $52,025
36%	Over $130,250	Over $158,550	Over $144,400	Over $79,275
39.6%	Over $283,150	Over $283,150	Over $283,150	Over $141,575

Capital Gains Tax Rates

Taxed as ordinary income	Short-term capital gains
20%	Long-term capital gains
10% (tax filers in the 15% income tax bracket)	Long-term capital gains

I don't want to imply that you should hold stock for longer than 12 months just to reduce your tax liability. There is no guarantee that a stock's share price will trade any higher 12 months and a day from now. Yet having this choice is one of the great tax advantages that capital gains have over ordinary income. You decide when to take your capital gains and therefore the tax rate that will be levied on the sales proceeds. Will you incur short-term or long-term gains? Will you pay higher or lower taxes? It's your choice. This is in contrast to ordinary income like interest and cash dividends, which are always taxed at the higher ordinary income tax rate and whose applicable tax rates you don't control.

Taking capital gains gives you the added option of postponing the sale of an appreciated stock. You can put off selling a stock until such a time when the tax treatment is more beneficial to you.

Remember that the rise in a stock's market price above its purchase price is only a paper profit until the shares are actually sold.
Would it be better for you to take the capital gain this year or
next? Only you know what is best as it relates to your specific tax
situation. Remember, you can participate in the gain of a company's stock price indefinitely without having to pay taxes on the
gains at least until a future date when you actually sell the stock.

■ How Do 1 Determine My Short-Term or Long-Term Capital Gains or Losses? ■

Capital gains and losses are based on the holding period and the
tax basis of the shares being sold.

The *holding period* is the elapsed time in calendar days beginning on the trade date of the purchase and ending on the trade
date of the sale. As mentioned earlier, stocks that were held for 12
months or less realize short-term gains or losses when sold, whereas
stocks held for over 12 months realize long-term gains or losses.
The proceeds from a stock bought on January 5, 2000, and sold
on January 4, 2001, would fall within the category of short term
and would be taxed as ordinary income. Trade dates are the key
dates for tax reporting. In general, the trade date of a sale determines the year in which your tax liability occurs. Stocks sold on
December 31, 2000, create tax liabilities in the year 2000 even
though the trade actually settles three business days later in the
year 2001.

The *tax basis* for calculating the amount of your gain or loss
is equal to the purchase price plus all commissions. Buying 500
shares at $20 with a $15 commission creates a stock position with
a tax basis of $10,015. Turning around and selling all 500 shares
13 months later at $30 with a $15 commission would result not
only in a terrific investment but also in a long-term capital gain of
$4,970 ($14,985 − $10,015). As you can see, the dollar amount
of any capital gain or loss is based on the difference between the
purchase price plus commission and the sales price minus commission. Therefore, if you bought stock at $20 and sold it at the
same price with a total commission of $30, you would actually re-
alize a capital loss of $30, which is the total commission paid.

Your original tax basis may not always default to the purchase price of the shares. The tax basis can be affected by stock splits, stock dividends, spin-offs, or company mergers and acquisitions. These types of changes are referred to as capital changes, the most common being stock splits. For example, if you had purchased stock several years ago at $50 a share and the company had since declared two separate 2 for 1 stock splits, the new basis of your shares would be $12.50 (the original price of $50 × ½ × ½). Any gains or losses would be based on this new amount. If you are convinced that there were capital changes in your stock but are unsure of the specifics, you should contact the investor relation's department of the company whose shares you hold or ask your online broker.

▪ What If I Don't Know the Tax Basis or Holding Period of My Shares? ▪

Several situations may occur that result in your not knowing the tax basis or holding period of your shares. You either lost your brokerage records, you inherited the stock, or you received shares as a gift. Under these circumstances it may be impossible to know the exact purchase date or price. In any of these cases, the IRS does not expect you to be 100 percent accurate, but it is your obligation as a responsible taxpayer to use all available resources now to arrive at an estimated basis. (You will also want to be certain that you can support the legitimacy of your estimate.)

Lost Statements and Confirmations

Let me put it bluntly: There is no excuse for losing statements and confirmations. Individual confirmation statements as well as a monthly statement accompany every executed trade. Both statements are sent to your address of record and contain all the information you need to prepare your taxes. Confirmation statements show clearly the number of shares purchased, the name of the company, the price, the trade date, and the commission paid. From this information you can calculate your tax basis and your holding period.

In addition to these specific statements, your online broker will also send a year-end statement, although this statement only lists the sales transactions for that year and doesn't show the original purchases. Therefore, it is important to keep your original confirmation statements. If you don't like having all that paper around, there is software available that allows you to download this same information directly from your online brokerage account onto your PC and makes figuring out your taxes at the end of the year much easier. One such software package that is used by many online investors is offered by Quicken.

If you happen to lose your records, you need to make the best estimates possible. Contact your online brokerage firm to request past statements that may show information about the original purchase. Keep this in mind: Your online broker will probably charge you a fee for this extra service, so it is important to keep your statements. If you're not successful in getting past statements from your broker, try to estimate a date of purchase. With this date in mind, track down the high and low trades for that day and take their average, and then use this average price for your tax basis. If the shares were purchased many years ago, don't forget to account for any capital changes that may have occurred.

Stock Received in an Inheritance

If you received shares of stock from an inheritance, it does not exclude you from your tax obligations. You still need to determine a tax basis for the shares. The good news is that it's not as difficult as you may think. In general, the tax basis on inheritance shares defaults to the current market value of the shares on the date of the original owner's death. You don't have to research the original owner's purchase information. The average share price of the high and low trades on the day of the benefactor's death is used for your tax basis. The holding period for the shares is automatically set as a long-term capital gain even if you sell the shares immediately.

Shares Received as a Gift

Figuring your tax basis on donated shares is a little trickier. You normally assume you'll use the same tax basis as the original owner would. However, if the market value of the shares is lower on the date of the gift, this lower price becomes your tax basis. What happens if the donor failed to keep records and doesn't know the original basis of the shares? Well, again, you must make reasonable estimates as to the original date of purchase and find the high and low trades for that day and take the average of the two, which then becomes your base. However, simply taking the average of the high and low prices for the estimated acquisition day is not enough. From this base you need to adjust for any capital changes. Not accounting for capital changes could cause you to incorrectly calculate your capital gains or losses. Who knows, you may find out through you research that you are owed additional shares because of an earlier stock split.

■ Identifying Shares—First In, First Out or "Versus Purchase" ■

How do you account for sales of shares that have been purchased at different times and prices? The IRS assumes that you sell shares out of your account under the accounting principle of first in, first out (FIFO), which means that you sell first the shares purchased first. For instance, you may have bought shares under the following time schedule: 200 shares at $20 on January 4, 1999; 200 shares at $22 on March 1, 1999; and 200 shares at $30 on December 10, 1999. If you subsequently sell 200 shares at $30, the IRS assumes that you are selling the shares that were purchased on January 4, 1999, the earliest shares. For tax-reporting purposes, the amount of the capital gain and the holding period is therefore based on the earliest trade. You are not permitted to take the average price of your shares as your tax basis. In the above example, you couldn't sell 200 shares and claim that the basis was $24, the average of the three purchase prices.

An alternative to FIFO is specific identification or "versus purchase." If you decide to sell specific shares, you need to identify these shares to your broker at the time of the sale. Your broker in turn must confirm your request in writing within a reasonable amount of time. You cannot go back to an earlier stock sale and identify specific shares because it is now beneficial to do so. You must designate the sale as "versus purchase" at the time of the sell order. You can identify versus-purchase shares being sold either electronically or orally. You could specify the shares online during the trade, send an e-mail to your online broker apart from the trade, or simply call your trading representative. The only information that you need to give to your broker is the trade date of the original purchase. For example, you simply notify your online broker, "I am selling shares versus purchase on December 10, 1999, at $30." To avoid any confusion, ask your online broker exactly how it would like to receive these versus-purchase instructions from you.

Benefits of Identifying Shares

The reason you want to go through the trouble of identifying shares is because it can save you money on your taxes. Identifying shares on sales of stock can reduce your tax liability in two specific ways. First, you can identify shares that have a higher cost basis and therefore produce smaller gains. A simple way to lower the amount of taxes is to sell shares with smaller gains. Second, you can identify shares to take advantage of tax benefits from capital losses because you're permitted to offset capital gains with capital losses.

Sheltering gains with losses is a complicated strategy that should be discussed with a tax advisor. However, in a nutshell, short-term losses offset short-term gains and long-term losses offset long-term gains. Your short-term gains of $3,000 and short-term losses of $3,000, for example, would offset each other. Because short-term tax rates are higher than long-term tax rates, it is generally more beneficial to take short-term losses in the same year that you have short-term gains. Because long-term gains already receive a more favorable tax treatment, it's not always prudent to take long-term losses in the same year in which you have long-term gains.

Losses can be carried forward but not back, and if you don't have any capital gains in a given year or if your capital losses exceed your capital gains, you can deduct your capital losses against ordinary income up to a limit of $3,000. For example, if you have capital losses of $5,000 in the year 2000 but no capital gains, you can deduct $3,000 against your ordinary income. If you are in the 36 percent tax bracket, this loss will decrease your year 2000 income tax by $1,080 ($3,000 × 36%). The remaining $2,000 can be carried forward to offset any gains in 2001.

When taking losses you must be aware of the *wash sale rule.* This tax law prohibits you from claiming a loss if you buy replacement shares in the same company either 30 days before the loss sale or 30 days after the loss sale. You do not lose the capital loss benefit entirely if you buy back shares within this 61-day window. Although you cannot claim the loss on the sale, you can add the disallowed loss to the basis of the replacement stock. The holding period on the replacement stock will then include the holding period of the stock you sold.

▪ TAXES AND YOUR STOCK OPTIONS ▪

Are you an options owner or an options writer? You need to know the difference to file your taxes properly. As we discussed earlier, an options owner buys either a put or a call with the inherent right to either buy (call option) or sell stock (put option) at a specified price known as the strike price. As an options writer, you are said to be short the options contract and therefore are the grantor of the option contract's right to either buy or sell stock to the options buyer. For granting this right you receive a payment known as the "premium." There are three possible outcomes to buying or selling option contracts, each with different tax implications. The following is a quick tax review for the long options holder and the short options writer.

Long Options Owner

1. You can sell the long put or call option contract for a capital gain or loss. Your holding period is determined by the amount of time that has elapsed from the trade date of the buy of the option contract to its sales trade date. More than 12 months would be considered a long-term capital gain. Your reportable gain or loss is based on net proceeds and including all commissions.

2. You can exercise the option contract. Exercising put options generates a stock sale. In this case you "put" stock to the person who wrote the option. The capital gain or loss is based on

your original cost basis of the underlying shares that are being sold. The gain or loss is either short term or long term, based on the holding period of the underlying shares. Deduct the cost of the option (premium plus commission) from the sales proceeds. Exercising call options produces a stock purchase. You "call" stock away from the option writer. Add the premium and commission of the option contract to the price of the shares being purchased to calculate your tax basis. The eventual gain or loss will be short term or long term depending on how long you hold the shares prior to any future sale.

3. You can let the option contract expire. In this case you simply have a capital loss based on total cost of the option (premium plus commission). Your loss is short term or long term depending on the length of time the option contract was held prior to expiration. Most option contracts expire within 12 months and are therefore short term.

Short Options Writer

1. You can buy back the option contract that you originally sold, which is also referred to as "closing the position." Purchasing back a put or call option contract relinquishes your obligation to fulfill the rights granted in the contract. If you sold (wrote) an XYZ January 20 call option for a premium of $4 and purchased it back two months later at $2, this closing transaction would cancel your obligation on the short call contract. In this case, you would have generated a short-term capital gain of $2 per contract, the difference between the premium you received ($4) and the premium you paid ($2). Your gain or loss is the difference between the sell premium and the buy premium plus commissions. A gain or loss is reported in the tax year of the closing transaction.

2. You can be assigned. In this case, the person who bought your options has exercised the rights of that option contract. As an assigned put option writer, you must buy stock. Stock is "put" to you. Your tax basis on these shares is the cost of the shares minus the premium received for selling the put option. Your holding period begins on the day after the shares are purchased. As a call option writer, you must sell stock. Stock

is "called" from you. Add the premium originally received for writing the option contract to the stock sale proceeds. Your gain is long term or short term depending on how long the underlying shares were held.

3. Your short option contract expires. You have guessed correctly on the movement of the underlying stock and the options owner does not exercise the option contract that you sold. In this case you have a reportable short-term capital gain in the amount of the premium received. The gain is always considered short term regardless of how long you held the short option. The gain is reported in the tax year in which the option expires.

Epilogue: The Closing Bell

■ MOVING AHEAD ■

From opening your account to the tax implications of your online trading, I have been able to cover many vital aspects of online trading. At times I'm sure that the material was not as exciting as you may have anticipated, but in the end I know it will make you a better online investor; in fact, I'm certain of it. We have all grown so accustomed to the excitement generated by online trading that most of us have forgotten about the unglamorous hard work that is required for responsible investing. It would have been easy for you to have jumped directly into trading without having done your homework first. You are very smart for wanting to learn more about how online trading works before jumping in completely.

As you move forward, I caution you to act deliberately. Think through your investment decisions thoroughly. Each time you log on to your computer and access your online account, realize that from that point on *you* are responsible for your actions. You alone are making the calls; with every click of the mouse you are setting your investment wheels in motion. Stick to the road map that you have laid out for yourself. Deviating from your charted course will cause delays in reaching your financial destination.

Online trading can become addictive, so remember that your actions hold financial consequences. After all, this is not Monopoly money you're playing with—it's your own hard-earned dollars! Don't get swept up in the online trading frenzy. You could discover at the end of the year that you have unknowingly traded your life savings away. It happens to many online investors, and if you're not careful, it can happen to you. I have seen too many so-called sophisticated and experienced traders lose the farm by trading recklessly. Before you know it, an innocent quick buy here and quick sell there can turn into 10, 30, 50, or an even greater number of unintended trades. With today's ease of access, you can find yourself unwittingly clicking through trades without any rationale.

Keep the information from the earlier chapters at the forefront of your trading decisions. Put into practice what has been discussed; give complete information on your account application, implement limit orders when appropriate, and use margin wisely. Above all, think before you act!

It has been my pleasure to review with you the fundamentals involved in online trading. My hopes and wishes for all of you are that you embark on a successful online trading experience. If this book helps you avoid the many roadblocks inherent with online trading, then I will consider it a tremendous success. If it gets you to stop and think before you take your next step, then I have done my job. Online investing is not a game and should not be treated as one! It is a highly regulated industry that has specific practices and processes that on the surface appear simple but at their core are complex. Take the trading markets seriously; your future wealth depends on it.

The stock market is not a place for the faint of heart and it is certainly not a place for the ignorant. As you move forward, educate yourself to the best of your abilities. Keep yourself current, not only on the companies that you invest in, but also on the online brokerage firms that you entrust with executing your investment decisions. The fact that you can open an online trading account so easily does not necessarily make investing easier. Keep this book handy in case you have questions about the application process, transferring your account, margin trading, trade processing, and other important issues. If you are unsure of anything, ask questions, because learning by your mistakes can be costly.

One thing about the market that will never change is that there will always be winners and losers. And unfortunately, no one has yet to devise the exact formula for winning on Wall Street. However, there is one ingredient to successful online trading that no one can dispute: A smart investor is a better investor.

The future of online trading continues to look promising. Technological innovations, particularly in wireless communications networks, seem limitless. The securities markets themselves are embracing technology to create more efficiencies and greater liquidity. In addition, more tools that once were available only to professional traders continue to be rolled out to the public investor. No one knows exactly where we'll be in five years. But wherever we are, exciting changes are imminent and there certainly won't be a dull moment. So from one online investor to another, I wish you good luck and good fortune.

APPENDIX A

Online Trading
Customer Exam

1. All of the following factors have contributed to the growth of online trading *except*
   a. the bull market.
   b. guaranteed trading profits.
   c. May Day (deregulation).
   d. the Internet.

2. TRUE or FALSE. Dirt cheap commissions are always the best criteria for selecting an online brokerage firm.

3. What type of stock quote displays the current bid and ask prices without the need to manually refresh the quote?
   a. Real-time quotes
   b. Delayed quotes
   c. Streaming quotes
   d. Level 2 quotes

4. Where can you go to find out if any customer complaints have been filed against your online broker?
   a. Your online broker
   b. NASD Public Disclosure Program
   c. Your online broker's competitors
   d. Web site chat rooms

5. NYSE Rule 405 is also referred to as
   a. transfer-of-assets rule.
   b. know-your-customer rule.
   c. margin maintenance rule.
   d. trade settlement rule.

6. All of the following account registration types may be eligible for margin trading *except*
   a. an individual account.
   b. an individual retirement account.
   c. a joint tenant account.
   d. a corporate account.

7. TRUE or FALSE. Only one signature is required on the new-account application form for a joint tenancy account in which only one person will be trading.

8. TRUE or FALSE. Anyone is eligible to open an online trading account as long as minimum initial account balances are met.

9. In which type of account registration does the deceased owner's interest in the account pass to the surviving owner?
   a. Corporate account
   b. Trust account
   c. Joint tenants with the right of survivorship
   d. Joint tenants in common

10. Whose Social Security number must be supplied on a Gifts to Minors Act account or a Transfers to Minors Act account?
    a. Donor's   c. A parent's
    b. Custodian's   d. Minor's

11. TRUE or FALSE. A call option contract gives the owner the right to buy the underlying stock at a specified price during the life of the contract.

12. The total cost of buying five ABC Inc. January 50 call option contracts at a premium of $2 plus a commission of $22 would be
    a. $522.   c. $1,022.
    b. $272.   d. $122.

13. The seller of a put option contract would be considered *(bullish, bearish)* on the underlying stock. (Circle the correct answer.)

14. TRUE or FALSE. Indicating on the options agreement that you would like to trade the most risky options strategies will ensure that you receive the highest options level.

15. The Securities Investor Protection Corporation (SIPC) insures assets in an account up to
    a. $500,000 in cash.
    b. $500,000 with minimum $100,000 cash.
    c. $500,000 with maximum $100,000 cash.
    d. $600,000 in stock and cash.

16. A signature guarantee can be obtained from all of the following *except*
    a. a bank.
    b. a mutual fund company.
    c. a notary public.
    d. an online brokerage firm.

17. Most online brokerage firms will accept for deposit all of the following types of checks *except*
    a. second-party checks.
    b. third-party checks.
    c. postal money orders.
    d. cashier's checks.

18. Which types of deposits are considered federal funds?
    a. Personal checks
    b. Certified checks
    c. Bank wires
    d. Credit card checks

19. Street name securities refer to securities that are held
    a. at your online broker's.
    b. at your home.
    c. at your bank.
    d. at the New York Stock Exchange.

20. TRUE or FALSE. A full account transfer via the ACAT from one online broker to another will disrupt your trading.

21. What are the three most common types of trading accounts?
    1. _____
    2. _____
    3. _____

22. Trades that are executed in a cash account are reflected in which category on your account balance statement?
    a. Cash core account
    b. Margin market value
    c. Short market value
    d. Cash market value

23. TRUE or FALSE. All trades that are placed in a margin account will be considered margin transactions and therefore charged margin interest.

24. A simple formula that can be used to calculate net worth or net equity is:
    Net worth/Net equity = (_____ positions + cash core balance) − (_____ positions + margin debit balance).

Questions 25 and 26—Calculate Net worth/Net equity

25. Cash core	$10,000	Net worth/Net equity	$_____
Margin debit	0	Cash market value	15,000
		Margin market value	20,500
		Long option value	5,000

26. Cash core	$ 0	Net worth/Net equity	$_____
Margin debit	10,000	Margin market value	70,000
		Long option value	20,000
		Short option value	15,000

27. What would be the result of a 2 for 1 stock split on 2,000 shares of stock priced at $50 per share?
   a. 4,000 shares priced at $50 per share
   b. 2,000 shares priced at $100 per share
   c. 4,000 shares priced at $25 per share
   d. 2,000 shares priced at $25 per share

28. TRUE or FALSE. Margin is the amount of cash or securities that must be deposited in order to secure a broker's loan.

29. What is the initial margin requirement set by the Federal Reserve Board called?
   a. Rule 405   c. Regulation T
   b. Regulation A   d. None of the above

30. With the Federal Reserve Board's initial margin requirement set at 60 percent, what would be the initial margin required on a purchase of $75,000 in marginable securities?
   a. $45,000
   b. $30,000
   c. $37,500
   d. $75,000

31. The minimum amount of margin equity that is required to be maintained during the entire life of a broker's loan is referred to as
   a. a Regulation T requirement.
   b. a market requirement.
   c. a house requirement.
   d. a house surplus.

32. With Regulation T set at 50 percent, calculate the Regulation T excess.

Cash core	$ 0	Net worth/Margin equity	$70,000
Margin debit	10,000	Margin market value	80,000
Regulation T		Regulation T (50%)	40,000
excess	$_____		

33. With house maintenance requirements at 30 percent, calculate house surplus.

Cash core	$ 0	Net worth/Margin equity	$70,000
Margin debit	10,000	Margin market value	80,000
Regulation T		Regulation T (50%)	40,000
excess	30,000	House maintenance (30%)	24,000
House surplus $_____			

34. Calculate the available-to-borrow amount and buying power for the following account.

Cash core	$ 0	Net worth/Margin equity	$70,000
Margin debit	10,000	Margin market value	80,000
Available to		Regulation T (50%)	40,000
borrow	$_____	House maintenance (30%)	24,000
Regulation T		Buying power	$_____
excess	30,000		
House surplus	46,000		

35. On the following account, at what level of margin market value will a customer be in violation of a house maintenance call? (Assume that all stock positions have a house maintenance requirement of 40%) $_____

Cash core	$ 0	Net worth/Margin equity	$40,000
Margin debit	30,000	Margin market value	70,000

Questions 36 and 37:

36. What is the house maintenance requirement on an account with the following stock positions? $ _____

Shares	Company	Price	Margin Market Value	House Maintenance Requirement
200	ABC Inc.	$40	$ 8,000	30%
300	XYZ Corp.	50	15,000	60

1,000	EZ Corp.	3	3,000	100
100	Big Inc.	20	200	30

Total Market Value = $26,200

37. Plugging in the house maintenance requirement calculated from question 36, would the account be in violation of a house call? YES / NO

Cash core	$ 0	Net worth/Margin equity	$14,200
Margin debit	12,000	Margin market value	26,200
		House maintenance requirement	$_____

38. The New York Stock Exchange is considered
    a. an auction market.
    b. a negotiated market.

39. Which of the following individuals transact business in the Nasdaq market?
    a. Specialists
    b. Two-dollar brokers
    c. Market makers
    d. All of the above

40. The bid price quoted on a listed security such as those traded on the New York Stock Exchange represents
    a. the lowest price at which someone is willing to sell stock.
    b. the highest price at which someone is willing to buy stock.
    c. the guaranteed price at which someone can sell stock.
    d. the guaranteed price at which someone can buy stock.

41. A listed security is quoted bid 30 and ask 30⅟₁₆, size 100 by 100. This tells you that there are
    a. 100 shares bid at 30 and 100 shares offered at 30⅟₁₆.
    b. 1,000 shares bid at 30 and 1,000 shares offered at 30⅟₁₆.
    c. 10,000 shares bid at 30 and 10,000 shares offered at 30⅟₁₆.
    d. none of the above.

42. A limit order to sell stock at 25 when the quote is bid 25 and ask 25⅛ may not be executed because
    a. there is stock ahead.
    b. the stock is trading in a fast market.
    c. the quote is a bad quote.
    d. all of the above.

43. Which one of the following is considered a 100 percent electronic trading marketplace?
    a. The New York Stock Exchange
    b. The regional exchanges
    c. The Chicago Board Options Exchange
    d. Electronic communication networks

44. A market order to buy stock when the stock quote is bid 20 and ask 20⅛ is guaranteed to be executed at what price?
    a. 20   c. 20⅛
    b. 20⁵⁄₁₆   d. None of the above

45. A limit order to sell stock at a price of 40 can be executed at what price?
    a. 40   c. 40⅛
    b. 40⁵⁄₁₆   d. All of the above

46. Under such conditions as hot IPO offerings, fast markets, or system delays, what type of order reduces the risk of buying or selling stock at an unanticipated price significantly away from the quoted market price? _____

47. When speaking with your online brokerage firm, you should always try to be P_____, P_____, and P_____.

48. When reporting capital gains or losses to the IRS, it is important to know both the _____ and the _____ for the shares that were sold.

49. The 1999 Internal Revenue Service Code stipulates that a long-term capital gain occurs when an asset that has been held for _____ is sold for a profit.
    a. 6 months
    b. 6 months and 1 day
    c. 12 months
    d. 12 months and 1 day

50. TRUE or FALSE. The greatest advantage of online trading is that you are certain to make money.

■ ANSWER KEY ■

1. B. Trading profits are never guaranteed.
2. FALSE. Select your online broker based on all criteria that are important to you.
3. C. page 32
4. B. page 42
5. B. page 48
6. B. page 59
7. FALSE. page 53
8. FALSE. page 52
9. C. page 54
10. D. page 55
11. TRUE page 60
12. C. page 61
13. Bullish. page 62
14. FALSE. page 63
15. C. page 64
16. C. page 65
17. B. page 74
18. C. page 72
19. A. page 76
20. TRUE. page 85
21. 1) Cash 2) Margin 3) Short stock. page 92
22. D. page 93
23. FALSE. page 93. Margin interest is only charged on debit balances!
24. Net worth/Net equity = (long positions + cash core balances) − (short positions + margin debit balances). page 98
25. $50,500. page 98
26. $65,000. page 98
27. C. page 100
28. TRUE. page 101
29. C. page 102
30. $45,000. page 102
31. C. page 102
32. $30,000. pages 104–6
33. $46,000. pages 104–6

34. Available to borrow = $30,000, Buying power = $60,000. pages 107–9
35. $49,999. pages 109–11. A $50,000 margin market value equity meets minimum house requirements.
36. $14,460. page 112. You must add up the maintenance requirement for each stock position ($2,400 + $9,000 + $3,000 + $60 = $14,460).
37. YES. pages 109–12. The account is in a house call violation of $260 (margin equity of $14,200 less the house requirement of $14,460).
38. A. page 120
39. C. page 131
40. B. page 120
41. C. page 121
42. D. pages 172–74. Limit orders are not guaranteed to execute. Market orders are.
43. D. page 129.
44. D. page 147. Market orders are executed at whatever the stock price is when the order is represented in the market.
45. D. pages 148–49. Limit orders are assumed "or better" orders.
46. Limit order. pages 148–49. Limit orders, if executed, must be done at that limit price or better. There are no surprises when it comes to the execution price.
47. Professional, Prepared, and Prompt. page 165
48. Holding period and tax basis. page 186
49. D. page 184
50. FALSE. Online trading is not magic. There are no guarantees when investing in the stock market!

APPENDIX B

Online Brokers

1st Discount Brokerage, Inc.	www.1st-discount.com
Mutual Securities, Inc.	
(Cowles Sabol)	www.mutualsec.com
A.B. Watley, Inc.	www.abwatley.com
Accutrade, Inc.	www.accutrade.com
Advisors Group, Inc. (The)	www.advisorsgroup.com
Alex Moore & Company, Inc.	www.livetrade.com
Amber Securities Corporation	www.swiftrade.com
America First Associates	www.aftrader.com
American Century Brokerage	www.brokerage.
	americancentury.com
American Express Co.	www.americanexpress.com/
	direct
Ameritrade, Inc.	www.ameritrade.com,
	www.ebroker.com
AmeriVest, Inc.	www.amerivestinc.com
Amerivet Securities Inc.	www.amerivet.com
AmSouth Investment Services,	
Inc.	www.amsouth.com
Andrew Peck Associates Inc.	www.andrewpeck.com
Arvest Investments	www.netvest.com/arv
Atlantic Financial of Mass.	www.af.com
Bank One Securities	
Corporation	www.oneinvest.com/home.html
BB&T Investment Services, Inc.	www.bbandt.com
Benjamin & Jerold Brokerage,	
Inc.	www.stockoptions.com
Benson York Group, Inc.	www.mostactives.com,
	www.buystocks.com
Bidwell & Company	www.bidwell.com
Brook Street	www.brookst.com
Brown & Company Securities	
Corporation	www.brownco.com
Bull & Bear Securities, Inc.	www.ebullbear.com
Burke, Christensen and Lewis	
Securities, Inc.	www.bclnet.com/fincenter.htm
Bush Burns Securities, Inc.	www.bushburns.com
Capital West Investment	
Group, Inc.	www.cwigroup.com/trading.htm

Charles Schwab & Co., Inc.   www.eschwab.com;
                                  www.schwab.com
Chase Manhattan Corp.   www.chase.com
CIGNA Financial Services, Inc.   www.cigna.com/cfs/broker/
                                  index.html;
                                  www.bhcihc.com/cig

Citicorp Investment Services   www.citibank.com/us/
                                  investments/home.htm
Comerica Securities   www.comerica.com/invest/dbol.
                                  html
Compass Bank   www.compassweb.com
Crestar Securities Corporation   www.crestar.com/creatatinvest
CyBerBroker, Inc.   www.cybercorp.com
Datek Securities Corp.   www.datek.com
Dain Rauscher (announced—
    not live)   www.dainrauscher.com
Delta Equity Services
    Corporation   www.deltaequity.com
Dime Securities, Inc.   www.dimesec.com
DLJ*direct*, Inc.   www.dljdirect.com
Downstate Discount Brokerage,
    Inc.   www.trade4less.com
Dreyfus Brokerage Services,
    Inc.   www.edreyfus.com
Dreyfus Investment Services
    Corp.   www.disc.mellon.com
E*Trade Securities   www.etrade.com
Emmet A. Larkin Company, Inc.   www.internettrading.com
Empire Financial Group, Inc.   www.lowfees.com
FarSight Financial Services, L.P. www.nfsn.com
Fidelity Brokerage Services, Inc. www.fidelity.com
Fifth Third Securities, Inc.   www.53.com/advisors/
                                  brokerage; ww.bhcihc.com
First Capital Brokerage
    Services, Inc.   www.firstcapitalbrokerage.com
First Flushing Securities, Inc.   www.firstflushing.com;
                                  www.firstrade.com
First Georgetown Securities, Inc. www.firstgeorgetown.com
First Security Investor Services www.bhcihc.com/fir

First Tennessee Brokerage, Inc.	www.firsttennessee.com/
Freedom Investments, Inc. (Trade Flash)	www.freedominvestments.com
Freeman Welwood & Co., Inc.	www.freemanwelwood.com
G H Securities, Inc.	www.ghsecurities.com.ky
G.W. & Wade Asset Management Company	www.gwwade.com
Grace (R. K.) & Co. (Cardinal Capital) (in development)	www.cardinalcapital.net
Heim & Young Securities, Inc.	www.heimandyoung.com
Herzog, Heine, Geduld, Inc.	www.maxule.com/htdoca/ trade1.html
Howe Barnes Investments, Inc.	www.netinvestor.com
Huntington Investment Company (The)	www.huntington.com
Instinet (announced—not live)	www.instinet.com
Investex Securities Group, Inc.	www.investexpress.com
Investin.com Securities Corp.	www.investin.com
Investrade Discount Securities	www.netvest.com/rg2
J B Oxford & Company	www.jboxford.com
Jack White & Company	www.jackwhiteco.com
Keystone Brokerage, Inc.	www.keyfin.com/kfb
Lintz, Glover, White & Co., Inc.	www.lintztrade.com
Lynx Capital Corporation	www.lynxcapital.com/trading. htm
M. One Securities, Inc.	www.mone.com
Madison Securities, Inc.	www.madisonsecurities.com
Marsco Investment Corporation	www.marscoinvestments.com
Mercantile Investment Services, Inc.	www.mercantile.com
Merrill Lynch	www.merrilllynch.com, www.ml.com
McDonald & Company (announced—not live)	www.laurelkay.com
Morgan Stanley Dean Witter Online	www.online.msdw.com
Mr. Stock, Inc.	www.mrstock.com
Muriel Siebert & Co., Inc.	www.msiebert.com

MyDiscountBroker.com/ Southwest Securities	www.mydiscountbroker.com
MyTrack	www.mtrack.com
National Discount Brokers	www.ndb.com
Nations Financial Group, Inc.	www.ffutures.com
NationsBanc	www.nationsbank.com/ investments
NBC Captial Markets Group, Inc.	www.nbcbank.com
New Times Securities Services, Inc. (in development)	www.newtimessecurities.com
New York Life Securities, Inc.	www.bhcihc.com/nyl
Newport Discount Brokerage, Inc.	www.newport-discount.com
Norwest Investment Services, Inc.	www.edart.com/nisi
Old Kent Brokerage Services	www.bhcihc.com/oka
Online Trading Inc.	www.onlinetradinginc.com
People's Securities Inc.	www.peoples.com/invest/ onlinetr.htm
Peregrine Financials & Securities, Inc.	www.peregrinefinancial.com
Peremel & Co.	www.peremel.com
Preferred Capital Markets, Inc.	www.deltatrader.com; www.tradeoptions.com
ProTrade Securities	www.protrade.com
Pyramid Financial Corporation	www.wyse-sac.com
Quick & Reilly, Inc.	www.quick-reilly.com
R.M. Stark & Co., Inc.	www.rmstark.com
Recom Securities, Inc.	www.trutrade.com
Regal Discount Securities	www.eregal.com; www.investrade.com
Robert Van Securities, Inc.	www.robertvan.com; www.robvanonline.com
Sagamore Trading Group, Inc.	www.time2trade.com
Salomon Smith Barney (Citicorp)	www.salomonsmithbarney.com
Scottsdale Securities, Inc.	www.scottrade.com

Scout Brokerage Services, Inc.	www.scoutbrokerage.com
Scudder Brokerage Services	www.scudder.com
Seaport Securities Corp.	www.sea-port.com
Searle & Co.	www.esearle.com; www.searlco.com
Securities Research, Inc.	www.securitiesresearch.com; esecuritiesresearch.com
Sloan Securities Corp.	www.sloansecurities.com
Southtrust Securities, Inc.	www.bhcihc.com/sou
State Discount Brokers	www.state-online.com
State Street Brokerage Services, Inc.	www.ssga.com
Stocks4Less	www.stocks4less.com
Summit Financial Services Group, Inc.	www.summitbank.com
Sun Trust	www.suntrust.com
Sunlogic Securities, Inc.	www.sunlogic.com
Suretrade, Inc. (Owned by Fleet Financial)	www.suretrade.com
T. Rowe Price Investment Services, Inc.	www.troweprice.com/brokerage/index.html
TF Partners (offered via Vanguard Capital)	www.taxfreebond.com
The Advisors Group, Inc. (TAG)	www.advisorsgroup.com
The R.J. Forbes Group, Inc.	www.forbesnet.com
Thomas F. White & Co., Inc.	www.computel.com; www.prodiscount.com
TradeCast	www.tradecast.com
Tradescape.com	www.tradescape.com
Tradestar Investments, Inc.	www.tradestar-trade.com; www.bhcihc.com/tsr
Trade-Well Discount Investing, LLC	www.trade-well.com
U.S. Clearing Corporation	www.mainatmarket.com; www.bsdmtweb.com
U.S. Discount Brokerage, Inc.	www.usdb.com
U.S. Rica Financial, Inc.	www.usrica.com
U.S. Securities & Futures Corp., Chicago	www.ussecurities.com

UBOC Investment Services, Inc.	www.investathome.com/ UBOCPages
Unified Management Corporation	www.umctrade.com; www.umcstock.com
UNISE Investment Corp.	www.unise.com
UVEST Investment Services	www.netbank.com/investments. htm
Vanguard Brokerage Services, Inc.	www.vanguard.com/vbs/online/
Vision Securities, Inc.	www.visiontrade.com
Wachovia Investments, Inc.	www.wachovia.com
Wall Street Access	www.wsaccess.com
Wall Street Discount Corporation	www.wsdc.com
Wall Street Equities, Inc.	www.wsei.com
WallStreet Electronica Online Trading, Inc.	www.wallstreete.com
Wang Investments Associates, Inc.	www.wangvest.com
Waterhouse Securities, Inc.	www.waterhouse.com
Web Street Securities	www.webstreetsecurities.com
Wells Fargo Securities, Inc.	www.wellsfargo.com/wellstrade
Westminster Securities Corporation	www.livebroker.com
Wilshire Capital Management, LLC	www.wilshirecm.com
Wit Capital Corporation	www.witcapital.com
York Securities, Inc.	www.yorktrade.com; www.tradingdirect.com
Your Discount Broker	www.ydb.com
Ziegler Thrift Trading, Inc.	www.ziegler-thrift.com
Zions Investment Securities, Inc.	www.zionsdirect.com

*The Commission staff compiled this chart from a variety of sources.

This chart may not represent every online firm. In addition, some of the information may have changed since its compilation.

RESOURCES

Books

After the Trade Is Made—Processing Securities Transactions. 2d ed. Davis M. Weiss (New York Institute of Finance, 1993).

Dictionary of Finance and Investment Terms. John Downes and Jordan Elliot Goodman (Barron's Educational Series, 1991).

PassTrak Series 7 Principles and Practices—General Securities Representative (Dearborn Financial Publishing, Inc.).

PassTrak Series 4 Principles and Practices—Registered Options Principal (Dearborn Financial Publishing, Inc.).

The Only Investment Guide You'll Ever Need. Andrew Tobias (Harcourt Brace & Company, 1998).

The 1999 Stock Traders Almanac. Yale Hirsch (The Hirsch Organization, 1998).

The Wall Street Journal—Guide to Understanding Money & Investing. Kenneth M. Morris and Alan M. Siegel (Lightbulb Press, 1993).

Internet Web Sites

American Association of Individual Investors www.aaii.com
American Stock Exchange www.amex.com
Bigcharts www.bigcharts.com
Bloomberg News www.bloomberg.com
Bullrally Total Investment Site www.bullrally.com
BusinessWeek Online www.businessweek.com
BusinessWire News www.businesswire.com

Chicago Board Options Exchange	www.cboe.com
Credit Suisse First Boston	www.csfb.com
Dow Jones Indexes	www.averages.dowjones.com
Econoday	www.econoday.com
Electronic Library	www.elibrary.com
Fairmark Press-Tax Guide for Investors	www.fairmark.com
Federal Trade Commission	www.ftc.gov
Forrester Research, Inc.	www.forrester.com
Gartner Group-Dataquest	www.gartnerweb.com
Gomez Advisors	www.gomez.com
Hoover's Online	www.hoovers.com
Investor's Clearinghouse	www.investoreducation.org
Island ECN	www.island.com
J.D. Power and Associates	www.jdpower.com
Jupiter Communications Research	www.jupitercommunications.com
Kiplinger	www.kiplinger.com
Nasdaq	www.nasdaq.com
National Association of Securities Dealers (NASD)	www.nasd.com
NASD Regulation	www.nasdr.com
National Center for Policy Analysis	www.ncpa.org
National Fraud Information Center	www.fraud.org
New York Stock Exchange	www.nyse.com
North American Securities Administrators Association, Inc.	www.nasaa.org
Options Institute	www.cboe.com
Philadelphia Stock Exchange	www.phlx.com
Quicken	www.quicken.com
Securities and Exchange Commission	www.sec.gov
SmartMoney	www.smartmoney.com
Standard & Poor's Personal Wealth	www.personalwealth.com
TheStreet.com	www.thestreet.com
USA Today	www.usatoday.com
U.S. Bancorp Piper Jaffray	www.piperjaffray.com
Worldly Investor	www.worldlyinestor.com

Articles, Periodicals, and Reports

Discount Broker Survey 2000: A Guide to Commissions and Services. Jean Henrich. *American Association of Individual Investors Journal* 22, no. 1 (January 2000).

Econoday 2000 Investment Calendar. Econoday Inc.

Figuring Your Tax Basis When You've Got No Statements & Taxes on Stock Options. Bill Bischoff. www.smartmoney. com, 3 March 1999.

Nasdaq goes for another tumble. Kimberly Blanton. *Boston Globe,* 13 April 2000.

1999 Securities Industry Factbook. Grace Toto and George Monahan, eds. The Securities Industry Association, 1999.

Online Brokerage Forecast, 1997–2002: Redefining the Brokerage Landscape. Paul D Johnson. IDC/LINK.

Online Brokerage: Keeping Apace of Cyberspace. Report by Commissioner Laura S. Unger. The Securities and Exchange Commission, November 1999.

Online Brokerage Quarterly Roundup, Third Quarter 1999. James Marks, Mark St. Marie, and Mitchell Y. Williams, CFA. Credit Suisse First Boston Corporation, 15 December 1999.

Stock Up. Margaret Opsata. Southwest Airlines *Spirit Magazine,* June 1999.

Statement by Chairman Arthur Levitt, Securities and Exchange Commission Concerning On-Line Trading, 27 January 1999.

Tax Guide for Beginning Investors. Kaye A. Thomas. Fairmark Press Inc., 24 December 1999.

Wall Street's hype machine—It could spell trouble for investors. Marcia Vickers and Gary Weiss. *BusinessWeek,* 3 April 2000.

You and the Investment World. New York Stock Exchange, 1998.

GLOSSARY

ACAT transfer Automated customer account transfer; the electronic transfer system developed by the National Securities Clearing Corporation to facilitate the transfer of assets and used by brokerage houses to expedite transfer of assets between institutions. A customer initiates an ACAT transfer by completing an account transfer form.

auction market Securities markets like the New York Stock Exchange and the American Stock Exchange where stocks are bought and sold through brokers who enter competitive bids to buy and competitive offers to sell; also referred to as a double-auction system because many buyers and many sellers come together in competitive bidding on the exchange floor as opposed to the over-the-counter market where trades are negotiated.

available to borrow The total amount of loan money available to a customer on a margin account for cash withdrawals or for additional securities purchases. Available to borrow is equal to the lesser of either the account's Regulation T excess or the house surplus.

buying power The total dollar amount available to a customer on a margin account for additional securities purchases; an amount equal to the lesser of an account's available-to-borrow figure divided by the Regulation T requirement or the house maintenance requirement.

cash account An account type in which stocks, bonds, mutual funds, and option contracts can be traded; often referred to as cash account. Securities purchased in a cash account must be paid for in full by the trade settlement date; money cannot be borrowed against securities in a cash account. Cash account figures do not reflect actual cash balances (see *cash core*).

cash core The amount shown on your balance statement that reflects the account's actual cash position. Cash received from check deposits, stock sales, interest payments, and dividends are credited to this account. Checks written off an account or debit card purchases are charged to the cash core. Collected cash balances reflect settled or cleared funds; uncollected cash balances reflect unsettled funds and are not cleared for withdrawal.

call option A derivative trading security based on an underlying investment instrument such as a stock, bond, or stock index that gives the owner or call buyer the right to buy the underlying stock at a specified price (strike price) any time up to the option's expiration date. For that right the *call buyer* pays what is called a premium; conversely, a *call writer* is one who sells the call option and therefore receives the premium.

capital gains/losses The difference between an asset's cost basis and its sale price. Assets sold at a profit are considered capital gains and those sold at a loss are considered capital losses. As of 1999, assets sold that have been held over 12 months are long-term capital gains/losses.

debit balance The amount shown on your balance statement that reflects the dollar amount of cash owed to your brokerage firm and subject to margin interest charges. It is also referred to as a *broker's loan* or a *margin loan*. Debit balances occur when securities purchases or cash withdrawals exceed the dollar amount held in cash core balances. Borrowing money from your broker to purchase stock is referred to as buying securities on margin.

delayed quote A securities quote that does not reflect the current bid and ask price at which a particular security can be bought and sold in the current market. Quotes can be delayed for two reasons: (1) as a matter of policy where all bid and ask prices are 15-minute delayed quotes; (2) the existence of fast markets where extreme trading volatility and volume make updating current bid and ask prices impossible.

Dow Jones Industrial Average The oldest continuing U.S. market index established by Charles H. Dow on May 26, 1896, and currently made up of 30 select blue chip U.S. stocks; the most quoted market indicator allowing investors to follow basic trends in the stock market. Companies in the Dow include AT&T, Coca-Cola, Exxon Mobile, General Electric, General Motors, McDonald's, and Walt Disney.

DTC transfer A system by which securities can be transferred between brokerage institutions via the Depository Trust Company (DTC); full brokerage account transfers may not be eligible for DTC transfer. A brokerage customer initiates a DTC transfer by contacting the firm that currently holds the securities. This transfer cannot be completed without a DTC number, which is obtained by contacting the brokerage firm that is receiving the securities.

electronic communication network (ECN) A purely computerized trading marketplace (also called alternative trading system) that collects, organizes, and matches (executes) customer buy and sell orders. At this time, the majority of stocks traded on ECNs are Nasdaq securities. Instinet, Island, Redibook and Spear, and Leeds & Kellogg are considered ECNs.

exercise The act of initiating the right inherent in an option contract. A call option buyer or call option owner exercises the right to buy the underlying stock at the specified strike price. The put option buyer or put option owner exercises the write to sell the underlying stock at a specified strike price.

expiration date The last day in which a call option owner can exercise the right to buy the underlying stock at the option contract's strike price; for put option owners, the last day to exercise the right to sell the underlying stock at the strike price. Stock options most often expire on the third Friday of the month designated in the option contract. Option contracts that are not exercised are considered to expire worthless.

fast market A trading condition caused by extreme market volatility or trading volume resulting in displayed quotes not reflecting actual market prices. Market orders placed on stocks trading in fast markets can be executed significantly differently than the last displayed quote. Hot IPOs or stocks with breaking news often trade under these conditions.

house call A margin maintenance violation occurring when a customer's equity balance in a margin account falls below house maintenance requirements. House calls must be met as soon as possible or according to the online broker's demand schedule by depositing additional cash or marginable securities.

holding period The amount of time that a security is held by its owner. It begins on the trade date (or date of purchase) and ends on the trade date of the sale. For tax purposes, this period is used to determine whether the sale of assets creates a long-term or short-term capital gain/loss.

house maintenance requirement The minimum equity requirement that must be maintained in a margin account while a broker's loan or debit balance is outstanding on a customer's account. It is determined by the online brokerage firm and can be set at any percentage greater than, but not less than, the NYSE maintenance requirement. Firms can raise house requirements at their discretion anytime.

limit order An order that instructs a trader to execute a buy or sell order at a specified price or better. This specified price is known as the limit price and for buy orders the execution price must be at the limit price or lower; for sell orders it must be at the limit price or higher. Limit orders are not guaranteed to fill but are guaranteed for price if executed.

long position A representation of ownership (assets). Purchases of stocks, bonds, mutual funds, or option contracts (other than to cover short positions) are considered long positions in an account. The values of long positions are added to your account balances in deriving total net worth.

margin Also referred to as equity, the amount of cash or securities that must be deposited by a customer to secure a broker's loan. For example, with Regulation T set at 60 percent, a stock purchase of $10,000 would require margin of $6,000 ($10,000 × 60% = $6,000).

margin account An account type in which stocks, bonds, mutual funds, and option contracts can be traded; often referred to as margin account. Securities can be paid for in full or in part (by borrowing money from your online brokerage firm); not all securities purchased in a margin account are eligible for margin loans. The Federal Reserve Board determines which securities a firm can loan money against. For example, securities trading under $3 or option contracts are not marginable.

market order An order that instructs a trader to execute a buy or sell order immediately at the best available price. Market orders are guaranteed to fill but are not guaranteed for price. Under normal market conditions, market orders to buy should be executed at the current ask price; market orders to sell should be filled at the current bid price.

Nasdaq National Association of Securities Dealers Automated Quotation System. A computerized quotation system providing bid and ask price quotations on many Nasdaq and some listed securities.

Nasdaq Composite Index A market value–weighted index (each company's security affects the index in proportion to its market value) measuring all Nasdaq domestic and non–U.S.-based common stocks listed on the Nasdaq. It is a broad-based index encompassing over 5,000 companies and is highly influenced by technology and Internet companies.

option level The designation found on an account indicating the type of permissible option orders (i.e., buying options, selling covered calls, or selling uncovered calls and combinations). Option levels are reviewed and granted by a firm's registered option principal according to strict guidelines based on a customer's experience, investment objectives, and financial condition (see Figure 3.1).

premium The amount of cash that an option buyer pays to an option seller; the price at which an option contract is quoted in the open market.

put option A derivative trading security based on an underlying investment instrument such as a stock, bond, or stock index that gives the owner or put buyer the right to sell the underlying stock at a specified price (strike price) anytime up to the option's expiration date. Conversely, a put writer is one who sells the put option.

registration type The designation on a new-account application as to how an account should be set up. Registration types of accounts include individual, joint tenancy, corporate, trust, partnership, Gifts to Minors, investment club, and individual retirement.

Regulation T Federal Reserve Board regulation that covers the extension of credit by brokerage firms to customers. It sets initial margin requirements for securities purchases and short sales and determines eligible and ineligible securities. It is currently set at 50 percent but can be raised at the discretion of the Federal Reserve Board.

Regulation T Fed call The initial cash or securities margin requirement issued under Regulation T. It requires that a customer deposit a specified amount of margin (cash or securities) based on the total market value of the securities purchase. For example, a margin purchase of $10,000 worth of stock with Regulation T set at 50 percent would generate a Fed call of $5,000 ($10,000 × 50%). Regulation T Fed calls must be met by the trade date plus five business days.

Rule 405 Also known as the know-your-customer rule, the New York Stock Exchange rule requiring brokerage firms to obtain essential facts pertaining to a customer's investment objectives, financial condition, and other securities holdings.

Securities and Exchange Commission (SEC) The federal agency created by Congress under the Securities and Exchange Act of 1934 to regulate and protect investors. It is made up of five commissioners appointed by the president of the United States. It supervises all national securities exchanges and over-the-counter broker-dealers; it enforces the Securities Act of 1933, the Securities Exchange Act of 1934, and the Investment Advisors Act of 1940, among others (see <www.sec.gov>).

Securities Exchange Act of 1934 Also called the Exchange Act, federal legislation that established the Securities and Exchange Commission. It protects investors by regulating the exchanges, the over-the-counter market, broker-dealers, disclosure of insider transactions, margin requirements set by the Federal Reserve Board, and client accounts.

short position A representation of an account's obligations (liabilities). Selling stock short or selling option contracts creates short positions. The values of all short positions are subtracted from your account balances in deriving total net worth.

short stock Selling shares of stock that you are not currently long; a short account transaction; a margin transaction whereby customers borrow shares of stock from their online broker to sell in the open market in hopes that the shares can be purchased at a lower price in the future and returned to the broker. A short seller profits when shares are repurchased at a price lower than the short sale price.

signature guarantee A stamp given by a fiduciary (bank or brokerage house) verifying a signature's authenticity that is most often requested by online brokers when instructions are given to change an asset's ownership or grant trading authorization to a third party. A notarized signature is not a signature guarantee.

SIPC Securities Investor Protection Corporation; a nonprofit corporation established by Congress under the Investors Protection Act of 1970. Brokerage customers' accounts are insured up to $500,000 in cash and stock (cash coverage limited to $100,000) in the event their brokerage firm declares bankruptcy. SIPC coverage does not include losses suffered from market risk.

Standard & Poor's 500 Index A service of the Standard & Poor's Corporation. The index is a broad-based market value–weighted index allowing investors to track large-cap U.S. market performance. Each stock's weight in the index is proportionate to its market value (number of shares outstanding times the stock price). Industry representation in the index is approximately 75 percent industrials, 8 percent utilities, 14 percent financials, and 2 percent transportation; 89 percent are NYSE stocks and 11 percent are Nasdaq stocks.

stock ahead Term used by traders to explain why a limit order could not be executed based on the fact that other orders at the same price were entered beforehand; limit orders get behind other limit orders.

streaming real-time quotes A price quotation that is continuously updated on your computer screen reflecting a security's current bid and ask prices. Quotes update independently and do not need to be "refreshed" as in the case of standard real-time quotes.

street name Term used to describe customer securities that are being held in a brokerage account. Securities are held in the name of the broker to facilitate transfer and shipment of shares in the event of a sale; customers maintain beneficial ownership. All securities held at an online broker's are considered street name securities.

strike price Also called exercise price; for call options, the price stipulated in the option contract at which the option owner can purchase the underlying security; for put options, the price at which the underlying security can be sold.

tax basis The price at which a security was purchased plus any brokerage commissions; used in figuring capital gains or losses. For shares received in an inheritance, it is the market value of the shares on the date of the original owner's death.

time and sales report A detailed display of minute-by-minute trading activity for a particular security; shows bid and ask prices with sizes, executed trade prices, and volume, and it indicates exchanges where trades were executed. The report is used by traders to review order challenges.

transfer in kind Term used in the transfer of assets to indicate that security positions specified in the transfer application should be transferred as is, not liquidated. Assets are assumed to be transferred in kind unless otherwise specified.

INDEX